Creating Christianity - A Weapon Of Ancient Rome

CREATING CHRISTIANITY

A WEAPON OF ANCIENT ROME

HENRY DAVIS

Published by Independent Publishing Network 2018

Revised and updated version published 2020

Copyright © Henry Davis 2020

The right of Henry Davis to be identified as the Author of this work has been asserted in accordance with the Copyrights, Designs and Patents Act 1988.

ISBN 978-1-78926-556-9 (Hardcover)

ISBN 978-1-78926-557-6 (Paperback)

ISBN 978-1-78926-558-3 (E-Book)

All rights reserved. No part of this book may be reprinted or reproduced or utilized in any form or by any electronic, mechanical or other means, now known or hereafter invented, including photocopying and recording, or in any information storage or retrieval system, without the permission in writing from the Author.

Contents

PREFACE	vii
PROLOGUE: ACADEMIA HAS A PROBLEM	ix
	xvii
1. THE GOSPELS	1
2. JOSEPHUS AND PHILO	13
3. THE GOSPELS AND JOSEPHUS: THE PARALLELS	29
4. FLAVIUS JOSEPHUS NEVER EXISTED	91
5. WHY THE NEW TESTAMENT WAS WRITTEN	137
6. 'ROYAL LANGUAGE'	161
7. THE MAIN AUTHOR - ARRIUS PISO	167
8. A FAMILY AUTHORSHIP	201
9. THE JEWS REJECTED THE STORY	229
10. THE '666' RIDDLE	247
11. ORIGIN OF THE POPES	275
12. CONCLUSION	309
TIMELINE OF EVENTS	321
NOTES & REFERENCES	325
SELECT BIBLIOGRAPHY	335

ABOUT THE AUTHOR

"Tyranny, as I was saying, is monarchy exercising the rule of a master over the political society; oligarchy is when men of property have the government in their hands; democracy, the opposite, when the indigent (poor, needy), and not the men of property, are the rulers….."

Wherever men rule by reason of their wealth, whether they be few or many, that is an oligarchy, and where the poor rule, that is a democracy."

-Aristotle

PREFACE

I owe a huge debt of gratitude to the many individuals (family and friends) who have helped and encouraged me during the process of writing this book, not only by checking the research but also through making me question the findings, to make sure my conclusions were both logical and informed. My sincere thanks also go to certain Cambridge and Oxford University professors for providing valuable feedback. As you have chosen to begin reading this book, I imagine you are either genuinely intrigued as to the information it presents, or, you may be looking to debunk yet another "conspiracy theory" regarding this subject, as I am fully aware that this information has been labeled as such. The history of this age is highly controversial, and the ancient evidence is not a quick read, and you may be unfamiliar with the many names examined in this investigation, for that reason, sometimes relevant evidence is repeated in order to explain these discoveries properly. As will be discussed in the book, in the time in which the New Testament and the works of the supposed Jewish Historian Flavius Josephus were written, the entire known world was being run by an oligarchy, where power rests with a small number of powerful people. There was no hope, or very little hope, of truthful information being included in anything that was written, because it all came from the same family who had hidden motives behind them. The reality was that the idea of all men being equal and free, and the concept of free speech was a very far-off goal for humanity.

I am aware that that last statement has a conspiracy ring to it, but the phrase, 'conspiracy theory', is an interesting one, the effect of its use can be to silence those who are the victims of a conspiracy or those who feel a conspiracy may be occurring. The expression, made popular by Sir Karl Popper in the 1950s, means we characterize an idea that appears impossible, as false, based on our own opinions or current knowledge. But we as a society know that people conspire, for example, it is widespread in politics, and taking the stance that all conspiracy theories are false and irrational is not logical, as it is simply not true. That is why it is so important to obtain as much information about a possible conspiracy as is possible, especially if there is a valid reason to do so, as the more information you have regarding a theory, the more adequately it may be verified or debunked. You may already be familiar with the major conflict this book focuses on, that being the Roman-Jewish War, which would be the greatest catastrophe in Jewish history before the Holocaust. If you are not familiar with that long religious, political war, which *was* a war, and *not* just a rebellion, as is so often stated, allow me to provide a brief introduction.

During the first century, Judea saw big political changes, and the people of Judea began fighting back against the injustice they were suffering under the rule of the Roman aristocracy. Judea was a client kingdom of Rome, and before 'Herod the Great' had been 'installed' by Rome to become 'King of the Jews', the rulers of Judea had cooperated with Rome in order to maintain their power. The Judean people were fighting back against the institution of slavery, the humiliation they were suffering because of their religion, and the extortionate taxes they were paying to the emperor, because of the corruption of the Roman governors of the countryside. In the year 66 CE, for example, a man named *Gessius Florus*, the last Roman procurator, who represented others in a court of law, in countries that continued to have a Roman civil law, stole vast quantities of silver from the Temple, declaring it was to be used as a tax payment for the emperor. The people were motivated to fight by the Jewish religious party known as the Pharisees, which would lead to the Pharisees gaining immense support from the people. The full-scale Jewish revolt against Rome would escalate into the main portion of the war, lasting from 66 CE to 70 CE, and a Roman general named *Titus Flavius Vespasian* would be sent by Emperor Nero to put an end to the revolt. The Romans defeated the Jewish people, however, complete victory would not be achieved by them until 73 CE, with their triumph at the Siege of Masada, a fortification in the Southern District of Israel. But back in Rome, by the year 68 CE, Emperor Nero, the man who we are told played the fiddle while Rome burned, persecuted Christians, and eventually lost the support of the rulers of the city, would become the victim of assassination.

Afterward, a year of civil war took place in Rome, as three different individuals tried to claim the throne. The historians of the time have told us that Nero's assassination meant the Judean people considered this as another sign of divine intervention, that God had finally killed the emperor who was trying to oppress them. In their minds, history was repeating itself, as Emperor Caligula had been assassinated earlier, and when he had given orders for his statue to be placed in the Temple of Jerusalem, the Jews refused to obey his orders, as they worshipped scripture, not statues. Caligula raged at them, "*So you are the enemies of the Gods, the only people who refuse to recognize my divinity,"* and threatened to destroy the Temple, only his sudden, violent death saved the Jewish people from a massacre. With the death of Nero, Titus Flavius Vespasian traveled back to Rome in the late summer of 70 CE to become emperor, and his son, Titus, who would succeed him a few years later, took charge of the armies in Judea. It was Titus at that point who would start the siege of the city of Jerusalem and finally end the main part of the war. During the summer of 70 CE, the Romans breached the walls of Jerusalem and began an orgy of violence and destruction, then afterward, they destroyed the Second Temple, and we are told that about one million Jews lost their lives against Rome.

However, there is far more to this war than we have been led to believe, and the facts behind the battle between the Roman and Jewish aristocracies, and the Judean people have led me to write this book. It explains how the creation of Christianity came about as a result of this war and is essentially divided into two parts:

The first part of this book provides an introduction to the increasing tension that was developing between the people of Jerusalem and the aristocracy of Rome. It also investigates the claimed parallels discovered between the work of the Jewish Historian, Flavius Josephus, and the ministry of Jesus as described in the Gospels. The parallels and connections between the Gospels and the work called 'The Jewish War', also referred to in English as 'The Wars of the Jews', have been noticed by scholars before, for example, by a man named Bruno Bauer, a German philosopher, theologian, and Biblical critic. But some connections are so obvious, one has to wonder why they had not been investigated further by those scholars who have noticed them, perhaps their personal beliefs allowed bias to come before logic. What brought these parallels to recent mainstream attention was a book called *'Caesars' Messiah'*, written by a scholar called *Joseph Atwill*. Joseph concluded that because the Gospels emerged during the reign of the Flavian Emperors, *Vespasian*, and *Titus* after Jerusalem was destroyed in 70 CE, that they must have been ultimately responsible for their creation. His conclusion was logical, as it was based on the evidence he had seen and could understand, *however*, his conclusion is inaccurate, and the second part of this book will explain why the parallels alone do not provide enough evidence of a Roman New Testament creation.

The second part of this book will go further into intricate detail regarding the aristocracy of Rome. It will explain the methods used to uncover alias names and family relationships between the Roman and Jewish aristocracies. The methods used were the same as those used by a man called *Sir Ronald Syme*, who is widely regarded as the 20th century's greatest historian of ancient Rome. He had used certain methods to uncover the genealogies of Roman royalty that had been obscured through the use of created names. The findings in the second part will show that the author of the *Gospel of Mark*, and the author of the *Book of Revelation* used both literary techniques, such as abbreviations and the numbers associated with the languages of the time, to reveal the name of the main author who oversaw the creation of the Gospels. These findings will show that illiterate laborers did not write the Gospels, and those responsible for the actual creation of Christianity were a powerful senatorial Roman-Jewish royal family called the *Calpurnius Pisos*, who were fully *supported* by the *Flavian Emperors* and the *Herodian Royal family*, as they were all related. These findings have been around for some time, but one of the reasons the information has not been taken seriously, and therefore, widely unknown, is because the original researchers did not present their findings very well at all. Unfortunately, it seems they relied on those who read about their findings to already have a thorough, expert knowledge of the events and time they were describing. The original researchers also described these findings as a 'literary code', which, understandably, makes people think this is another absurd conspiracy theory. I remained skeptical until I heard about a discovery that revealed the Spanish King, *Ferdinand II of Aragon*, had used a 500-year-old secret code to give orders and instructions for military action. This secret code contained over 200 special characters and was used by the king to communicate with his military commander, *Gonzalo Fernández de Córdoba*. A total of 88 different symbols and 237 "combined letters" were used to create the code, and it is believed that encrypted letters were a common system in Italy at the time the king wrote this. Even *Julius Caesar* used code, known as the 'Ceasar cipher', in his private correspondence, and it was used to protect messages of military significance.

Whatever your reasons for deciding to read this book, I hope you find the facts presented here incredibly eye-opening, you may even find them very provocative. What I have been able to do is verify the information presented in the discoveries described above, and I will explain such things as the meanings behind certain words, the literary techniques used by the

Roman aristocracy, including how the various languages worked, and I will take you on the investigative journey which led to my final conclusions.

PROLOGUE: ACADEMIA HAS A PROBLEM

I will begin by first highlighting some very important points that will explain my reasons for studying this period in history, and, therefore, compelling me to write this book. Within academia, there is an understanding that no ancient author should ever be viewed as always telling the complete truth without any omissions or bias. However, when controversial information is discovered about certain subjects, as in the issues being investigated here, the above understanding seems to take a backseat. Preconceptions regarding the period of the Roman-Jewish War, and the authors who recorded the events, need to be put aside, as what will hopefully become clear is the fact that:

1) the authors <u>were not</u> who they claimed to be.

2) <u>were not</u> writing in an honest and forthright manner.

3) had ulterior motives leading them to mislead the reader or listeners.

4) <u>were</u> closely related to each other, and therefore, were writing in concert with each other.

5) were <u>not</u> writing in a time where *everyone* could publish for public consumption; this was not the case, there was no published freedom of speech that existed in those times. Only royals could publish works for the public.

6) <u>were</u> using literary devices and other methods in which to deceive the masses.

Although there were no specific rules regarding who could publish written works for public consumption within the Roman Empire, both historical and religious, the only people that would have been able to do so, were those who were educated and wealthy. Published ancient literature was the product of those who were in power, and in-depth intricate research has uncovered controversial facts regarding the story of a particular individual that has eluded biblical scholars for an extraordinary amount of time, that individual is the famous Christian Messiah, Jesus. The information presented in this book cannot be discovered by reading ancient texts and simply believing what you read, as Sir Ronald Syme once stated in his paper, 'People in Pliny', "*The written record has little more to disclose than the families of Seneca* (Roman philosopher and statesman) *and Agricola* (father in law of Tacitus) *or the pedigree of the Antonine emperors. One has recourse* (resort to a person or thing for help) *to inscriptions and the study of nomenclature* (the system of using personal and family names to create new names).." He was saying that simply reading classical works on a superficial level is not enough if someone wishes to learn all the information necessary to have a complete understanding of ancient history. Sir Ronald Syme was a British historian by profession and was known for his mastery of intricate detail, he studied and taught at Oxford University and was a famous scholar of classical Rome and very well respected by his peers. In his book 'Emperors and Biog-

raphy: Studies on the Historia Augusta', Syme gave ten ways to examine the nomenclature of ancient history, and although his book deals specifically with the nomenclature within the *Historia Augusta*, which is a collection of biographies of the Roman Emperors, the same methods have been used to reveal the names created using nomenclature in the first and second centuries CE.

The ten ways Syme gave are as follows:

1) Indistinctive Names, 2) Imperial Gentilicia, 3) Names from earlier Vitae, 4) Recurrent and favorite names, 5) The names of the Authors, 6) Names of Classical Authors, 7) Names from Literature, 8) Names of fun and Fantasy, 9) Perverted Names, 10) Fictitious Characters; meaning their names or attributes, or both, resemble eminent families in the Roman aristocracy.

The true authorship of the Historia Augusta, its actual date, reliability, and its purpose, have been a source of controversy amongst historians and scholars. It has been analyzed using computer algorithms, and the conclusion of those studies revealed that there was only one author instead of the six it has been attributed to. In his book, '*Emperors and Biography*', Syme stated: "*When the attempt is made to expose a fraud, attack on all fronts is to be commended.*" He concluded that, on a superficial level, the Historia Augusta was a deliberate fraud, and to understand what it really presents, different studying methods must be applied and was saying that, as historians, we cannot dismiss any methodology or piece of evidence, because a piece of information which may not seem vital, can, prove crucial. Sir Ronald also produced a book that would cause controversy within the academic world, as it undermined the accepted view of Roman history, that book was called the 'Roman Revolution'. It provided a new, intense analysis of the Roman state in terms of the political ambitions of the leading families, and summarised the ruthless and brutal manipulation used by Emperor Augustus to establish a monarchy under the appearance of restoring the old Republic. He showed that republican Rome was ruled by an oligarchy, in this case, where a small group of powerful people, related by blood and marriage links, are in control.

Syme's book undermined the established understanding of Roman history presented by *Theodor Mommsen*, a German classical scholar, politician, and archaeologist, who was regarded as one of the greatest classicists of the 19th century. Syme wrote "*The Roman constitution was a screen and a sham*", which horrified those who had studied the work of Mommsen, but Syme was saying that Emperor Augustus', (previously known as Octavian), supposed restoration of the Republic was a pretense on which he had built a monarchy based on personal relationships and the ambition of Rome's political families. Syme's expertise regarding famous Romans allowed him to practice what is known as *prosopography* at the highest level, which is the investigation of common characteristics of historical people by the collective study of their lives and multiple career analyses. It is Syme's expertise that has helped historians make further discoveries, including those concerning the senatorial family, the Calpurnius Pisos, as presented in this book. Syme wrote many extremely important papers on ancient Roman history and the individuals who lived at that time. He wrote articles that were published in 'The Journal Of Roman Studies', and well-known books within academia called 'The Roman Papers'. The material found in these journals or periodicals is, more often than not, written by those researchers who have approached the subject in a very professional and intelligent way. Knowing which researchers analyze ancient history in a logical way, some of whom have been referenced in this book, as opposed to a predominantly emotional way, will help future researchers greatly.

Sticking to a literal meaning regarding ancient writings gives us innumerable contradictions, and a topic such as how, why, and by whom a ruler was killed would be obscured, especially if the winner gets to write the history, but it's often the deliberate contradictions or wrong information that can clue us in to a hidden message. Take, for instance, the written statements regarding Emperor Titus Flavius' death, after the destruction of Jerusalem, some said that his brother Domitian had a hand in his early death, but the Babylonian Talmud (Gittin 56b), the primary source of Jewish religious law, claims that after Titus destroyed the Temple in Jerusalem, a gnat flew into his nostril and gradually ate away his brain. Many of the stories available for us to read credit those in the power circles of Rome with an intimate knowledge of plants, something that is associated with the ancient *"right to rule"*, in ancient Egyptian culture, for example, iris flowers played a role as symbols of victory, rule, and power. Some biblical scholars who have spent decades studying the history surrounding the Christian religion, have noticed certain peculiarities but don't piece together other discoveries or cannot see past the massive amount of propaganda produced by the Church, the most powerful organization that has ever existed. The church's apologetics were inserted into the introductions of all great books to explain away anything that did not support a historical Jesus. It is only in the last century that it has become possible to publish without most books going through a Christian filter. *Bruno Bauer* was the first person to study ancient texts as literature and published his findings in his book titled *Christus und Caesaren (Christ and the Caesars)*. Bruno revealed the main difficulties of the historical events of Jesus' life as described in the Gospels and made the claim that the Romans had authored the New Testament and that the Romano-Jewish historian Flavius Josephus was the inventor of Jesus. Bauer's work contained the most complete collection of problematic points in the biography of Jesus Christ, and he broke down the parts and made various comparisons between texts that had similarities, his conclusions led him to state that Rome had authored the New Testament.

He was the first major researcher to find that material in the New Testament was taken from other sources, and he made comparisons of entire phrases and concepts from other sources that were used – and he gave examples. Bauer makes a statement regarding Seneca, the Roman Stoic philosopher, statesman, and dramatist, "... *Seneca is mentioned nowhere in the parallel passages of the New Testament. Neither is Plato when a basic passage is borrowed from him.*" What Bruno was saying is the authors of the New Testament used material from other authors and did not give them an acknowledgment or credit for that usage. Regarding material being *borrowed* from other sources, he says, "*But the concurrence in style found between the main tenets of Seneca and the parallel passages in* the New Testament remains in all these considerations, a sure proof that the authors of these parallels like, e.g., the first ones with whom we began this chapter, had before their own eyes, the writings of the Roman sage (i.e., Seneca). Fleury compared only the parallels between Seneca's short sentences or keywords and the Bible, but if one considers the stylistic form of composition and diction on both sides, one will realize that on the part of the Roman, content, and form develop as originals and have their natural motivation, whereas, in the New Testament, given material is sharpened to make new points."* Bruno was saying he had observed that even though some of the same phrases were used, the context was changed, and that is what someone will see repeatedly in such writings. (**ref** – 'Christ and the Caesars', Bauer, Bruno, 1877, translated into English by Frank E. Schacht. Alexander Davidonis, 1998, published by Charleston House Publishing.)

Other respected individuals that shared the same views as Bruno Bauer include *John William Colenso* and *William Edward Hartpole Lecky*. William, an Irish historian, essayist, and political theorist quotes *"from the vast mass of evidence which has been collected from the writings of Catholic divines and from decrees of Catholic councils, during the space of many centuries; so the descriptions in the Bible from the complaints of the prophets are an exact replica of what was going on in Rome and Constantinople, during the creation of the Bible, and in Europe till quite recent times.* John Colenso, defined as the 'Queen's Bishop', as it was Queen Victoria herself who sent Colenso on a mission to 'enlighten' Africa from the locality of Natal and Zululand, was a British mathematician, theologian, Biblical scholar, and social activist who did similar research into the Church's claims. It was whilst translating the Bible, done in consultation with Zulu converts, that many questions were raised to which Colenso had difficulty in answering truthfully. He also found the Bible contained many things that were at odds with new scientific discoveries, and, although he was taught that *"the Bible is none other than the word of God...absolute, faultless, unerring, supreme,"* his mind began to fill with doubts. Colenso published his *'Commentary on St Paul's Epistle to the Romans'* in 1861, which enraged fellow Bishops who called it *"a revolt against the faith of Christendom"*, he would attract even more anger when he wrote his *'Critical Examination of the Pentateuch'* (the first five books of the Old Testament Bible).

He told a friend that although he believed wholeheartedly in God, *"the Pentateuch, as a whole, cannot personally have been written by Moses, or by anyone acquainted personally with the facts which it professes to describe, and, further, that the Mosaic narrative, by whomsoever written, and though imparting to us, as I fully believe it does, revelations of the Divine Will and Character, cannot be regarded as historically true."* Colenso's book was first published in South Africa, but his fellow Bishops were determined to stop it from being published in England. The Church persecuted him in civil courts up to the House of Lords, to ruin him for exposing its claims as a fraud, but he assembled his facts in such a masterly form that even a Bishop-ruled House of Lords had to accept his statements as the truth. The Old Testament was edited, most likely by the family being investigated in this book, and was rewritten at a later date to include items that make it appear that those texts had foretold the coming of Jesus. For example, there are some earlier copies of the Old Testament that are different and do not have items that were added later, such as *Isaiah Chapter 53*.

Speaking of claims, we are told, in the form of two contradictory accounts, one by Christian historian *Eusebius*, and the other by an individual named *Lactantius*, a tutor to Constantine's son, that Constantine saw a 'vision' in the sky which led to his conversion to Christianity. Eusebius says that Constantine saw this vision in 312 CE, just *before* the Battle of the Milvian Bridge, which was essentially a battle between Constantine and Emperor Maxentius over the throne of Rome. Constantine looked up to the sun before the battle and saw a cross of light above it, and with it, a message saying *'in this sign, conquer'*. Lactantius, however, says that Constantine and his army saw a great cross in the sky whilst in Gaul, *before* setting out towards Rome. Many people, including scholars, who have researched the history of Christianity, have come to the opinion it did not exist until the time of *Emperor Constantine*, which has led some to conclude that it was created by him. The evidence in this book will show that it did not *really* exist before Constantine's time, but those behind the creation of this religion were his ancestors, what Constantine did, when he became emperor, was revive it for political purposes; the real reason for the creation of this religion in the first place.

As will be shown, Christianity was 'dead' from about the year 120 CE until Constantine revived it just after 310 CE. We read that in 325 CE he called the First Council of Nicaea and called upon 318 Catholic Bishops to separate the 'divinely inspired' writings from those of questionable origin, which is a debated statement, but, as will be shown, it is debated because many logical historians, unfortunately, are still under the impression that the key figures involved with Christianity were being honest about their identity. One example would be *Eusebius*, who scholars believe exaggerated the extent of persecution enforced under Emperor Diocletian, to create the image of "martyrs". But if that is the case, what else did these "Christian historians" lie about, and can they be trusted? In 367 CE, a man named *Athanasius*, Bishop of Alexandria, published a list containing the 27 books that currently comprise the New Testament, and those same books were later sanctioned at the Council of Hippo in 393 CE and in 397 CE by the Council of Carthage. It is interesting to note that 'St. Athanasius' wrote, *"should we understand sacred writ according to the letter, we should fall into the most enormous blasphemies."* He is saying that it is a great sin to read the Bible literally, and the supposed Christian scholar, Origen, and 'St. Gregory', also held that the Gospels were not to be taken in their literal sense. There were many books not included in the New Testament, including, *The Book of Enoch, The Book of Jubilees, The Infancy Gospel of Thomas, The Life of Adam and Eve,* and *The Apocalypse of Peter*, to name a few. The selection process was a lengthy one that finally ended when there was almost universal agreement on which books made up the New Testament in the fifth century, and many books went back and forth on and off the list during those four hundred years, depending on who was making the decisions.

The problem surrounding Constantine's conversion, and whether the decision as to what books would make up the New Testament did begin at the Council of Nicaea, are just a few of the numerous issues surrounding the history of that time. The claim that the Council of Nicaea began the process of deciding what scriptures the New Testament would consist of seems to come from a statement by *Francois-Marie Arouet*, aka, "Voltaire". Voltaire states in his *Dictionnaire Philosophique* (1764) that *"It is reported in the Supplement of the Council of Nicaea that the Fathers, when they had no idea how to determine which were the questionable or apocryphal books of the Old and New Testament, piled all of them disorderly on an altar; and the books to be rejected fell to the ground. It's a pity this nice method has fallen into disuse nowadays."* This statement comes across as Voltaire noting that this is a silly way the Council supposedly chose the relevant books. Voltaire appears to have got his statement from an appendix in Jesuit scholar Philippe Labbe's *Sanctissima concilia* (1671). However, the main source seems to be the *Synodicon Vetus*, an anonymous medieval Byzantine work, which gives a concise history of church councils up to around 887 CE, and its account of Nicaea concludes: *"The canonical and apocryphal books it distinguished in the following manner: in the house of God the books were placed down by the holy altar; then the Council asked the Lord in prayer that the inspired works be found on top and – as in fact happened – the spurious on the bottom."*

This account of what happened is unconvincing, however, was Voltaire trying to tell us something, as an observation in his *Philosophical Dictionary*, published in 1764, relates to the discoveries detailed in this book. In his dictionary, when talking about how learned men are surprised that no Roman historian speaks of the extraordinary events described in the Gospels, such as the sky becoming dark in the daytime during the crucifixion of Jesus, meaning Rome must have been plunged for three hours in darkness, he says, "*The same persons also find some difficulties in the gospel history. They remark that, in Matthew, Jesus Christ tells the Scribes and Pharisees that all the innocent blood that has been shed upon earth, from that of Abel the Just down to that of Zachary, son of Barac, whom they slew between the temple and the altar, shall be upon their heads. There is not (say they) in the Hebrew history any Zachary slain in the temple before the coming of the Messiah, nor in His time, but in the history of the siege of Jerusalem, by Josephus, there is a Zachary, son of Barac, slain by the faction of the Zelotes. This is in the nineteenth chapter of the fourth book. Hence they suspect that the gospel according to St. Matthew was written after the taking of Jerusalem by Titus.*"

The above observation in 1764 is remarkable by Voltaire and comes into the realm of conjecture, which is the technique of textual criticism to find the most logical answers. It takes an experienced expert with an in-depth knowledge of the period, language, and style of the time, to undertake a close study of the text in its cultural and historical context. As many scholars and academics will agree, all history is partly conjectural as not all information from the past is still here, so it is vitally important to work with what we do have. One of the difficulties in investigating ancient history is that many primary sources are inaccurate, muddled, based on hearsay, or intended to mislead, and the majority are in some way incomplete or tainted by prejudice and self-interest. When the above statement is the case, you must make your best guess about what happened, but the best guess needs to be based upon your knowledge of the historical situation, which means using the facts we *do* have, coupled with an understanding of the way the world is. It is no secret that the Bible falls apart when properly scrutinized, and the Jesus of the Gospels has remained elusive even to experts, some of which of course have produced many books on the subject. This book, however, will present new information explaining how the answers have been right in front of us the entire time, and how past scholars have been conducting their research based on the assumption that the writers of that time were being honest, and were who they claimed to be. This book will sympathetically show that the Jesus described in the Gospels could not have existed and that Christianity did not become a proper religion until *after* Emperor Constantine, and Emperor Theodosius, began making it the official religion of Rome.

The information presented aims to explain the *Calpurnius Pisos'*, *Flavian's*, and *Herodian's* involvement in Rome's war against Jerusalem, and in particular, their conflict with the prominent Jewish sect called the *Pharisees*. The troubles between the Roman aristocracy and the Pharisees persisted for many years, and it is at that point the New Testament circulated. That is a key factor in unraveling the mystery surrounding the origin of Christianity, to realize that before the New Testament emerged, Judea was at war with Rome over religious and political issues. Many conservative scholars and academics still view the war as just a rebellion and also reject the idea that the New Testament could ever be a Roman creation, possibly because many scholars are themselves religious. It has been argued that the Romans were not smart or knowledgeable enough regarding the Jewish writings to have created religious literature like this, but the Calpurnius Piso family were related to the family of Herod the Great, as will be shown, meaning they were descendants of both Roman and Jewish royalty. That means this family was highly educated and possessed the knowledge to create the New Testament story, as their relatives were the ones in control of the Jewish religious texts, I would even argue that the Herodians assisted the Calpurnius Pisos in the creation of the scriptures. Another argument against Roman authorship is that the Romans knew one thing well, and that was how to fight. I have to agree on that point, but the Roman aristocracy *was* very intelligent, there is no way they would have been able to build an empire and maintain it, without the knowledge and power to do so. Another argument comes in the form of just why Rome would *persecute* the very people who were following what they had written, but, as noted above, claims of persecution are not what they appear to be.

I would like to raise a few points that have been very important factors throughout my investigation —

1) there is not one word explaining how these scriptures were obtained or proving their honest origin, and nothing was allowed to leak out as to the method used to compile the collection of doubtful tales made up of crude religious or phallic stories.

2) all mentions of persecution come after the fact and after the New Testament emerged, and come from Roman historians.

3) all mentions of Christians themselves, or Christos, and Chrestus, came from Roman historians, again, after the New Testament emerged.

4) scholars and academics have not identified who the authors of the Gospels were. The consensus is that their names are 'Mark', 'Matthew', 'Luke', and 'John', but because the Koine Greek word, *Kata*, appears within the titles of the Gospels, we know they are not the authors because a different form of Greek defines the term 'author'.

5) the individual named 'Paul' never claimed to have met Jesus, but claimed to have received his information from Jesus *'speaking to him'*. For a historical investigator, being told that someone received information from an individual who is dead does not count as reliable evidence. There is also no reliable evidence that a Christian sect existed before the New Testament emerged, even Paul says nothing about them.

6) there are no direct Jewish sources or any other sources outside Rome for a historical Jesus of the Gospels.

Another key point to take into consideration is the controversy surrounding the discovery of the Dead Sea Scrolls, the ancient Jewish literature discovered in the caves of Qumran in the Judaean Desert, near the Jordan River. This was an important discovery, as it was thought these scrolls may have contained a missing link concerning this time in history. However, the find became controversial when the Roman Catholic Church kept these scrolls out of the public eye for almost 50 years, and information about them was on a *"need to know basis"*. Today that would not be acceptable for such an important find, and my thoughts on this are that if the scrolls provided evidence for early Christianity, the Catholic Church would not have hesitated to tell anyone.

If uneducated common men did write the scriptures, then many of the issues within the Bible result from a lack of knowledge. But if those in control of the Roman Empire, and everything published within it, were responsible for their creation, then the reason for this new religious law becomes one of a desire to maintain power. If that is the case, then, as this information will show, it is clear the Gospels were written in a way that gave the perception the scriptures were written by common people, with the supposed grammar errors being written on purpose, to present names. As mentioned, the aristocracy was in control of all publishing within the empire, and was very knowledgeable about religions, philosophy, and the Jewish religion and had close supporters to help them. Although there was no specific rule in place limiting who could publish literature, the only people who had the means to do so were *Nobles, merchants, and high-ranking people.* In the book 'Jewish Literacy in Roman Palestine', Professor of Jewish Studies, Catherine Hezser stated: *"within the Jewish lower society, the average literary rate must be considered lower than the Roman average, significantly less than 10-15 percent"* which perhaps gives us a figure of approximately 5-6 percent. (**ref** – Catherine Hezser, 'Jewish Literacy in Roman Palestine', page 496.)

That means the chances of illiterate laborers being able to publish this literature, and get away with it, are highly unlikely. One problem they would have faced was obtaining the resources to reproduce the literature if destroyed, which would have been the case considering the claimed persecutions. As Assistant Professor of early Christianity, ancient Judaism, and Roman archaeology, *Robyn Faith Walsh* states in her book 'The Origins of Early Christian Literature': *"To assume sources like the Synoptics emerged from the folk speech of established early Christian groups presumes a social environment for these writers that agitates against what is known about ancient authorship practices. It privileges a presumed social formation (religious communities) over an axiomatic one (networks of literate specialists) without demonstrating why such a move is warranted. Moreover, religion is not a matter of "more or less" in this scholarly construction; it is a matter of "only": the author's assumed religious community is the only considered social context, leaving more plausible associations-like broad networks of elite cultural producers -largely unexamined."*

There zero evidence for any supposed followers of Jesus being illiterate or literate, but if we consider for a moment that the first followers of Jesus may have been Palestinian Jews, and if we think about the fact The Dead Sea Scrolls show a high degree of Jewish literacy, then the first followers could well have been literate enough to produce quality works. But the Dead Sea Scrolls say nothing of Christianity or Jesus, and, as I have said, the way the Catholic Church hid them away is suspicious. The scriptures we have today are of unknown authorship and they can not be the product of the common classes – so who wrote these "eyewitness accounts" after a very troubled 40-year gap?

1. THE GOSPELS

The Torah was a holy book that the Jews guarded and cherished with their life, and they shared these manuscripts all over Ancient Israel, except Jerusalem as the Romans had destroyed the Jewish presence there. The different sects in Judea, the *Pharisees*, the *Scribes*, the *Sadducees*, the *Essenes*, and the *Zealots*, held varying beliefs about their religion. The *Essene* sect, who lived in Qumran on the West Bank of the Judean Desert, likely followed the rebellion because of their messianic expectations. When the Romans occupied Qumran, the Essenes stored manuscripts in the caves for fear of them being destroyed. Eventually, Qumran was conquered in 68 CE, and archeological remains show that the Romans burnt this area to the ground, and, after the destruction of the Second Temple in 70 CE, they then turned their attention to Masada to complete their victory in 73 CE. The conquering of Qumran forced the Jews to try and save the scrolls by hiding them in the caves, those scrolls are known today as the Dead Sea Scrolls. Much like today, during that time there were no actual rules in place concerning who could produce literature for the people within the Roman Empire, but there was no freedom of speech either. Only 1-2% of the population could read and write, those being *Nobles*, *merchants*, and *rich individuals*, and the *royalty* of the day had to agree with all the literature being circulated, otherwise, the author would not live long. Considering that slaves copied these various books or book rolls one by one, means only high society people had the powers to achieve this. What is interesting, is this research shows that at that time only those of royal status wrote public literature. Following the war, Rome took command of all the Churches and Temples, which means that the Roman emperor of the time, *after* the war, would have had to allow and agreed to any holy writing being read out and distributed in and around the empire, and in the other territories under Roman authority. This limits just who would have been able to write religious texts.

The early Christian literature becomes suspicious regarding this, as so far, no concrete information regarding the author's identities has been provided, only speculations. Within the Roman Empire, the emperor controlled all publishing, the lives of philosophers and where they lived, access to the Royal Library of Alexandria in Egypt, and all places of religious interest. Writers had a great influence on people and so the emperor tried to control what was available, with bookshops often being raided and undesirable books destroyed. Emperor Augustus ordered private houses to be searched for books he took a dislike to, so writers had to be careful when writing about powerful people in Rome, as the punishment meant death. As we learn from the writer *Juvenal*, a Roman poet active in the late first and early second century CE, the best thing to do was wait until someone died before you criticized them. By the time of the fourth century CE, Rome had 28 large libraries where citizens could read books for free, however, government officials, called prefects, selected the books that appeared in these libraries, in this way the government could control what information was available. Supporting information regarding the 'rules' around literature come from *Appian* in his '*Civil Wars*'. Written approximately 160 CE, he says,

"Laena (under instructions from Antony) cut off Cicero's head... He also cut off the hand with which Cicero had written his attacks on Antony... The head and hand of Cicero were suspended for a long time from the rostra in the forum where formerly he had made speeches".

Another example comes from *Tacitus*, the Roman historian, and politician, in his book *The Annals of Imperial Rome*, where, in 118 CE, he says, "*The Senate ordered his books to be burnt by the aediles*". But they survived, first hidden and later republished... *the stupidity of people who believe that today's authority can destroy tomorrow's memories*". This is a statement regarding when the Roman historian *Cremutius Cordus* criticized the power of the emperors. All public literature went through a '*Roman filter*', and to maintain this control, the emperor used secret police called the Frumentarii. These officials of the Roman Empire were originally wheat collectors but acted as the 'secret service' of the Roman Empire in the second and third centuries, and their loyalty was to the emperor. But with these 'rules' in place, it brings us back to the discoveries regarding Flavius Josephus and the New Testament itself. The evidence seems to suggest the authors of the Gospels would need to be literate enough to create writings for public use, but they would also need to have the means to reproduce them if under threat of being destroyed. If literate high priests wrote the Gospels, records clarifying this should exist, possibly. If illiterate peasants gave these eyewitness accounts, then those who were literate would need to have written them, so the question, again, is, who were the authors? The first thing to understand when researching the Gospels is that the word '*kata*' appears with the name following it.

For example –

'ΤΟ ΚΑΤΑ ΜΑΤΘΑΙΟΝ ΑΓΙΟΝ ΕΥΑΓΓΕΛΙΟΝ'.

Which means

'The According To Matthew Holy Glad Tidings'.

The verb, **'Glad-Tidings'**, is translated, in the King James Bible, as **'To Preach The Gospel'**. The English word **'Gospel'**, is created from the Anglo-Saxon **'god-spell'**, meaning **'good news'** or **'tidings'**. But **'Glad-Tidings'** occurs in the King James Bible and translates as 'ευαγγελιον' (**evangélion**), which is the classical Greek word meaning **'good news'**.

The word **'kata'** κατα in Greek designates the source, not the author, a different form of Greek would designate the author, such as **'archegos'** αρχηγος. So when these names were attached to the accounts, somebody was claiming the names were the sources for the authors, not the authors themselves. But they cannot be eyewitnesses, as Matthew copies Mark using the same words, and if you were an eyewitness, why would you use the words of someone who is not an eyewitness? This is what the *'New Oxford Annotated Bible'* has to say on the matter:

"Scholars generally agree that the Gospels were written forty to sixty years after the death of Jesus. They are not eyewitness or contemporary accounts of Jesus's life and teaching. Even the language has changed. Though Greek had become the common language used by groups whose primary languages were different in the eastern Roman Empire, and inscriptions and fragments of Greek translations of the Hebrew Bible show that Greek was used

among Jews within Judea, Jesus, his disciples, and the crowds would have used Aramaic, a Semitic language closely related to Hebrew, which it had replaced as the principal spoken language of Palestine. Despite scholarly efforts to detect an underlying Aramaic original for Mark or Matthew, it is probable that all the evangelists wrote in the common (koinē) Greek of their day. Further, the vast majority of Hebrew Bible citations in the New Testament are taken from the Greek translation of the Hebrew Bible (the Septuagint)." (**ref** – 'The *New Oxford Annotated Bible New Revised Standard Version*', page 1380) – For an article investigating when the Septuagint was created, please visit www.henryhdavis.com.

Secondly, as mentioned above, the Greek word for Gospel is 'ευαγγελιον' (**evangélion**), which again, as shown above, means 'good news'. According to the standard theological dictionary, the word "*Gospel*" means the good news of military victory. If we look at Mark's Gospel closely, we can see that being the case:

Jesus has authority over **Doctrine** (1:21-22, 27)

Jesus has authority and victory over **'Demons'** (1:23-27, 34, 3:11)

Jesus has authority and victory over **'Disease'** (1:31, 34, 40-45, 3:10)

Jesus has authority and victory over **'Sin'** (2:5-12)

Jesus has authority over the **Sabbath and Traditions** (2:23-28)

Jesus has authority and victory over **'Satan'/Strong Man** (3:23-27)

Jesus has authority and victory over **'Storms'** (4:35-47)

Jesus has authority and victory over **Death** (5:35-43)

When reading the above, if for a moment we put the word **Rome** in place of the word **Jesus**, we can see that these victories become the military victories of Rome after the Roman-Jewish War. The Jewish presence in Jerusalem was destroyed and Rome had authority over that land, so the *military victory* meaning of 'Evangelion' applies to the Gospels. When we come to the chapter which examines the parallels between Josephus and the Gospels, this fact will hopefully become even more apparent. The Gospels claim to be four very separate stories or reports written independently by four different individuals, but when we consider the information above, we can see how they were constructed and, therefore, understand what they are.

'**Mark**' and '**Matthew**' are works of literature, and were created using the structure that makes up the **Torah** (The Old Testament). The Torah, the traditional and sacred book of the Jews, that is made up of five sacred books, appears to have been used as the basis for creating the five parts in these Gospels. That means someone used the origin story presented within the Torah to create the origin story of Jesus. They used the theme of Exodus, which means leaving Egypt, to create the passage about Jesus visiting Egypt, simply a reversal of what appears in the Torah. The book of **Numbers** is, according to the story, an account of how God ordered a counting of the people (a census) of the twelve tribes of Israel. After counting all the men who were over twenty and fit to fight, the Israelites began to travel in a well-ordered division. In **Hebrew,** it means the **'book of the wilderness'**, and that leads to the passage in which Jesus goes on into the wilderness. Next, we have **Deuteronomy**, the important section in the fifth book of the **Torah**, in which '**Moses**' gives law to the **Israelites** on the mountain. In '**Mark**' and '**Matthew**' we see the story of the '**Sermon on the Mount**', in which Jesus gives a new law. Finally, we have the **Book of Leviticus,** the third book of the **Torah**, which is the account of the '**sacrifice**' which was used to create the story of the '**crucifixion**'. In the book of **Exodus**, '**Moses**' is told to go to Egypt and come back from Egypt, and that part was used to describe how Jesus' father is told to go into Egypt, because of the destruction of the children. So one story is used as a literary structure to create another story, and if that is the case, it is not a historical account.

OLD TESTAMENT	MATTHEW
Gen: 45-50 Joseph takes old Israel down to Egypt.	**2:13** Joseph brings new Israel down to Egypt.
Exodus:1 Pharaoh massacres boys.	**2:16** Herod massacres boys.
Exodus:4 "All the men are dead..."	**2:20** "They are dead..."
Exodus:12 From Egypt to Israel.	**2:21** From Egypt to Israel.
Exodus:14 Passing through water (baptism).	**3:13** Baptism.
Exodus:16 Tempted by bread.	**4:4** Tempted by bread.
Exodus:17 Do not tempt God.	**4:7** Do not tempt God.
Exodus:32 Worship only God.	**4:10** Worship only God.

Examining The New Testament

Now, you may be familiar with the following arguments regarding why there should be a mention of Jesus outside of the New Testament, but for those who are not, I will present a few of them. The New Testament contains some two dozen scriptures in which Jesus is said to be famed far and wide and performing miracles. For example, in 1 Corinthians, 500 people supposedly saw him resurrected, and at his death there were *earthquakes, the sun darkens,* and the saints *rise out of the ground* and wander through the streets of Jerusalem:

"And the graves were opened, and many bodies of the saints

which slept arose, and came out of the graves after his resurrection, and went into the holy city, and appeared unto many."

This unique event is not recorded in the historical record of the day, the question is, why? The period in which this event happened is one of the best documented in history, so I think it's very reasonable to assume that the above event would have been noticed. Jesus was also, supposedly, rampaging through the streets, going into the temples, and feeding 5,000 people with fishes and loaves of bread, and this area was a very busy trade route, but even if people did not mention him, it's reasonable to think that the other issues that were going on at the time would have been noticed. It is written that the curtain of the temple was torn in two from top to bottom at Jesus' death (Matthew 27:50-51), meaning there was damage to the Jewish temple. That should have been recorded somewhere other than the Bible, as the Jews would have been very protective of their Temple if somebody had entered there in an aggressive manner such as this. In another incident, Jesus threatens to '*destroy the temple*' (Matthew 26:61), and he's calling the Jews sons of Satan, which was blasphemy and deserved the death penalty. Again, it can be expected that the Jews would have recorded that incident, but even the supposed persecution of the Christians by 'Paul', who was **Saul** at the time, does not make it into the historical record.

An individual who should have recorded something of these events, a man named **Philo Judea of Alexandria** (Judaeus), a Jewish historian who was living at that exact time and who was part of the wealthiest family on the planet, says nothing, but his '*logos*' (word of God) idea appears in the New Testament.

Philo was an important historian at this time, but in his works, he does not write about a Jesus that would be seen as the Messiah of the Gospels. The only similarity is his Incarnate Word: *the Logos*, which was significantly developed by the Greeks as the 'Living Word of God', and Philo describes the words that end up in the New Testament.

Philo wrote:

"The Logos of the living God is the bond of everything, holding all things together…"

The New Testament says:

"And he is before all things, and in him, all things hold together." – Colossians 1:17

Another perhaps trivial point, but a valid one, is regarding the three kings, or 'the Biblical Magi', also referred to as the 'Three Wise Men', who make only one appearance in the Gospels, the Gospel of Matthew. These wise men felt that the birth of Jesus was important enough to visit him, even bringing gifts, but we have no record of them or from them regarding this visit, so what happened? It is by considering all of these factors and putting them into the context and culture of *that* time, that the only possible way this story would have been able to gain credibility, is for it to be the product of those who controlled the creation of religious laws. The Old Testament is a set of laws, and the New Testament gave new laws, which is why the story of Jesus does not present itself as it should in history, especially considering other recorded events. Jesus' story parallels past ancient messiah stories and uses attributes from other gods worshipped around the empire. Those gods include the Etruscan god **Usil**, *who walked on water*, the Egyptian god **Osiris**, *who came forth from the tomb*, **Dionysus/Bacchus**, *the god of wine*, and the Greco-Egyptian god **Aesculapius/Serapis**, *the god of healing*. The next step then in this investigation is to examine the background information regarding the first-century historians, *Flavius Josephus* and *Philo Judea of Alexandria*. Understanding the background of these two individuals will hopefully make it easier to understand the discoveries investigated in the following chapters.

2. JOSEPHUS AND PHILO

To examine the events described in the New Testament, we must first research and consider what was happening within the Roman Empire at that time, to do that, we need to begin with the work of the following historians.

Philo Judaeus or Philo of Alexandria

Philo was born between 15 and 10 BCE and died between 45 and 50 CE. He was a Greek-speaking Jewish philosopher who became the most important representative of Hellenistic Judaism and was regarded by Christians as a forerunner of Christian theology. Little is known about the life of this individual Philo, the names of his parents are unknown and what we know either comes from himself or the brief bit of information that Josephus provides us with. It appears he came from a family of nobility and wealth, and Josephus says his family surpassed all others in the nobility of its lineage, it's possible he was a son or grandson of Herod the Great. We are told his father or paternal grandfather was granted Roman citizenship by dictator Gaius Julius Caesar, although it is unclear which one. His father played a prominent role in Palestine before moving to Alexandria. His brother Alexander Lysimachus was a tax administrator in charge of customs in Alexandria and the wealthiest man in the city, which means he must have been one of the richest men in the Hellenistic world. Josephus says he gave a tremendous loan to the wife of King Agrippa I and he contributed the gold and silver which covered nine giant gates of the Temple in Jerusalem. Alexander also seems to have been very influential in Roman imperial circles, being an old friend of Emperor Claudius and having acted as the guardian for the emperor's mother. Philo was an eclectic philosopher who borrowed ideas from the Platonists (followers of Plato), Stoics (followers of Hellenistic philosophy), and Cynics (an ancient Greek philosophy). Yet he remained loyal to both his Jewish faith, regarding Mosaic scripture (named after Moses) as a source of religious revelation, and the philosophic truths put forward by the Greeks. According to Philo, the Greek philosophers 'borrowed from Moses' and received their insights from the God of the Jews, even finding subtle and obscure differences in the biblical sagas.

This is where Philo's "**Logos**" idea comes in, which is a term inspired by the Stoics, and according to Philo, "**Logos**" the Greek for *'word'* or *'reason'* was the same as **divine reason**. The *Logos* or *Word* originated from God and communicated with his creations, so the "**Logos**" spoke to Moses from the burning bush, and it was the Logos that infused the righteous High Priest. When an individual experienced *a "religious ecstasy"* it meant the *Logos* had entered that person's soul. Philo described the nature of God's link between people in his *Who is the Heir of Divine Things?* 42.205-6.

"And the Father who created the universe has given to his

archangelic and most ancient Word a pre-eminent gift, to stand on the confines of both, and separated that which had been created from the Creator.

And this same Word is continually a suppliant to the immortal God on behalf of the mortal race, which is exposed to affliction and misery; and is also the ambassador, sent by the Ruler of all, to the subject race.

And the Word rejoices in the gift, and, exulting in it, announces it and boasts of it, saying, 'And I stood in the midst, between the Lord and You; neither being uncreated as God, nor yet created as you, but being in the midst between these two extremities ... For I will proclaim peaceful intelligence to the creation from him who has determined to destroy wars, namely God, who is ever the guardian of peace".

Given the time when Philo lived, and the status he had, we should have an excellent witness to events in Judaea and the Jewish diaspora, the dispersion of the Jews beyond Israel, in the first half of the first century CE. He was the perfect person to provide an account of the activities of a man claiming to be the Messiah and performing the miracles described in the Gospels, but there is nothing. Philo came from a noble and wealthy family and his ancestors and family had social connections with the priesthood in Judea. His family was connected with the Hasmonean/Herodian dynasty and the Julio-Claudian dynasty in Rome. He also visited the Temple in Jerusalem during Passover (detailed in his writing *On Providence*). So I find it puzzling to believe a man such as Philo never heard about a man such as Jesus, who caused as much of a scene as he did. We know Philo lived at the time that "Jesus of Nazareth" entered the world because he was an old man when he led an embassy from the Jews in Alexandria to the court of Emperor Gaius Caligula in the year 39-40 CE. *Marcus Julius Alexander*, the nephew of Philo, by his brother Alexander, was married to Berenice, the daughter of King Herod Agrippa I, tetrarch (or governor) of Galilee and Peraea, 39-40 CE. When *Herod Antipas*, the villain of the Jesus story was exiled, Marcus ruled as *King of the Jews* from 41 to 44 CE. Another nephew, Julius Alexander Tiberius was the "apostate" (which is someone who abandons religion), and a Prefect of Egypt, and also the Procurator of Judaea from 46 to 48 CE. Philo also wrote apologetics that defended the Jewish religion and also wrote about contemporary politics, with about thirty manuscripts and at least 850,000 words still surviving. He also wrote about the major characters of the *Pentateuch*, mentioning *Moses* more than a thousand times. In **Acts 5:18-40**, we read about the miraculous escape from a royal prison of a gang of apostles, and **Acts 12:2-7** describes the second angel-assisted flight of Peter, even though chained between soldiers and guarded by *four* squads of troops. With Philo's connections to the House of Herod, is it unreasonable to think Philo would have heard about this?

Flavius Josephus

Josephus, or to use his original name, **Yosef ben Matityahu**, is considered the most important historian in Western Civilization, who produced four major writings: *The Jewish War* (circa. 75 CE), *Antiquities of the Jews* (circa. 94 CE), *Against Apion* (circa. 97 CE), and *The Life of Flavius Josephus* (circa. 99 CE). From what he says, he was born around 37-38 CE, as a religious Jew, but he appears to have a strange background for an individual of his status and time. He claims that at the age of 16 he sampled the three sects of Judaism in this era, the **Essenes**, the **Sadducees**, and the **Pharisees**. Spending three years living as a hermit under **Bannus**, a member of one of the ascetic Jewish sects active in Judaea around the time of Christ, he decided to become a Pharisee whilst in the desert (*Josephus, Life*, 2). But spending three years in the wilderness sounds suspicious, it's difficult to accept that he still had time to sample these sects and gain a proper understanding of them. He also claims to be from the royal family, on his mother's side, her being descended from the **Royal Hasmonean** priests family (the family of **Herod the Great**), the family running the Maccabean Kingdom. Introducing himself in Greek as **Iosepos**, son of **Matthias**, he describes himself as a cosmopolitan who is familiar with many countries and cultures. When he was 14, he states, "*the high priests and principal men of the city*" came to him to ask his opinions about the law (*Josephus, Life*, 2). This is very similar to **Luke 2:42**, where Jesus is found in the temple, sitting among teachers, listening to them and asking questions, "*and all who heard him were amazed at his understanding and his answers*".

He visited **Poppaea** in Rome, the wife of Emperor **Nero**, and goes to negotiate with Emperor Nero for the release of 12 Jewish priests, as we know, Jesus had 12 Apostles. It appears he spent two years in Rome and returned to Judea when on the verge of war (Josephus, Life, 3). But he says he opposed the war, which he believed the Jews would lose, and tried to persuade the rebels not to fight (Josephus, Life, 4), this sounds like he tried to 'downplay' his role in the revolt. He also appears to have had a foot in both worlds, one in the Zealot rebel Jewish world, and the other in the cosmopolitan international world which Rome dominates. Josephus also contradicts himself when his different works cover the same period. The clearest example is his descriptions of his military exploits in Galilee in the early stages of the war. According to **The Jewish War**, the Jewish generals were assigned to different regions, Josephus being put in command of the Galilee. He presents himself as an excellent general, fortifying the cities, raising an army, and training it along Roman lines. However, the bandit leader, *John of Gischala*, a leader of the Jewish revolt against the Romans, undermined his position (Josephus, Jewish War, Book 2, Chapters 20-22). In his **The Life** (bio/vita) **of Flavius Josephus** though, he tells a somewhat different story, he says the Galilee had not yet revolted against Rome, and Josephus, accompanied by two priests, went to persuade them to lay down their arms. Josephus also goes into greater detail about the internal fighting and factionalism in Galilee (Josephus, Life, Book 7). Josephus' **Life** (bio/vita) seems to be not so much a bio, but more of an apologia, or a formal written defense of his opinions and conduct.

A quote from Tessa Rajak, Josephus, The Historian and His Society, p. 147, says:

"It contains some biographical information, but it is largely

concerned with defending his actions in Galilee, which had been attacked while he was living in Rome. It would seem that Josephus wrote Life/Vita to justify himself, it is less reliable than The Jewish War, but there are those that believe that Life/Vita is more credible".

The books *The Jewish War* and *The Antiquities of the Jews* both cover the period from the Maccabean revolt to the start of the Jewish war, the Maccabees were a group of Jewish rebel warriors who took control of Judea and founded the Hasmonean dynasty. But *The Jewish War* and *The Antiquities of the Jews* contain contradictions that cannot be explained by Josephus' attempt to justify himself. In the book *The Jewish War*, Josephus says 10,000 Jews died in a riot after a Roman soldier exposed himself to the crowd of worshippers, during the festival of Passover. While in *Antiquities of the Jews*, he says 20,000 Jews died and they do not agree on how the soldier exposed himself (*Josephus, Jewish War*, Book 2, Chapter 12, *Antiquities of the Jews*, Book 20, Chapter 5), but this may be explained with new details he received. In 67 CE, General Vespasian invaded Galilee and besieged Jotapata where Josephus was in command. *The Jewish War* claims Vespasian received word that if he captured Josephus all Judea would fall into his hands, so he ensured that he could not escape. When Jotapata fell and his men committed mass suicide, Josephus surrendered to Vespasian. He then claimed to be a prophet and prophesied that Vespasian would become emperor (*Josephus, Jewish War*, Whiston Book 3, Chapter 8, Section 9), two years later Josephus' 'prophecy' came true and he says they released him. But historians have expressed skepticism about the historicity of the prophecy that Josephus gave to Vespasian.

It resembles how, about 2000 years earlier in Egypt, his namesake, Joseph, was released from captivity by the king (Pharaoh), because of his successful 'prophetic' gifts. In 67 CE, Emperor Nero was still alive and Vespasian was not an obvious candidate for becoming emperor, so Josephus could not have guessed it would happen. If Josephus' prophecy did not happen, then there *must* be another explanation for Josephus' release and very good treatment by Vespasian and Titus, despite Josephus writing he had his men pour boiling oil and fenugreek on the Romans during the siege of Jotapata (*The Jewish War*, Book 3, Chapter 7, Verse 29.) He may have offered to betray the Jews and work for Vespasian to save his own life and later invented the prophecy as a cover-up, but that hardly seems to account for the amount of imperial appreciation shown towards him. Josephus tells us that when Jerusalem believed he was killed at Jotapata, the whole city mourned for a month. Upon finding out he was still alive, had betrayed them, and gone over to the side of the Romans, they became more determined to fight (*Josephus, Jewish War*, Book 3, Chapter 9). This is hard to believe, but yet another problem with Josephus as an eyewitness is that the emphasis is on his own experiences in the war. He describes the war in Galilee, in detail, but not so much what happened in the areas where the other generals were assigned (*Josephus, Jewish War*, Book 2, Chapter 20). *The Jewish War*, therefore, is more of a 'Josephus war memoir', rather than a comprehensive history of the war. Josephus also claims Titus did not want the Temple destroyed (*Josephus, Jewish War*, Book 6, Chapter 4). However, the Fourth Century

Christian historian **Sulpicius Severus** contradicts this, perhaps citing a lost passage from Tacitus' Histories, he wrote that Titus wanted to destroy the Temple. Josephus even appears to contradict himself when he wrote in The Antiquities of the Jews that:

> "Titus took the temple and the city, and burned them." (Josephus, Antiquities of the Jews, Book 20, Chapter 10)

Is it possible that in The Jewish War Josephus was 'covering up' Titus' role in the temple's destruction? From the Roman perspective, the destroying of the temple represented the victory of the Roman gods over the intolerant and exclusive God of the Jews. But Josephus did not believe Judaism had been discredited, and he tried to explain it in the same way that the prophets had explained the destruction of the first temple, by Nebuchadnezzar. God was again punishing the Jews for their sins, by letting the temple fall (Josephus, Jewish War, Book 4, Chapter 6). Titus had not defeated Yahweh, according to Josephus, he was Yahweh's 'instrument' or 'tool' for punishing his rebellious people. (Feldman, L.H., "*Josephus: Interpretative Methods and Tendencies*" in Evans, C.A. and Porter, S.E. (editors), Dictionary of New Testament Background (Illinois: IVP, 2000), p597) 'After the death of Titus, Josephus found a new support in **Epaphroditus**, who is said to have had a 30,000 volume library. Josephus may have had access to this library, since, in his later works, his knowledge of Jewish and Pagan literature had improved.' (Feldman, "Josephus: Interpretative Methods and Tendencies", p592-593, Josephus, Antiquities of the Jews 2:2:1, 2:4:2, 2:9:5, 6:4:1, 6:8:1, 7:8:5).

In his final work, **Against Apion**, another apologetic work, he argued that the Jews were an ancient people who should make respectable in the eyes of Greco-Roman culture, which regarded the old as worthwhile. Josephus made another valuable contribution by citing historians, like the Egyptian **Manetho**, and preserving passages that would have otherwise been lost.

A Specific Understanding of Jewish Prophesies

Josephus brings to history a specific understanding of the Jewish Prophesies and how the Jews are being cursed because of their rebellion against Rome. This is something that many people have noticed, he is describing the same curse that Jesus does, in terms of the end of the covenant between God and the Jews. The *War of the Jews* reports, through Josephus about himself, that he was a member of all 3 of the Jewish sects, as previously mentioned, and they all had somewhat different beliefs. Again, as mentioned earlier, he was an **Essene**, a **Sadducee,** and a **Pharisee**, at certain points in his life, which is very hard to believe. If you were to look at the scrolls, leaving a particular sect did not seem like something you could do at that time, because you would get killed. Josephus claims this background, and also says he was an emissary to Rome, sent as a diplomatic representative on a special mission. He goes to Rome and meets Emperor Nero and his wife, Poppaea, and they give him presents and he seems to be familiar with court manners. When the war breaks out between the Romans and the Jews, despite this relationship he has with Rome, they make him the general of the Jewish military forces in Galilee.

Remember, Josephus is a *high priest* of *royal descent* and is using a diplomatic approach with Roman royalty. Considering the above information, it is unlikely that they would make him a general in the Jewish military forces, it's possible but highly unlikely.

So here we have a Priest, who is not just any Priest, he is from the family of **Matthias**, which would be the **Hasmonean Royal family**, so he has a very powerful ancestry. Now, because he claims to have been an **Essene**, a **Sadducee**, and a **Pharisee**, it's important to understand and compare these different sects:

The **Sadducees** rejected the Oral Law as was proposed by the Pharisees, and rather they saw the written **Torah** as the sole source of **divine authority**. The written law, in its depiction of the priesthood, confirmed the power and enforced the leadership of the **Sadducees** in Judean society.

According to **Josephus**, the Sadducees believed that:

There is no fate, God does not commit evil, man has free will; "man has the free choice of good or evil", the soul is not immortal; there is no afterlife, and there are no rewards or penalties after death. The Sadducees did not believe in the resurrection of the dead, whereas the Pharisees did.

The **Pharisees** believed that:

God would send the Jews a messiah who would bring peace to the world and rule from Jerusalem. They also believed that all circumstances that affected the lives of Jews were divinely ordained. The Sadducees rejected the notion of spirits or angels, whereas the Pharisees acknowledged them.

The **Essenes** held themselves to a higher standard of being religious – including voluntary poverty, abstinence, and other forms and degrees of severe self-discipline. Additionally, they lived in a tighter community (Jerusalem had an "Essene Quarter"). Some of them took a more radical approach to this communalism and established the community of **Qumran**, which produced the **Dead Sea Scrolls**. They appear to have had heightened respect for Moses, a strict interpretation of the law, and for following their own sacrificial system.

We also have the **Zealots** who believed that change could only be effected in the ruling powers (i.e. Rome) through force, and likely had no real religious leader.

It is important to compare these various sects with modern-day Christianity, with its varied denominations. This would mean in today's understanding, that Josephus would perhaps have been a member of the **Catholic Church**, the **Methodist Church**, and would be a **Jehovah's Witness**, going from one belief to another. That would be impossible for Josephus to do, with his position as a 'High Priest' and being from the Royal Hasmonean family, who were following the **Saducean** belief, it would have been very odd for that time. When the war between the Jews and the Romans breaks out, he and his forces are captured by the Romans, **Vespasian**, and **Titus Flavius**, but before they capture him something odd happens. According to Josephus, he was trapped in a cave with 40 of his men, and Vespasian and his son Titus asked the group to surrender, but they refused. Josephus suggests they play a mathematical game to see who would commit suicide first, and, in the end, Josephus is the last person alive, along with another individual. They decide not to commit suicide and are captured, and now Josephus claims to go into a religious trance and he comes out of it and they take him to Vespasian. Josephus informs Vespasian that he will be Caesar, but they say they will take him to Emperor **Nero**, but Josephus says no, Nero is dead, you will be Caesar. Vespasian is surprised by the prophecy, but it turns out to be correct, and they say Josephus appears to be a prophet and Josephus says God's good favor that had been given to the Jews, the covenant described in the Torah, is gone and the covenant is now with Rome. This is a complete rewrite of the Jewish prophecies, and mainstream historians being skeptical about the historicity of Josephus' prophecy to Vespasian, makes Josephus even more suspicious as a reliable source.

Josephus even wrote that his revelation had taught him three things-that God, the creator of the Jewish people, had decided to "**punish**" them, that "**fortune**" had been given to the Romans, and that **God** had chosen him "**to announce the things that are to come**." Josephus is saying that all the Jewish prophecies looking to Messiahs, who would be the ancestor of *'David'*, predict the **Flavian Caesar reign**. David, who in the Hebrew Bible is the second King of the United Kingdom of Israel and Judah, is, according to the biblical narrative, a young shepherd who first gains fame as a musician and who later kills Goliath. In Josephus' writings, the story continues with them saying that Josephus is a prophet, and they consider him useful, and so they brought him into their world. Following the war, they brought him back to Rome, gave him a wife, and gave him a townhouse in the Emperor's Palace, and they asked him to write the official version of the war, which became what's known in history as **The War of the Jews**. That book has always been linked with the origins of Christianity because the prophecies that Jesus makes about the future are "understood" as having been correct and having come to pass, after all, Josephus recorded them. What Josephus wrote is the same concept being described within the Gospels, all the Jewish prophesies are being connected to this person Jesus Christ, who is pro-Roman and is clearly against the Pharisees. The one thing that seems to confuse many people is the '**son of man**' who Jesus refers to, who will come in the future, and there will be some apocalyptic events which will take place, the question is, who is this 'son of man'? Josephus even writes at the dramatic conclusion of The War of the Jews, that the Jews rebelled because they were expecting a different Messiah, the Son of David, but according to **Josephus**, the 'son of man' and 'messiah' is the **Flavian Caesar**.

Josephus was also the first person to make mention of an individual who is thought to be the Jesus of the Gospels, however, the authenticity of what Josephus wrote is hotly debated. Here is what Flavius Josephus writes:

"Now there was about this time Jesus, a wise man, if it be lawful to call him a man; for he was a doer of wonderful works, a teacher of such men as receive the truth with pleasure. He drew over to him both many of the Jews and many of the Gentiles. He was [the] Christ. And when Pilate, at the suggestion of the principal men amongst us, had condemned him to the cross, those that loved him at the first did not forsake him; for he appeared to them alive again the third day; as the divine prophets had foretold these and ten thousand other wonderful things concerning

him. And the tribe of Christians, so named from him, are not extinct at this day".

So here we have a clear mention of someone named Jesus that fits with the accounts mentioned in the Gospels, and appears to come from a person in a position of authority. This statement appears in his 'Antiquities of the Jews' in Book 18, Chapter 3, section 3 (Whiston's translation). The statement, known as the '**Testimonium Flavianum**', is actually talking about an individual known as Jesus ben Damneus, or Jesus son of Damneus, who was a Herodian-era High Priest of Israel in Jerusalem. Further, scholars have argued that this mention likely resulted from the accidental insertion of a marginal note added by a copyist between the time of Origen of Alexandria, an early Christian scholar, and Eusebius, a historian of Christianity. Scholars have also argued that anything within the works of Josephus that appear too Christian, were added by later Christians. However, I will present my argument at the end of the book explaining why that cannot be the case, as understanding why the above statement was <u>not</u> a later addition, and why it was worded the way it was, requires understanding the information explained in the rest of the book.

3. THE GOSPELS AND JOSEPHUS: THE PARALLELS

NOTE

If you are already familiar with these parallels, please feel free to continue to the next chapter.

As explained earlier, the books of '**Mark**' and '**Matthew**' present an example of a typology that will continue throughout all of the Gospels. The author(s) of the Gospel of '**Mark**' has taken stories from the **Old Testament** and placed them into their story of the pre-ministry of **Jesus**; if you are unsure of what typology is, it is simply basing one character upon another and is found throughout the Hebraic literature in the Old Testament, to link one prophet to another prophet.

The author(s) of the Gospel of '**Mark**' have taken **names, locations**, and **concepts** from the **Old Testament**, and used them in their story about **Jesus Christ**, and these stories appear in the same sequence. When comparing one story to the other, the **Old Testament** with the **New Testament**, you can see that **Moses** was directly connected to the character the author of '**Mark**' is writing about, that character being **Jesus Christ**.

Moses was chosen as the example of Jesus because he was the first savior of Israel, and by connecting Jesus directly to Moses, it can be portrayed that Jesus Christ is also a savior of Israel. This shows that the early life of the character Jesus Christ is fiction and not original or historical, which means the events in his early life have been taken from another book, which means the rest of his ministry must be questioned.

Investigating Further

When examining the rest of Jesus' ministry, it becomes clear that it is *all* taken from another book. The ministry of Jesus parallels the military campaign of the Roman **Titus Flavius**, and, as mentioned before, Flavius Josephus recorded the events and activities from the Roman military campaign in Judea, involving Vespasian, and Titus, who was partly responsible for the destruction of Jerusalem in 70 CE. I say partly because he did not act alone regarding this event, but for now, we will focus on the parallels below.

Helpful Resources

To see the parallels discussed below for yourself, it is highly recommended that you obtain either the online versions or print versions of both the **Gospels** and the **Loeb Classical Library translation of The Jewish War** and **Whiston's translation of The War of the Jews by Josephus**; Whiston was a professor of mathematics at Cambridge University and published his translation of Josephus' work in 1737. His translation is the only single volume widely available, however, the Greek manuscripts he used are now not considered the best. The Loeb Classical Library, conceived by James Loeb in 1912, was originally published in London, UK, but is now published by Harvard University Press. Both translations will allow you to go step by step and see the connections examined below which cannot be considered a coincidence, only deliberate, because mathematically there are too many of them. It is also very important to remember, as Joseph Atwill himself has stated, that this examination of the parallels between the *Gospels* and *The Wars of the Jews* **cannot** go outside of the immediate text that is being examined. That means the examination is confined to precise areas of text, which is how a disciplined examination of this subject matter should be conducted.

BEFORE JESUS' MINISTRY BEGAN

Beginning with **John 4:7-21**, at **Mount Gerizim**, Jesus describes himself as "**living water**", and this is the *exact* spot where the war would come to and can be considered ironic, just like a story called '**Cannibal Mary**' in *The Wars of the Jews* during the siege of Jerusalem, and the "*living bread*" in the Gospels, as will be examined below. Josephus' **Wars of the Jews**, **Book 3**, **Whiston Chapter 7**, **Section 32**, **Page 307-309** mentions **Mount Gerizim** and the Jews being starved to death and dying of thirst by the Romans. These are the only two places that the Mount is mentioned in the Bible or Josephus, and it is also the only time in which Jesus refers to himself as "*living water*".

In the passage of **John** above, it appears, from what we are about to examine, that Jesus is said to be predicting the Roman destruction of Mount Gerizim and Jerusalem.

> The events begin at the same location for both Jesus and Titus, the **Sea of Galilee**.

I am inclined to hold the view that a place called Nazareth, which would become associated with the Jesus character, did not exist until the fourth century CE. One reason is that no other source, other than the New Testament, confirms this place existed before the first century CE. However, we cannot use an effective *'argument from silence'* or *'absence of evidence'* here, as we *do* have mentions of Nazareth, the question is, can we trust the sources? The other reason is that the word *'Nazarene'* (as in Jesus the Nazarene) is a Greek form of the Hebrew word netzer/netser, meaning **'branch'**. The location of Nazareth eventually came into question, and the authors of the Gospels must have known this would happen. Because of this, Helena, the mother of Emperor Constantine, used her "faith" and had a "vision" that the place they needed to build Nazareth was Japha. That was because the campaign of Titus started in Japha/Jaffa, which means the battles that Jesus has in Nazareth in the Gospels, symbolizes Titus at Japha/Jaffa in *The Wars of the Jews*.

But it would seem that the authors of the Gospels tried to confuse matters by having four Gospels instead of just one. But what is known, is that 'Nazarene' or 'Nazorean' was the name of an early Jewish sect, which was an off-shoot of the Essenes.

They had no particular relation to the city of Nazareth, but their name may mean '**truth**', or '**branch**', as mentioned above, with the plural of netzer/netser becoming 'Netzoreem'. There is no mention of the Nazarenes in any of St. Paul's writings, although Paul is himself accused of *being* a Nazorean in *Acts of the Apostles*, even though we are told he is from Tarsus; although 'Paul' does not mention many biographical details of Jesus, so we could argue why he should mention this location. The importance of why the authors chose to use the word 'Nazarene' in regards to the Jewish religion will be explained later in this chapter; an in-depth article on this issue can be found at www.henryhdavis.com.

Mark. 1:14-19, Matthew 4:18-21, and Luke 5:1-11

Jesus – At the Sea of Galilee, Jesus comes and tells his disciples *'Follow me, and I will make you become fishers of men.'*

Titus – This is mirrored by the experience that Titus has. He won a great ship battle against the Jews, and according to **Josephus**, in **The War of the Jews, Whiston Book 3, Chapter 10, Verse 1-9**, the Jews escaped in their boats into the **Sea of Galilee**. Titus' men pursued them in their own faster boats and upturned them or destroyed them. The Jews fell into the sea and Josephus writes *"and for such as were drowning in the sea, if they lifted their heads up above the water, they were either killed by darts, or caught by vessels"*.

The parallel here is that the soldiers were trying to catch the Jews in the sea, in other words, they were '**fishing**' for the Jewish rebels in the **Sea of Galilee**. After the battle, the lake water was covered with dead floating Jewish bodies.

Titus essentially said to his men *"don't be afraid, follow me"*, so his men went out into the sea to attempt to destroy the Jewish rebels who are in their fishing boats. The boats are sunk, the Jews attempt to swim to safety and the Romans catch the men like they were fish. But it is important to realize that the typological connection that was mentioned before in '**Mark**', to connect **Jesus** to **Moses**, ends *directly before* this part, then just a few lines later we have this parallel connection between **Jesus** and **Titus**. It is also very important to note that the connection between **Jesus** and **Moses** is something that scholars *do not* dispute and that the connection was deliberately created. But the '**Sea of Galilee**' connection above is the **same location** *and* it is at the **beginning** of the events of both of these individuals. Josephus even mentions the 'Coracin fish' of Capharnaum, and Jesus is said to have performed 'mighty works' in 'Chorazin', but these towns rejected his work.

But let's continue...

Jesus – The next parallel event, after the *fishing for/catching men* parallel, is in **Luke 4:31-34** and **Mark 1:21-28**, where Jesus goes to **Capernaum** and casts out a demon, but not before the demon was to recognize him as God.

Titus/Josephus – In Josephus' **Wars of the Jews**, Book 4, **Chapter 7** and his autobiography **Life Of Flavius Josephus**, 72, **402-403**, Josephus writes about a 'John' beginning to tyrannize (as if possessed by a demon) in **Capernaum**, where he also announced to the Jews that Titus was the Messiah.

Jesus – The next parallel event we find is in **Matthew 8:14-17**, **Mark 1:29-34** and **Luke 4:40-41**. In an unnamed town, Jesus cast out demons that inhabited the whole town and they recognized him as the savior.

Titus – In Josephus' **Wars of the Jews**, **Book 3**, **Chapter 9**, in the town of Tiberius, Titus was called savior and, according to Josephus, cast out all the demons infecting the whole town.

Jesus – The next parallel event is in **Mark 1:35-39** and **Luke 4:42-43**. Jesus talks about the "*good news*", in Greek, the word is '*Evangelion*', as mentioned earlier.

Titus/Flavians/Josephus – According to Josephus' **Wars of the Jews**. The same word was used by The Flavians to announce big events and military victories.

Jesus – The next parallel event is in **Matthew 9:1-8**, **Mark 2:1-12** and **Luke 5:22-26**. When Jesus asks the question "*Which is easier, to say your sins are forgiven or rise up and walk*"?

Titus –The question is answered satirically in Josephus, **War of The Jews**, when Titus is being talked out of letting some Jewish prisoners go he says, "*It is easier to say rise and walk than to forgive*".

Jesus – The next parallel event is in **Matthew 12:1-8, Mark 2:23-28** and **Luke 6:1-6**, when Jesus says he *"keeps the Sabbath holy better than the Pharisees"* and *'heals the right hand of someone in the temple while on the Sabbath'*, *"it is better to save life than to lose it"*.

Titus – In Josephus' **Wars of the Jews**, Titus said he was better at keeping the Sabbath than the Jews. And on the Sabbath when a Jewish prisoner stretched out his right-hand begging not to be killed, Titus says *"it's better to save a life on the Sabbath than to lose it"*. On the Sabbath, Titus sends Josephus who offers the Jews "his" (*Titus'*) *right hand* ("security of Rome") to surrender, but they refuse because they cannot go for peace on the Sabbath.

Jesus – The next parallel event is in **Matthew 5:1-12** and **Luke 6:22**. Jesus reassures two followers who were being hated and cast out for him.

Titus – In Josephus' **Wars of the Jews**, Titus reassures pro-Roman Jewish priests, Jesus and Animus, after they were being hated and cast out.

Jesus – The next parallel event we find is in **Matthew 8:5-13** and **Luke 7:1-9**. It describes a Roman Centurion, whose faith in Jesus is so great, he believes that Jesus can heal his slave without going into his house. He likens Jesus to a Roman soldier who orders those under him to come and go.

Titus – In Josephus' ***Wars of the Jews***, Titus tells his men there is no need to go into the city because God is acting as a Roman soldier and causing the Jews to kill themselves. When the Gospels describe an illness or demonic possession of a Jew, it refers to the "fever" that caused them to rebel against Rome, "healing" them means either conversion or death.

Jesus – The next parallel event is in **Matthew 11:2-19** and **Luke 7:33-35**. John the Baptist is possessed by a demon and tax collectors are said to be friends, which must be an inside joke because the Flavians were the most notorious tax collectors in history.

Titus – In Josephus' ***War of the Jews***, the rebel John is said by Josephus to have a demon of wickedness.

Jesus/ Titus – The next parallel event is in **Matthew 8:28-34**, **Mark 5:1-20** and **Luke 8:26-33**, where we have the story of the **Demons of Ghidorah**. This story is an *exact parallel* to the **Battle of Ghidorah** that **Titus** had, and in the story, you can read what happens to the herd, where they rush to, and how they drowned.

Mark 5:9 and **Luke 8:30** tells of Jesus asking for the name of a demon and casting out a demon named **"Legion"**, and the demon says *"we are many"*. The demon asks to be sent to the pigs on a hillside and then the whole heard of pigs, about two thousand, all rushed down the side of the hillside, into the lake and drowned.

In Josephus' **War of the Jews**, he describes a legion of Jews with a demonic (rebellious) spirit against Rome-

Titus reaches **Gadara**, and a **legion** of **Jewish militants** (rebels), called **Sicarii**, who are led to a revolt by the rebel leader John, began to rush around and rush to the hills like '*swine possessed by demons*', after being attacked with Roman darts. These rebels run and fall off the cliff into the River Jordan, and there were so many dead bodies floating in the river, the army could not cross it, and **both** accounts say the bodies totaled about **two thousand**. Josephus also said "*from one head this wickedness came forth*", and that the first group affected a second group that became just as bad. It may be fair to speculate that '**swine**' was how the authors thought of the **rebels**. In Josephus' story, after the battle, the Jewish leader **hides in the tombs**, and in the **Gospels**, the **demon hides in the tombs**, and in Josephus' story there is **one rebel leader** and in the Gospel, **there is one demon**. Josephus wrote the names of two of the rebel leaders were **John** and **Simon**. Also, an interesting point to make is that '**Gadara**' is defined by Josephus as 'possessing' territory, 'which lay on the frontiers of the Sea of Galilee'.

Also, all of the four great ancient **uncial codices**, which contained the entire text of the Old and New Testament (Greek Bible), record **Gadara**, the only thing different is the form in which the location is presented. In the Gospel of '**Matthew**', the location is presented as '**Gadarenes**', in the **Codex Vaticanus**. In the Gospel of '**Mark**', the **Codex Vaticanus** has '**Gerasenes**', but the **Codex Alexandrinus** and **Codex Ephraemi** have '**Gadarenes**'. In the Gospel of '**Luke**', Gadara is presented in the **Codex Alexandrinus** has '**Gadarenes**' and the **Codex Sinaiticus** has '**Gergesenes**'.

Jesus – The next parallel event we have is in **Matthew 8:23-27**, **Mark 4:35-41**, and **Luke 8:23-26**. Jesus is said to have power over wind and rain.

Titus – In Josephus' ***Wars of the Jews***, it says the same thing.

Jesus – The next parallel event is in **Matthew 16:13-19**, **Mark 8:27-29**, and **Luke 9:18-20**, where Jesus claims to be '*The Christ of God*', in **Matthew**, '*the son of the living God*'.

Titus – In Josephus' ***Wars of the Jews***, Titus says he is "*the son of the living God*".

ON THE ROAD TO JERUSALEM

Jesus – The next parallel event is in **Luke 9:51-56**. This is where Jesus left Galilee for Jerusalem and sent messengers ahead of him. They went into a Samaritan village to get things ready for him, but the people there would not receive him.

Titus – In Josephus' ***Wars of the Jews***, it says that Titus left Galilee and headed straight for Jerusalem. He sends his messengers in advance to warn Jews to surrender, otherwise it may be too late, but the Jews refuse to surrender.

Jesus – The next parallel event is in **Luke 9:59-62**, where Jesus scolds one of his followers for wanting to bury his dead and tells them to follow him.

Titus – In Josephus' **Wars of the Jews**, after a defeat, Titus tells his soldiers not to bury their dead, but to follow him.

Jesus – The next parallel event we find is in **Luke 10:1-22**. Jesus sends out the seventy-two and says "*All things have been committed to me by my Father. No one knows who the Son is except the Father and no one knows who the Father is except the Son and those to whom the Son chooses to reveal him.*"

Titus – In Josephus' **Wars of the Jews**, it is an address by Titus about his destruction of Galilee and his sending of troops to Jerusalem and the hidden identity of the God and his father Vespasian.

Jesus – The next parallel event is in **Luke 10:25-37** the story of the Samaritan left half-dead.

Cestius Gallus – In Josephus' **Wars of the Jews**, whilst on the road to Jerusalem, **Cestius Gallus**' army had been attacked by a group of rebel Jews, and their mules and other belongings were taken away. Cestius meets this legion on the way to Jerusalem and goes to the good people of Samaria to get his army fixed up.

The Good Samaritan is a story in the Gospel which describes someone who has been on the road to **Samaria**, he's attacked by a group of robbers and they **steal his mule** and **they beat him up**.

At this point in the ***War of the Jews***, **Cestius Gallus** appears with the 12th Legion, and Josephus recounts how well they have been refurbished. The 12th Legion was **attacked by a group of Jewish rebels on the road**, in the pass of **Beth Horon**, which is in **Samaria**. The rebels **stole the Legions mules**, **stripped them of their clothes and goods**, and left them **half dead**. Cestius, who is described as coming through **Samaria**, refurbished the Legion and is now walking with them to **Jerusalem**. **Josephus** and the **Gospels** use the same Greek word for '**robbers**' 'leistes' λησταις.

So the story of the **Good Samaritan**, which has had many things written about it, regarding what it means and what exactly Jesus is talking about, appears to be a representation of *Cestius Gallus* refurbishing a legion, and then going forward to wage war against the Jews.

OUTSIDE JERUSALEM

Both of these individuals arrive outside Jerusalem and they pause. In the case of Titus, he pauses because he needs to organize his triumphant entrance into the city. The same is true for **Jesus**, but it is not clear why he does not just walk in at this particular point, but he does not, he stays outside the city and is involved in several events. But, when you compare the events between **Jesus** and **Titus**, when they are *out-*

side of Jerusalem, the connections between the two become very clear.

Jesus – In **Luke 11:5-12**. Jesus says, *"Suppose you have a friend, and you go to him at midnight and say, "Friend, lend me* **three loaves of bread** *a friend of mine on a journey has come to me, and I have no food to offer him"…. "Or would you give him a scorpion when he asks for an egg."*

Titus – Josephus' **Wars of the Jews Book, Book 5, Chapter 2** also documents the three legions outside of Jerusalem, the three loaves of bread are needed to feed the three armies, and the scorpion mentioned is the name of a Roman artillery piece also called a ballista.

Jesus – The next parallel event is in **Matthew 12:25, Mark 3:20-30,** and **Luke 11:17-20**, where Jesus says the house of Satan (which, as is become clearer, is Jerusalem) is divided against itself and cannot stand.

Titus – In Josephus' **Wars of the Jews**, as the army is still outside the walls of Jerusalem, says that the house of Satan (the Jews) is divided and cannot stand.

Jesus – The next parallel event is in **Matthew 12:22-30, Mark 3:20-27,** and **Luke 11:21-23**. It says a man with armor and weapons will meet someone and be overcome.

Titus – In Josephus' **Wars of the Jews**, it says the same thing.

Jesus – The next parallel event is in **Matthew 12:38-42** and **Luke 11:29**, which records the crowds increasing.

Titus/Josephus – Josephus' **Wars of the Jews** says the same thing. When Titus arrives outside the city, his army is attacked by Jews who fight him first outside the city walls.

Woe saying Jesus.

Now there is a parallel that we can call the '*Woe Saying Jesus*'. In both **Josephus** and the **Gospels** you have the character called **Jesus**, who goes into a long recital of woes, he uses the word woe repeatedly. This Jesus character in Josephus has many connections to the character in the Gospels, and many scholars have written about them. But what hasn't been recognized, is that the woe saying Jesus appears at the **same place** in both accounts.

The Josephus Jesus –

The Jesus in Josephus enters Jerusalem during a pilgrimage festival, and he delivers a **Woe Oracle** against Jerusalem and is seized by the leading citizens. Both the **Josephus Jesus** and the **Jesus in the Gospels** are **beaten** and later **scourged** (whipped as a punishment). Neither one of them answers a direct question during the interrogation, they are both taken to the Roman procurator, and both of them prophecize their death and then both of them die. This is another direct connection between Josephus and the Gospels and is a very clear example of typology. The author(s) of the Gospels at this point appear to be creating this character Jesus Christ in the Gospel and using characters from Josephus to create the context. But there is a distinct connection following that event between the so-called "***innocence being beaten worse than the guilty***", which is a very unusual concept in itself, and in both books, it occurs immediately following the '**woe saying Jesus**'.

Jesus – So, we have the parallel event in **Luke 11:43-52**, **The "woe-saying" Jesus**.

Titus - Josephus' **Wars of the Jews**, **Book 6**, **Chapter 5**, describes an individual called *Jesus ben Ananias* doing the following things, which are identical to the Gospel Jesus: **1)** they enter Jerusalem during a festival **2)** they deliver an oracle against the temple **3)** they are seized by leading citizens **4)** they are beaten and later scourged **5)** they offer no answer to interrogations **6)** they are taken to the Roman prosecutor **7)** they are called madmen **8)** they prophesy their death and **9)** they die.

Jesus – The next parallel event is in **Matthew 22:15-19**, **Mark 12:13-17 and Luke 12:53**. Jesus said that the Jews were trying to trap him.

Titus – Josephus' **Wars of The Jews** says the same thing.

Jesus – The next parallel event is in **Matthew 24:45-51** and **Luke 12:47-48**. Jesus says the innocent will be **beaten worse than the guilty**.

Titus – Josephus' **Wars of the Jews** says the same thing.

Jesus – The next parallel event is in **Matthew 7:13-14** and **Luke 13:22-30**, where Jesus talks about the narrow gate at the city wall, and the master of the house will get up and close the door.

Titus – In Josephus' **Wars of the Jews**, Titus is described as saying the same words. Also, both texts describe the city before entering. We read a description of where the Roman siege apparatus has given the Jews only a very narrow door, and Josephus then records the points of a compass that described how this door has been shut, and Jesus has a story that has these exact concepts.

The Fig Tree

A trivial parallel, but a parallel nonetheless.

Jesus – The next parallel event, which is in **Matthew 7: 17-19** and **Mark 11:12-14**, has Jesus cursing a Fig-Tree, saying if it does not bear fruit then it should be cut down and thrown in the fire.

Titus – In Josephus' **War of The Jews, Book 5, Chapter 3, Verse 2** Titus, who is intending to pitch his camp nearer to the city, gave orders for the whole army to level the distance and to cut down all the fruit trees, "*...he gave orders for the whole army to level the distance, as far as the wall of the city. So they threw down all the hedges and walls, which the inhabitants had made about their gardens and groves of trees; and cut down all the fruit trees, that lay between them and the wall of the city...*"

Jesus – The next parallel is in and **Luke 14:28-30**, where Jesus discusses how to best build a tower.

Titus – In Josephus' **Wars of the Jews**, **Book 5**, **Chapter 7**, Titus does build a tower specifically outside the wall of Jerusalem.

Jesus – The next parallel event is in **Luke 14:31-32**, Jesus says every king before going into battle asks for peace and will send messengers to ask for peace.

Titus – In Josephus' **Wars of the Jews**, **Book 5**, **Chapter 9**, Titus sends a delegation to find peace.

INSIDE THE CITY

Jesus – The next parallel event is in **Luke 19:39-41**. Luke describes Jesus' entrance into the city and Jesus saying *"if disciples were to be quiet, then the stones themselves would cry out"* and that if they (the Jews) only knew today the things needed for peace, but now it has been hidden from their eyes.

In Josephus' **Wars of the Jews**, it describes Titus' entrance into the city, where stones being hurled by catapults 'cried out'. In the Gospels, you have the triumphant entrance of **Jesus**, and the people cry out **"the son has come"**. You then have an odd moment where Jesus is told by the Pharisees to make these people quiet down, but he says *"oh no if they were quiet* **the stones themselves would cry out**". Then Jesus goes on and states that something has been **"hidden from your eyes."** Theologically, and generally, this statement does not make a lot of sense, **'the stones themselves would cry out'**, **'something has been hidden from your eyes'**, what exactly does Jesus mean?

It is only when this story in the Gospels is read parallel to, and **in context** with what **Josephus** wrote in **War of the Jews**, at that **exact point**, that the meaning becomes clear, but only when you read **Josephus**. At this point, a reader could be forgiven for thinking that Josephus made his **"mistake"**. Titus has his entrance into the city, then at this point, Titus fires a stone from a catapult and it goes right into the city, and the Jews have a watchman who cries out when he sees the stone coming. But Josephus did not write that the watchman said a "**stone is coming**", which is what we would expect him to say. What Josephus wrote, and what is presented in the writing, in **Chapter 6 page 789** of the copy of Whiston's Josephus used in this example, was that the watchman cried out "**the Son comes/cometh**", which would appear to be a "mistake". But, when placed in context, this becomes fascinating, and many scholars have tried different ways to explain this "mistake".

Many scholars have been unable to make sense of the statement, "**the Son comes/cometh**", and have resorted to 'correcting' the Greek word '**υιος**' or '**huios**', which is '**son**', with a speculative substitute word that improves the reading for them, but is not true to the original word. Or they have claimed that an alleged mispronunciation of Hebrew words by the rebels explains why Josephus, writing in Greek, supposedly misreported "**the stone comes**" as "**the Son comes**". Many modern translators have simply written that the watchman states that the "**stone is coming**", but what Josephus wrote was "**the Son comes/cometh**", and the Greek Manuscripts say "*theSon cometh*".

Here is what is written in Whiston's translation:

"...As for the Jews, they at first watched the coming of the stone, for it was of a white color, and could therefore not only be perceived by the great noise it made, but could be seen also before it came by its brightness; accordingly, the watchmen that sat upon the towers gave them notice when the engine was let go, and **the**

stone *came from it and cried out aloud in their own language,* **"THE SON COMETH."**

In his detailed note on this passage, the 18th-century translator, Whiston, states:

"What should be the meaning of this signal or watchword, when the watchmen saw a stone coming from the engine, "The Son Cometh," or what mistake there is in the reading, I cannot tell. The MSS. both Greek and Latin, all agree in this reading: and I cannot approve of any groundless conjectural alteration of the text from **huios** to **ios, that not the son or a stone, but that the arrow or dart cometh**, as hath been made by Dr. Hudson, and not corrected by Havercamp. Had Josephus written even his first edition of these books of the War in pure Hebrew, or had the Jews then used the pure Hebrew at Jerusalem, the Hebrew word for a son is so like that for a stone, ben and eben, that such a correction might have been more easily admitted. But Josephus wrote his former edition for the use of the Jews beyond Euphrates, and so in the Chaldee language, as he did this second edition in the Greek language; and bar was the Chaldee word for son, instead of the Hebrew ben, and was used, not only in Chaldea, etc., but in Judea also, as the New Testament informs us: Dio also lets us know, that the very Romans at Rome pronounced the name of Simon the son of Gioras, Bar Poras for Bar Gioras, as we learn from Xiphiline, p. 217. Roland takes notice, "that many will here look for a mystery, as though the meaning were, that the Son of God came now to take vengeance on the sins of the Jewish nation;" which is indeed the truth of the fact, but hardly what the Jews could now mean: unless possibly by way of derision of

Christ's threatening so often that he would come at the head of the Roman army for their destruction. But even this interpretation has but a very small degree of probability. **If I were to make an emendation by mere conjecture, I would read petros instead of huios, though the likeness be not so great as in ios; because that is the word used by Josephus just before, as has been already noted on this very occasion, while ios, an arrow or dart, is only a poetical word, and never used by Josephus elsewhere, and is indeed no way suitable to the occasion, this engine not throwing arrows or darts, but great stones, at this time.**"

Here Whiston points out that "**ios**" is a poetical word that Josephus never uses elsewhere, and the word is not even suitable for the context, as the Roman engine is throwing large stones, not darts or arrows. Some have argued that sound-alike Hebrew words were the reason for Josephus writing "**the Son Comes**", but the problem with that explanation is that first-century Jews spoke Aramaic, not Hebrew. In the *next line* Josephus has written that the **stone** was crying out, and Whiston again very faithfully translates it. In the text, it says "**the stone cries out**", this is followed by a description of the Romans being aware that the Jews can see the stone and so they **blacken it**, they **hide it** from their sight. It is incredibly difficult to believe that Josephus would make the only real error in grammar in his entire book at this exact point in the storyline that the "**Son comes**" in the **Gospels**. The only logical answer at this point is that "the Son Cometh" is referring to how Titus views himself as 'the son of God', because his father Vespasian was deified as a god, and Josephus also wrote, "they are hidden from your eyes". It also makes no sense as to why Josephus would write this, why would he think that the watchman said "*the Son cometh*", considering the context of the moment, the context, of course, being that stones were being hurled.

In the Loeb translation (*Jewish War*, Book V, Verses 268-272, pages 284-285) it reads "**Sonny's coming**":

"*τη πατριω γλωσση βοωντες* "*ὁ υἱός ͑ερχεται.*"

"*...Watchmen were accordingly posted by them on the towers, who gave warning whenever the engine was fired and* **the stone** *in transit, by shouting in their native tongue,* "**Sonny's coming**"; *whereupon those in the line of fire promptly made way and lay down, owing to which precautions* **the stone** *passed harmlessly through...*"

The explanatory note here states:

"*Probably, as Reland suggests, ha-eben ("the stone") was corrupted to habben ("the son").*

Again, this does not explain why the word 'stone' appears just before and a few lines after the incorrect word.

Jesus – The next parallel event we have is in **Luke 19:43-44**. Jesus '**predicts**' the city of Jerusalem being encircled by a wall and says "*Your enemies will pile up earth against your walls and encircle you and close in on you and shall not leave one stone upon another*", this is in the so-called '*abomination of desolation*'.

Titus – In Josephus' **Wars of the Jews**, **Book 5**, **Chapter 12**,

Titus did raise and encircle the city of Jerusalem with a wall and then destroyed every stone.

John's Revelation – In **John's Revelation 16:18 (The Book of Revelation)** it reads – *"And there were noises and thunderings and lightning; and there was a great earthquake, such a mighty and great earthquake as had not occurred since men were on earth."*

Josephus – In Josephus' *War of the Jews* **Book 4, Chapter 4, Verse 5**, Josephus writes *"for there broke out a prodigious storm in the night, with the utmost violence, and very strong winds, with the largest of showers of rain, with continued lightning, terrible thunderings, and amazing concussions and bellowings of the earth, that was in an earthquake. These things were a manifest indication that some destruction was coming upon men."*

Jesus – The next parallel event is in **Mathew 21:12**, **Mark 11:15-19**, and **Luke 19:45-47**, where Jesus drives out the robbers from the temple.

Titus – In Josephus' *Wars of the Jews*, **Book 6, Chapter 5, Verse 1** at this exact point, before destroying the temple, Titus gets control of the area in front of the temple and refers to the group that he's driving out with the same Greek word "ληστων" or '**liston**' that Jesus uses, which indicates that they are robbers or thieves.

Jesus – In **Matthew 24:15-16** and **Daniel 9:26-27** (Hebrew Bible), Jesus predicts that the **abomination of desolation**, which is an event that **Daniel the Prophet** predicted, will come to pass. The Hebrew Bible refers to a prince who will destroy the city of Jerusalem, along with the temple and sacrifices – *"and on the wings of abominations shall come one who makes desolate." "From the time that the daily sacrifice is abolished and the abomination that causes desolation is set up, there will be* **1,290 days***."* **1,290** days, or three and a half years, is the exact period of Titus' military campaign in Judea, according to Josephus, and he records that the abomination of desolation occurred at this **exact point**.

The passage ends with Jesus talking about the coming of the **'Son of Man'** and promising that *"this generation will not pass away until all these things have taken place"*. In that time a generation was considered **40** years of a lifetime among Jews, and so the destruction of the Temple happened within the lifetime of **that** generation. **The Abomination of Desolation** came to pass with the actions of Titus Flavius, but the above indicates that Josephus wrote this parallel to indicate that the 'prophecy' of Daniel came to pass with the destruction of Jerusalem, which also connects to the old Bible as well. At this point so far, we have parallel events which include the *fruit tree*, the **Son comes**, and the **stone crying out**. We then have the things that cannot be disputed, the **encircling of Jerusalem with the wall, the driving of the thieves and robbers away from the area directly in front of the temple**, and the **abomination of desolation**. It is simply impossible for these unique events and parallels to be a coincidence. But the crucial point to realize is that these events take place in the **same sequence** in **both books**. That cannot be possible unless it was deliberately done and the authors of the two books were either the same person or people working very closely together.

The Passover lamb, a Last Supper

The following passage refers to **The Passover Lamb**, a Last Supper, where the **son of Mary** (Jesus) becomes a human Passover lamb. This event is the *same concept* as an incident in the **Wars of the Jews** called 'ced **Cannibal Mary**'. The similarities between the "**son of Mary**" described in the *Wars of the Jews*, and the "**son of Mary**" in the **Gospels**, are too precise to have been the product of circumstance, the subject, the context, and placement are the same. **The Passover Lamb** and **Cannibal Mary** are what can be referred to as an *allegory*, meaning it is a story, poem, or picture that can be interpreted to reveal a hidden meaning, typically a moral or political one. This was regarded as a science in Josephus' time and educated readers were expected to be able to understand another meaning within *religious* and *historical literature*. The 'Apostle Paul', for example, stated that passages from the Hebrew Scriptures were allegories that looked forward to Christ's birth.

The famous passage "Cannibal Mary" in Josephus

The following passage by Josephus (*Jewish War*, VI, 193) is using allegory to reveal something else about Jesus. According to the New Testament, **Jesus** is the **human Passover lamb**, and in the passage of '**Cannibal Mary**', it says that the **human Passover lamb is a myth for the world,** whose killing is going to be seen as an **atrocity by gentiles** that will create bitter **hatred against the Jews.** This is precisely what happened in the Bible, Jesus was killed when he became a human Passover sacrifice (lamb) and the Jews received the blame. But by knowing the history surrounding that time, and by what we have examined above, it appears this is the message the Bible describes. It describes a *"curse"* that was put on the Jews by the Romans for their constant rebellion. It is saying that because of the Jews, the Passover Lamb (Jesus) will be killed and the world will blame the Jews. If this religion was a creation of the Roman aristocracy, then we may be correct in thinking their plan backfired, because there are plenty of Jews still around today. If this was the plan, why are Christians worshiping a Jew and not Titus, a Roman Caesar today? Well, they are, because **Pope**, meaning 'father' in Greek, is another title for **Caesar**, and is Caesar's successor. It has been mentioned, on more than one occasion, that the ruling Pope has claimed that the title of Pope is the continuation in the line of Caesar of the Roman Empire.

Here is a statement from Pope Boniface VIII –

*"The papal theory ... made the Pope alone God's representative on Earth and maintained that the Emperor received his right to rule from the successor of 'St. Peter'... It was upheld by Nicholas 1., Hildebrand, Alexander III., Innocent III., and culminated with Boniface VIII. At the jubilee of 1300, when seated on the throne of Constantine, secured with the imperial sword, wearing a crown and waving a scepter, he shouted to the throng of loyal pilgrims: "**I am Caesar – I am Emperor**".*

It's important to remember that there needs to be an explanation for who the '**son of man**' actually is. Some people say it is **Jesus**, and he's talking about himself, but the problem is that Jesus does not come back after the war when he makes these pronouncements, because there would have certainly been some record of it. So the only candidate for this comeback, after the war, is the Roman Caesar, and at the end of the war, Titus tried to get the Jews to call him God because at that time Titus was known as the '*son of God*' because his father **Vespasian** was given the title God by the Roman Senate. The 'son of God' title was written on Titus' sacred arch in Rome, so it would seem the plan was to make the Jews think that the 'son of man' that Jesus was predicting was a Caesar, but that idea was never accepted. The original Jewish Messiah was not a passive cosmopolitan person, he was a Jewish Messiah warrior. The person we read about, however, seems to be a fictional character, and despite popular belief, the 'son of man' who was predicted to come is the Roman Caesar Titus.

Examining the

'Passover Lamb' Last Supper

The passage begins with Josephus speaking in the first person, where he describes the difficulty he is having in writing about an exceptionally gruesome event caused by the famine that occurred during the Roman siege of Jerusalem –

"But why do I describe the shameless impudence that the famine brought on men in their eating inanimate things, while I am going to relate a matter of fact, the like to which no history relates? It is horrible to speak of it, and incredible when heard. I had indeed willingly omitted this calamity of ours that I might not seem to deliver what is so portentous to posterity. But that I have innumerable witnesses to it in my own age..."

Then after, he describes the event:

"There was a certain woman that dwelt beyond Jordan, her name was **Mary**; her father was Eleazar, of the village **Bethezob**, which signifies the **House of Hyssop**. She was eminent for her family and her wealth, and had fled away to Jerusalem with the rest of the multitude, and was with them besieged therein at this time. The other effects of this woman had been already seized upon, such I mean as she had brought with her out of Perea, and removed to the city.

What she had treasured up, besides as also what food she had contrived to save, had been also carried off by the rapacious guards, who came every day running into her house for that purpose. This put the poor woman into a very great passion, and by the frequent reproaches and imprecations she cast at these rapacious villains, she had provoked them to anger against her; but none of them, either out of the indignation she had raised against herself, or out of commiseration of her case, would take away her life; and if she found any food, she perceived her labors were for others, and not for herself; and it was now *become impossible for her anyway to find any more food, while the famine* **pierced** *through her very* **bowels** *and marrow.*

When also her passion was fired to a degree beyond the famine itself: nor did she consult with anything but with her passion and the necessity she was in. She then attempted a most unnatural thing; and snatching up her son, who was a child sucking at her breast, she said, "O thou miserable infant! For whom shall I preserve thee in this war, this famine, and this sedition? As to the war with the Romans, if they preserve our lives, we must be slaves. This famine also will destroy us, even before that slavery comes upon us. Yet are these seditious rogues more terrible than both the other. Come on: be thou my food, and be thou a fury to these seditious varlets, and a by-word to the world, which is all that is now wanting to complete the calamities of us Jews".

As soon as she had said this, she slew her son, and then **roasted** *him, and ate the one half of him, and kept the other half by her concealed. Upon this the seditious came in presently, and smelling the horrid scent of this food, they threatened her that they would cut her throat immediately if she did not show them what food she had gotten ready. She replied that she had saved a* **very fine portion of it for them**, *and withal uncovered what was left to her son. Hereupon they were seized with a horror and amazement of mind, and stood astonished at the sight, when she said to them*

"This is mine own son, and what hath been done was mine own doing! **Come eat of this food (body), for I have eaten of it myself!** *Do not you pretend to be either more tender than a woman, or more compassionate than a mother; but if you be so scrupulous,*

and do abominate this my sacrifice, as I have eaten the one half, let the rest be reserved for me also."

After which those men went out trembling, being never so much affrighted at anything as they were at this, and with some difficulty, they left the rest of that meat to the mother.

It does appear that there are no witnesses to this speech that Mary gives before she kills her son, so the dialogue may have been invented by Josephus, even though the passage seems to have been based on an actual event. But this same concept appears in the Gospels, and to understand the satire within this passage, you need to first understand the phrase "**Bethezob, which signifies the House of Hyssop**". **Beth** is the Hebrew word for '**house**' and **Ezob** is the Hebrew word for '**hyssop**', hyssop being the plant that Moses commanded the Israelites to use when marking their houses with the blood of the sacrificed **Passover lamb**. That mark identified the houses the Angel of Death would *"pass over"*, and so the phrase **House of Hyssop** brings to mind the first **Passover sacrifice**. It is written that God also instructed Moses to prepare the Passover sacrifice by **roasting it in a fire**, it's head with its legs and it's entrails. This relates to this women 'Mary' in Josephus, slaying her son and roasting the body. So, in the passage from the **Wars of the Jews**, Mary's son can be seen as a symbolic Passover lamb, because it shares the same details.

In **Mark 14:22-27**, during the meal, Jesus asked the disciples to eat of his flesh –

"Also during the meal, he took a Passover biscuit, blessed it, and broke it. He then gave it to them, saying, take this, it is my body".

This parallels the eating of the body of the son of Mary in Josephus, and he also connects his Mary to the Mary in the New Testament by another detail he records. He describes the famine as having **"pierced through Mary's very bowels."** In the New Testament, the **piercing through** is predicted for just one person, Jesus' mother **Mary-**

*"Then Simeon blessed them, and said to Mary his mother, behold this child is destined for the fall and rising of many in Israel, and for a sign which will be spoken against (yes, a sword will **pierce through your own soul** also; that the reasonings in many hearts may be revealed.")* **Luke 2:35**

As we can see, both Mary's had their heart pierced. **Psuche** ψυχη, the word translated in the New Testament as '**soul**', can also mean '**heart**', or '**the seat of emotions**'. **Splanchna** σπλαγχνα, the Greek word that Josephus uses to describe the part of Mary that was pierced through, is translated as '**bowels**', but is, in fact, a synonym for '**psuche**', and can mean either '**inward parts**', especially the **heart, lungs, liver,** and **kidneys.** But like 'psuche', it can mean "**the seat of the emotions**", so they are different words, but the words mean the same thing. The most important play on words is found in Josephus when Mary is speaking to her "miserable child", wherein she says "... *be thou a fury to these seditious varlets and a byword to the world, which is all that is now wanting to complete the calamities of us Jews.*" But why would a mother who has eaten her son expect him to become a byword to the world? Also, if taken literally, Mary's words seem confusing and unclear, why would her child become a *fury* to the *varlets*, or, in other words, the Jewish rebels against Rome, by being cannibalized? And why would this "*complete the calamities of us Jews*"?

It just does not make sense in that context.

But within the context relating to Jesus, the meaning of the phrase becomes clear. The author is not just ridiculing Christ, he is saying that Jesus will "*complete the calamity*" of the Jews by becoming a '**byword to the world**', and that the spread of Christianity will "complete" the destruction of the Jews. This interpretation indicates that Christianity was designed to promote anti-Semitism. A group that produced anti-Semitism would have both helped Rome prevent the messianic Jews from continuing and spreading their rebellion, and punished them by "poisoning" their future.

The New Testament has numerous passages that seem deliberately intended to cause Christians to hate Jews, and there are clear examples of this technique throughout the New Testament. The chapter in **Wars of the Jews**, **Book 6**, **Chapter 3**, **Section 4** that contains the "son of Mary" passage, comes to an end with Titus, who, having been told the story of the mother who ate her son's flesh, delivers a sermon on the meaning of the sordid affair. Titus uses the word '**repent**' in his sermon, which is interesting. '**Repent**' is, of course, one of the keywords of Jesus' ministry, and Titus using it brings the parallels even closer. Jesus states repeatedly, *"Repent, the Kingdom of God is at hand"*, but what sin does he want the Jews to repent for? Jesus never answers this question, but from what I can understand, in terms of history, the Jews have done nothing wrong in this situation. What they did do was attempt to stand up to the Romans who were trying to force the Jews to worship them as gods, and continue the system of slavery. In that case, the sin of which Jesus wishes the Jews to repent becomes obvious, it is their rebellion against Rome.

These parts of The Gospels are dark humor, which comes as no surprise when the Latin literature during the Roman Flavian period is examined. They appeared to love their black comedy of the cannibalism that occurred during Titus' siege of Jerusalem, a siege that happened to have occurred on The Passover. Eating the flesh became another prophecy Josephus recorded as coming true, just like the other apparent 'prophecies'. This is why the sacrament, a ceremony regarded as imparting spiritual grace in the Christian Church, particularly in the **Roman Catholic** and many **Orthodox Churches**, is supposed to be symbolizing flesh and blood. It is symbolizing the act of cannibalism because Jesus died, and no record of him returning alive has ever been recorded, so in any other context, this act would be classed as disgusting. But as seen above,

Josephus goes into great detail about a '**Mary**' at the siege of Jerusalem, who he allegorically sets up as '**Mary**' the mother of **Jesus**, and also possibly as a mockery of **The Passover Lamb**. The son of Mary in **Josephus**' writings and the son of Mary in the **Gospels** are the only two human Passover lambs in literary history.

The Crucifixion

There is no parallel to the crucifixion in Josephus' *Wars of the Jews*. Instead, it is in his autobiography, **The Life Of Flavius Josephus**, which discusses the time when Josephus saw **three** of his friends on crosses and asked **Titus** to take them down, which he did, but only **one** lived. This parallels the **Bible**, where there are **three men on a cross** and **one survives**, and both are taken down by a Joseph, with the name **Josephus** being another version of **Joseph**. So again, we see a parallel in both books, this time a **crucifixion of three**, where one survives and **Joseph of Arimathea** (or **Joseph bar Mathia** in **Josephus' story**), takes them down from the cross. Then the conclusion of the Gospels is the prophecy that Jesus makes concerning **Simon** and **John**. Simon will be taken where he **does not want to go, bound, and given a death to glorify God**, and **John will be spared**, and at the conclusion of **Josephus**, the rebel leaders **Simon** and **John** are captured. **John is given never-ending imprisonment** and **Simon's** experience is the same as the prophecy that Jesus gave. The next parallel concerns the length of time of Titus' campaign and Jesus' ministry, in which both lasted **three and a half** years.

That is an examination and introduction to the parallels found within the main story of the Gospels and Josephus' books *Wars of the Jews* and *The Life of Flavius Josephus*. There is undoubtedly an odd connection between the military campaign of **Titus** and the ministry of **Jesus**, and in terms of these parallels being a coincidence, I don't see that as a possible answer, due to the number of them. It tells me that something is not right, that the Jesus of the New Testament appears at this stage to indeed be a fictional character. The events and similarities, when they are compared side by side, point to the conclusion that Jesus' ministry is based upon this Roman individual, **Titus**.

Jesus rising from the dead

The four contradictory Gospel stories of the events at the empty tomb, become one un-contradicted story, if read intertextually, meaning the relationship between texts, especially those of literature, which are similar, reveals that Jesus did not rise from the dead. To begin with, **Mary Magdalene** mistakes **Lazarus'** empty tomb for the empty tomb of **Jesus**, which then creates a lot of confusion. **John's** version occurs first because it is still dark, then **Mark's** version begins *after* **Matthew's**, but *before* **Luke's**. Lazarus was supposedly raised from the dead just a week before Jesus died, leaving an open tomb with burial clothes next to Jesus' tomb (**John 11:44**), and **Lazarus'** tomb is a parallel of **Jesus'** tomb, also, the Sudarium funeral cloth, which is mentioned three times in the Gospels, was never used by the Jews, only the Romans. Since it was dark, it would have been possible to go to the wrong tomb, but of course, we have to take into account that this appears to be made up by the Roman/Jewish aristocratic authors and their knowledge of Judaism. What we have is a four-part puzzle that can be understood in two ways, one is where readers who believe in the story will believe the passages indicate that Jesus rose from the dead. The other is those who don't believe in the story can understand what is happening. As Joseph Atwill has stated, the odds of four different authors accidentally describing their version's of the first visit, beginning with **John's**, then **Matthew's**, followed by **Mark's**, and finally **Luke's** are:

4 x 4 x 4 x 4 or one chance in **256**.

And since the combined story has a total of **21** story elements, the chain of multiplication to determine the probability that four distinct authors could record these exact facts by chance would be –

4 x 3 x 2 x 2 x 2 x 3 x 2 x 2 x 4 x 3 x 2 x 4 x 3 x 2 x 4 x 2 x 3 x 2, or one chance **in 968**.

It is highly unlikely that the first visit story was by four separate authors working apart. It has to have been either one author or multiple authors working closely together, because of all the contradictory things **Mary Magdalene** has to do in the first visit story, it is only possible for there to be four distinct **Mary Magdalenes**. There can indeed be more than one **Mary Magdalene**, just like there can be more than one **Jesus**, for example, **Jesus Barabbas** who was let go at the trial instead of the Messiah Jesus. **Mathew** and **Luke** have different genealogies for Jesus, making him two different people, and

Mary Magdalene is unable to recognize **Jesus** and confuses him with a **gardener** (**John 20:15-16**). Scholars have never known why this is, but the answer is that this passage is a part of the '**Root**' and '**Branch**' system of the **Judaic messianic lineage**, which is a vast literary device that runs through the Gospels and three of Josephus' books. But because it extends over several different books, it is hard to discover. As noted above, this literary device is not unusual in Hebraic literature, it is, for instance, similar to how the **Abraham** saga is continued in the book of **Samuel** and the **Book of Kings**. Through a series of distinct passages, one character becomes associated with another character using parallel acts or locations and through similar language.

The purpose of this particular satire is to say that the "**Root**" and "**Branch**" of the **Judaic messianic lineage** have been destroyed, and a "**Roman lineage**" has been "grafted on" in its place. This satirical literary creation begins in the book of **Malachi**, the final book of the **Old Testament**, Malachi meaning "my messenger" in Hebrew, and was used to express the attributes of the prophet **Elijah**. This is because in Judaic literature it was predicted that the Messiah would be preceded by the appearance of Elijah, who would act as the messenger of his coming:

"But I shall send you Elijah the prophet before the coming of the great and dreadful day of the lord" **Malachi 3:23**

This final passage in the book of **Malachi** predicts a coming disaster for the "wicked", one that will leave them destroyed by fire and with neither "**root**" nor "**branch**":

> "For behold, the day is coming, burning like an oven, and all the proud, yes all who do wickedly will be stubble. And the day which is coming shall burn them up, says the Lord of Host, and will leave them neither root nor branch" **Malachi 3:19**

Josephus records that the **first part** of this prophecy, concerning the "**wicked**" being "**burned up**", happened during the war with the Romans. He also records that the **second part** of the prophecy-they would be left with neither "**root**" nor "**branch**"-was also fulfilled during Titus' campaign, though not so openly.

This is clearly stated in the following quote from **Pliny the Elder**, who later died during the eruption of Mount Vesuvius (79 CE), and dedicated his "Naturalis Historia" to **Titus**:

> "The balsam shrub is native to Judea but was brought to Rome by "the Vespasian emperors" and it now serves Rome and pays tribute along with its race (i.e. Judeans). The Jews did violence to it as also to their own lives, but the Romans protected it in response, and there has been warfare over a bush!"

The Roman historian **Tacitus** also has his horticultural analogy:

> "destroy the vine and destroy also the branch."

Paul also joins with the following from **Romans 11:24**:

"For if thou were to cut out of the olive tree which is wild by nature, and were to be grafted contrary to nature into a good olive tree: how much more shall these, which be the natural branches, be grafted into their own olive tree?"

There is also the analogy made to describe the 'pruning' of the Jewish warrior **Eleazar**, during the siege of Jerusalem, an analogy being something comparable to something else. This is the case when, following the killing of Jesus, **Titus** begins to be '**Jesus of Christianity**'. First, we notice that Mary's mistaking the Messiah for a "**gardener**" and asking if he has "**carried him away**", can be considered ironic. This is exactly what happened to **Eleazar**, who is "**carried away**" by a "**gardener**" on the **Mount of Olives**. The authors have **Mary** *'mistake'* the individual for a "**gardener**" because this creates a satirical prediction in what has already occurred through the war. So it is a mirror image of the Bible story, because while **Jesus** is mistaken *for* a "**gardener**", who has **not** "**carried the Messiah away**", **Titus** becomes a "**gardener**" who **is** mistaken **for Jesus** and who ***does*** "**carry away**" the **Messiah**. In **John 21**, after **Titus** becomes **Jesus**, in the meal with the disciples they are eating the same "**loaf**" that was eaten during the "feast of Lazarus", i.e. real flesh, although fictional flesh in the Bible, but **not** fictional in the Siege of Jerusalem's cannibalism which Josephus wrote about.

To understand that the "**wicked**", or in other words, the **messianic rebels**, were to be left with no "**root**" or "**branch**", it must be understood that what we are examining is perhaps the most complex literary satire that has ever been created. The satire centers around Titus' '**pruning**', or, in other words, attempting to '**domesticate**' the Jewish Messiah **Eleazar**, who was "carried away" on the **Mount of Olives**. We know that the Romans wanted the Jews to think of them as their God or Messiah, and, after the war with the Jews, that is what the Romans wanted to bring back with them, the title of **Messiah**. When Titus "prunes" the Jewish Rebel **Eleazar**, who was "**carried away**" on the Mount of Olives, the event is the prophetic and satirical ending of the New Testament. It is the moment that foresees Titus switching himself for the Jewish Messiah, which occurs in **John 21**.

As noted above, **Root** & **Branch** were Judaic metaphors used to indicate the messianic lineage, for example, the **Genesis Florilegium** states:

"*...until the Messiah of righteousness, the branch of David comes, because to him and his seed was given the Covenant of the kingdom of his people...*"

This root and branch of messianic imagery, which is found in the **Dead Sea Scrolls**, is a continuation of its use by the prophet **Isaiah**, concerning the coming Messiah, as the following translation from another fragment of the scrolls shows:

"...Isaiah the prophet...the thickets of the forest will be felled with an ax and Lebanon shall fall by a mighty one. A staff shall rise from the root of Jesse, and a planting from his roots will bear fruit...the branch of David..."

This reads like the Gospel of '**Luke**', just before he outlines the fictional genealogy of Jesus, as the case strongly appears to be:

"The ax is already at the root of the trees, and every tree that does not produce good fruit will be cut down and thrown into the fire (**Luke 3:9**).

Romans 11 speaks of grafting into the tree:

"... But if some of the branches were broken off, and you, although a wild olive shoot, were grafted in among the others and now share in the nourishing root of the olive tree, do not be arrogant toward the branches. If you are, remember it is not you who support the root, but the root that supports you..."

The authors of the New Testament continue the messianic 'root' and 'branch' metaphor, though with a different perspective. Within the New Testament, the 'root' and 'branch' imagery is presented in the context of there being a transformation into a different lineage, that lineage being of the new Messiah. The "**branches**" are described as either being "**pruned**" or "**grafted onto**", and Jesus predicts (echoing the book of Malachi), that those "**branches**" that do not abide in the **new Judaism** he brings, will be "**burned**":

"*If anyone does not abide in me, he is cast out as a branch and is withered; and they gather them and throw them into the fire*".
John 15:6

Josephus builds on the root and branch imagery in the New Testament by creating a series of related parallels. As we have seen so often, these parallels contain puzzles that reveal the names of unnamed characters, and in **every** case, the name of the unnamed character is **Eleazar/Lazarus**. The parallels involving **Eleazar/Lazarus** indicate that Eleazar was the name of the individual that the messianic rebels looked to as the "**root**", which is foreseen by Judaic prophecy. Judging from the satire, it appears this individual may have existed and have been the spiritual leader of the rebellion. Just like all the other typological passages, the "**root**" and "**branch**" satire can be recognized by determining the related order in which the events occur, even though they are described in different books. As Joseph Atwill has stated, it is the same technique required to solve "**the puzzle of the empty tomb**" above, where the four empty tomb texts have to be arranged in chronological order to understand the combined story the texts have created. Josephus provides the reader with a path to realizing the events are related to each other through their words. To understand the "root" and "branch" satire, it is important to recognize that the satire uses the same construct as that used throughout the **New Testament** and **Wars of the Jews**, those are the **parallel locations** and **conceptual parallels**. Also, some of the principles from the Roman sciences of botany and Homeopathic medicine are used in the "**Root**" and "**Branch**" satire, because the Romans believed that whatever made you sick could sometimes cure you. Roman botany considered that by introducing tamed specimens into a colony of wild plants, an offspring and tamer plant would result. **Pedanius Dioscorides**, the chief Physician and botanist accompanying Vespasian and Titus into Judea, was familiar with both of these scientific principles that are key elements in this "**Root** and **Branch**" satire. Pedanius was famous for pioneering the first documented use of anesthesia and the first medical use of electric shock therapy, using electric eels to generate the current. He also wrote a textbook on botany that became the basis for modern herbalism and identified hundreds of medicinal plant roots, *"many very serviceable roots"*, as he put it, that had not previously been known to medical science. As one of Rome's leading scientists, Pedanius would have advised Titus on what Josephus calls the *"useful science"* (**Antiquities of Jews, Book 8, Chapter 2**,) of '**expelling demons**' from apparently "**insane people**".

One of the elements of the "Root" and "Branch" satire, is the strange plant that Josephus calls, **rue**, which has a root by the name of '**Baaras**'. This root, '**Baaras**', has the power to "dispel demons", which is defined by Josephus as the "spirit of the wicked". The fact that Josephus mentions a plant named '**rue**' is significant because rue is one of the plants that Pedanius studied and wrote about. In his textbook on Herbalism, he explains the dangers of the wild or mountain rue, and the benefits of the domesticated or garden rue, which grew near Fig trees and could be safely used in tinctures and infusions. Pedanius' gardening technique is essentially the central part of the Roman pacification strategy, documented in the "**Root**" and "**Branch**" satire. The Romans attempted to "**domesticate**" the Jewish people by "**pruning**" the "**root**" of their demonic wickedness, that "**root**" being the messiah or rebel leader **Eleazar/Lazarus**, and then "**grafting**" in the root that is **Jesus**, which has the power to "dispel demons". A quote from Titus, recorded by the fourth-century Christian writer **Sulpicius Severus**, after the fact, mentions his understanding of the importance of the "root" to the Jews and Christians.

Titus is said to have first summoned a council and deliberated whether or not he should destroy such a mighty temple...

"*the destruction of the Temple was a prime necessity, in order to wipe out more completely the religions of the Jews and Christians, for they urged that these religions, though hostile to each other, nevertheless sprang from the same sources, the Christians had grown out of the Jews, if the root were destroyed, the stock would easily disappear.*

Analysis of the "Root and Branch" satire

To begin the analysis, it's important to first note the elements from the New Testament that are used in the "root" and "branch" satire. These concepts are created from the messianic prophecies of the "**root of Jesse**" and "**branch of David**" in the **Old Testament** and **Dead Sea Scrolls**.

The Root and Branch elements contained within the New Testament are:

1)

The messianic lineage is described as being "**pruned**"

2)

There is a prediction that the messianic lineage

will be "**grafted**" onto.

3)

Jesus' capture occurs on the **Mount of Olives**

4)

Three are crucified but **one** survives

5)

Joseph of Arimathea takes the survivor down from the cross.

Now let's examine each of the above elements in the actual passages, in turn, that make up the whole satire. The following passage takes place at the fortress **Herodian** and occurs *before* the siege of **Jerusalem**. It tells the story of an **Eleazar/Lazarus** who, like his namesake at the siege of **Masada**, commits suicide.

For clarification, the following is a list of the concepts in the passage which are elements in the entire satire:

First location: **Thecoe** (Tecoa) & **Herodian**

1. **Eleazar/Lazarus**

2. Pitched camp at **Thecoe**

3. **Refusal to Surrender**

4. **Suicide**

"Nor was it long ere Simon came violently again upon their country; when he **pitched his camp** at a certain village called **Thecoe**, and sent **Eleazar**, one of his companions, to those that kept garrison at **Herodium**, and in order to persuade them to surrender that fortress to him. The garrison received this man readily, while they knew nothing of what he came about; but as soon as he talked of the surrender of the place, they fell upon him with their drawn swords, till he found that he had no place for flight, when he **threw himself down from the wall into the valley beneath; so he died immediately**." (**Wars of the Jews Book 4, Chapter 9**)

The following passage is also part of the satire:

The name of the Messiah that was captured on the Mount of Olives, was **Eleazar/Lazarus**. One of the reasons that make the "root" and "branch" satire so difficult to comprehend, is that it uses the solutions to **other** puzzles as elements. In other words, you must first solve the puzzle that reveals the "certain young man" captured on the **Mount of Olives** was indeed named

Eleazar/Lazarus, to be able to move forward and see the even larger story that the captured Eleazar is part of.

For clarification, the following is a list of the elements in the story that are part of the satire:

Second location: **Mount of Olives**

1. **Eleazar/Lazarus**

2. Pedanius (Physician)

3. Pedanius hangs Eleazar/Lazarus **down from his hand** as he "carries him away."

4. Capture occurs on the **Mount of Olives**

5. The fact that Eleazar is ordered to be "**pruned**".

"Now after one day had been placed since the Romans ascended the breach, many of the seditious were so pressed by the famine, upon the present failure of their ravages, that they got together, and made an attack on those Roman guards that were upon the **Mount of Olives**, and this about the eleventh hour of the day, as supposing, first, that they would not expect such an onset, and, in the next place, that they were then taking care of their bodies, and that they should easily beat them.

But the Romans were apprised of their coming to attack them beforehand, and, running together from the neighboring camps on the sudden, prevented them from getting over their fortification, or forcing the wall that was built about them. Upon this came on a sharp fight, and here many great actions were *performed on both sides; while the Romans showed both their courage and their skill in war, as did the Jews come on them with immoderate violence and intolerable passion.*

The one part were urged on by shame, and the other by necessity, for it seemed a very shameful thing to the Romans to let the Jews go, now they were taken in a kind of net, while the Jews had but one hope of saving themselves, and that was in case they could by violence break through the Roman wall. And one whose name was **Pedanius**, *belonging to a party of horsemen, when the Jews were already beaten and forced down into the valley together, spurred his horse on their flank with great vehemence, and caught up a certain young man belonging to the enemy by his ankle, as he was running away. The man was, however, of a robust body, and in his armour, so low did Pedanius bend himself downward from his horse, even as he was galloping away, and so great was the strength of his* **right hand**, *and of the rest of his body, as also such skill had he in horsemanship.*

So this man seized upon that his prey, as upon a precious treasure, and carried him as his captive to Caesar, whereupon Titus admired the man that had seized the other for his great strength, and ordered the man that was caught to be punished (with death) for his attempt against the Roman wall, but betook himself to the siege of the temple, and to pressing on the raising of the banks."
(War of the Jews Book 5 Chapter 2,)

The following passage is one of the most important in the works of Josephus, as in it he records his parallel to the **crucifixion of Jesus in the New Testament**. It occurs **after** the siege of Jerusalem, but **before** the passage describing **Eleazar's/Lazarus'** capture and release at **Macherus**. Its relating position to the other events in the "**root**" and "**branch**" satire is crucial, but to make this more difficult to see, the event is recorded in **Josephus' Vita/Bio/Life** and **not** in *Wars of the Jews*. However Josephus provided details to understanding when his crucifixion scene occurred in relation to the other events in the satire, and he did so with this statement-

> "Moreover, when the city of Jerusalem was taken by force, I was sent by Titus."

This indicates the event occurred **after** the capture of the "certain young man" on the Mount of Olives by Pedanius, but **before** the siege of Macherus, which occurred **after** Titus left Judea. This related placement is also crucially important for the overall parallel sequence between Jesus' ministry and Titus' campaign. In other words, as is presented in the **New Testament**, the "**Three are crucified**, **one survives**" episode occurs **after** the capture on the Mount of Olives but **before** the condemning of the punishment of **Simon/Peter** and the sparing of **John**, which Titus learned of by letter after he had left Jerusalem. (**Wars of Jews** Book 7, Chapter 2)

The following list contains the elements that are used in the "**Root**" and "**Branch**" satire from the passage below, which describes three Jews who are crucified and one who survives at **Thecoa**.

Third location: **Thecoa** (translated as 'Village of the Inquiring Mind'). In the satirical version in the Gospels, the place is called **Golgotha** (translated as 'Hill of the Empty Skull')

1. **Three** are crucified but **one** survives

2. **Joseph Bar Matthias** takes survivor down from the cross

3. Pitched camp at **Thecoa** (Inquiring Minds)-(Empty Skull, **Matthew 27:33**)

4. **Physician**

"Moreover, when the city of Jerusalem was taken by force, Titus Caesar persuaded me frequently to take whatsoever I would of the ruins of my country, and did that he gave me leave so to do. But when my country was destroyed, I thought nothing else to be of any value, which I could take and keep as a comfort under my calamities, so I made this request to Titus, that my family might have their liberty and I had also the **holy books** *by Titus' concession. Nor was it long after that I asked of him the life of my brother, and of fifty friends with him, and was not denied.*

When I also went once to the temple, by the permission of Titus, where there were a great multitude of captive women and children, I got all those that I remembered as among my own friends and acquaintances to be set free, being in number about one hundred and ninety; and so I delivered them without their paying any price of redemption, and restored them to their former fortune. And when I was sent by Titus Caesar with Cerealins, and a thousand horsemen, to a certain village called **Thecoa, in order to know whether it were a place fit for a camp,** *as I came back, I saw many* **captives crucified,** *and remembered* **three** *of* *them as my former acquaintance. I was very sorry at this in my mind, and went with tears in my eyes to Titus, and told him of them; so he immediately commanded them to be taken down, and to have the greatest care taken of them, in order to their recovery, yet* **two** *of them died under the physician's hands, while the* **third** *recovered."* (**The life of Flavius Josephus Chapter 75, Pages 417-421**)

So we can see that two died and one survives, and following Titus' return to Rome, Josephus describes a valley next to the fortress Macherus, in which a "magic root" that could dispel demons grew.

The following is a list of the elements in that passage that are used in the satire:

Fourth location: **Baaras**

1. A **root** that can "**dispel demons**"

2. The fact that this "**root**" must be **hung down from the hand** of its captor, as he "**carries it away**"

"*Now within this place there grew a sort of* **rue** *that deserves our wonder on account of its largeness, for it was no way inferior to any fig tree whatsoever, either in height or in thickness, and the report is,* **that it had lasted ever since the times of Herod, and would probably have lasted much longer, had it not been cut down by those Jews who took possession of the place afterward.** *But still in that valley which encompasses the city on the north side, there is a certain place called* **Baaras**, *which produces a root of the same name with itself its color is like to that of flame, and towards the evenings it sends out a certain ray like lightning.*

It is not easily taken by such as would do it, but recedes from their hands, nor will yield itself to be taken quietly, until either the urine of a woman, or her menstrual blood, be poured upon it; nay, even then it is certain death to those that touch it, unless anyone take and **hang the root itself down from his hand, and so carry it away**. It may also be taken another way, without danger, which is this: they dig a trench quite round about it, till the hidden part of the root be very small, they then tie a dog to it, and when the dog tries hard to follow him that tied him, this root is easily plucked up, but the dog dies immediately, as if it were instead of the man that would take the plant away, nor after this need anyone be afraid of taking it into their hands. Yet, after all this pains in getting, it is only valuable on account of one virtue it hath, that if it be only brought to sick persons, it quickly drives away **those called demons**, which are no other than the **spirits of the wicked**, that enter into men that are alive and kill them, unless they can obtain some help against them." (**Wars of the Jews**, Book 7, Chapter 6)

-The sentence highlighted above, *that it had lasted ever since the times of Herod, and would probably have lasted much longer, had it not been cut down by those Jews who took possession of the place afterward,* I feel relates to the Calpurnius Piso Family and the Flavians taking possession of Jerusalem after the war, but that information will be explained later in the book.

Immediately following the description of the magic root, Josephus describes another incident involving an **Eleazar/Lazarus** at one of the Herodian fortresses, **Macherus**.

The following elements from the passage are part of the entire satire:

Fifth location: **Macherus**

1. **Herodian Fort**

2. **Eleazar/Lazarus**

3. The fact that Eleazar/Lazarus is **carried away in his armor**

4. The fact that Eleazar/Lazarus **survives his crucifixion**

*"Now a certain person belonging to the Roman camp, whose lame was Rufus, by birth an Egyptian, ran upon him suddenly, when nobody expected such a thing, and **carried him off with his armour** itself, while in the meantime, those that saw it from the wall were under such an amazement, that Rufus prevented their assistance, and carried **Eleazar** to the Roman camp. So the general of the Romans ordered that he should be taken up naked, set before the city to be seen, and sorely whipped before their eyes. Upon this sad accident that befell the young man, the Jews were terribly confounded, and the city, with one voice, sorely lamented him, and the mourning proved greater than could well be supposed upon the calamity of a single person.*

*When Bassus perceived that, he began to think of using a stratagem against the enemy, and was desirous to aggravate their grief, in order to prevail with them to surrender the city for the preservation of that man. Nor did he fail of his hope, for he commanded them **to set up a cross**, as if he were just going to hang **Eleazar** upon it immediately, the sight of this occasioned a sore grief among those that were in the citadel, and they groaned* vehemently and cried out that they could not bear to see him thus destroyed. Whereupon Eleazar besought them not to disregard him, now he was going to suffer a most miserable death, and exhorted them to save themselves, by yielding to the Roman power and good fortune, since all other people were now conquered by them. These men were greatly moved with what he said, there being also many within the city that interceded for him because he was of an eminent and very numerous family, so they now yielded to their passion of commiseration, contrary to their usual custom. Accordingly, they sent out immediately certain messengers, and treated with the Romans, in order to a surrender of the citadel to them, and desired that they might be **permitted to go away**, and **take Eleazar along with them**." (**Wars of Jews, Book 7, Chapter 6**)

The famous depiction of the **siege of Masada** is also part of this satirical theme.

It's elements are:

Sixth location: **Masada**

1. **Herodian fort**

2. **Eleazar**

3. **Not surrendering leads to suicide**

...This fortress was called Masada.

"It was one **Eleazar**, a potent man, and the commander of these **Sicarii** that had seized upon it. He was a descendant from that Judas who had persuaded abundance of the Jews, as we have for-

merly related, not to submit to the taxation when Cyrenius was sent into Judea to make one" (in 6 CE) (**War of Jews, Chapter 7 – 8, Pages 252-253**)

Finally, Josephus records his last story regarding **Eleazar**, this time he is located in Rome. Although included in the **Antiquities of the Jews**, we can be certain the event occurred in the presence of Vespasian's sons. We know this because Vespasian's son, Domitian, did not travel to Judea, this fact establishes the event took place *after* Titus had returned to Rome.

In the passage, Eleazar is using a magic root to remove demons from captives.

Its elements within the satire are:

Seventh location: **Rome**

1. **Eleazar/Lazarus**

2. **Magic Root**

3. **Demons cannot pass through water**

"*And he left behind him the manner of using exorcisms, by which they drive away demons, so that they never return, and this method of cure is of great force unto this day, for I have seen a certain man of my own country, whose name was* **Eleazar**, *releasing people that were demoniacal in the presence of Vespasian, and his sons, and his captains, and the whole multitude of his soldiers. The manner of the cure was this: He put a ring that had a foot of one of those sorts mentioned by Solomon to the nostrils of the demoniac, after which he drew out the demon* through his nostrils, and when the man fell down immediately, he abjured him to return into him no more, making still mention of Solomon, and reciting the incantations which he composed.

And when **Eleazar** would persuade and demonstrate to the spectators that he had such a power, he set a little way off a cup or **basin full of water**, and commanded the demon, as he went out of the man, to **overturn it**, and thereby to let the spectators know that he had left the man, and when this was done, the skill and wisdom of Solomon was shown very manifestly: for which reason it is, that all men may know the vastness of Solomon's abilities, and how he was beloved of God, and that the extraordinary virtues of every kind with which this king was endowed may not be unknown to any people under the sun for this reason, I say, it is that we have proceeded to speak so largely of these matters." **(Antiquities of the Jews, Book 8, Chapter 2)**

To begin to understand the "**root**" and "**branch**" satire, we need to note that all the passages above involve a character named "**Eleazar**". In the passages that occur at **Herodian**, **Macherus**, **Masada**, and **Rome**, Josephus names the character openly. In the case of the "young man" who was "carried away" at the Mount of Olives, the puzzle has already been shown above that leads to this conclusion. The crucified man who survived at **Thecoa**, and the "**magic root**" of **Baaras**, are also part of the satirical system regarding **Eleazar**. In other words, all the **Eleazars** are parts of a single overall satirical literary event, just like '**Mary**' and the **Passover sacrifice**. The passages work together to create a story describing the Roman capture of the messianic "root" of the Jews, that "root" being **Eleazar** and then their "**pruning**" of him and transforming him into **Jesus**, the demon-dispelling Messiah. The parallel that indicates that **Eleazar** is the "**root**" is shown openly, but the reader must remember the method by which Josephus states someone may capture the magic root **Baaras**, that is, the "**son**", without killing himself:

> "...it is certain death to those that touch it, unless anyone take and hang the root itself **down from his hand**, and so carry it away."

This is the precise method used by **Pedanius** to obtain **Eleazar** on the **Mount of Olives**:

> "...so low did Pedanius bend himself downward from his horse...and so great was the strength of **his right hand**...So this man seized upon that his prey, as upon a precious treasure, and carried him as his captive to Caesar."

Just like his depiction of the "**magic root**", Josephus' embellished description of Pedanius' capture of the "certain young man" on the Mount of Olives stretches the truth. This means that the literary structure shows us that the tales are not literal history, and therefore, we should indeed look for another type of meaning. In this instance, the parallel methods by which they are captured identifies, metaphorically, that **Eleazar** is like **Baaras**, a dangerous "**root**". This identification is also made easier by the name of the root '**Baaras**', which means '**son**', and the satirical capture by Pedanius of the Jewish Messiah, who is the "**root**" to the **messianic rebels**, contributes to the overall satirical theme. Because Pedanius was the Romans' most renowned root specialist, he would have been the one chosen to handle such a dangerous one. The meaning of the tale of the 'magic root of **Baaras**' (son), within the "**Root** and **Branch**" satire, is also easy to understand. It documents the existence of a metaphorical "root" (**son**), that had the power to remove demons, obviously that 'root' being the **Jesus** of the **New Testament**, the only person in history with such power. The Romans would graft this demon dispelling "root" (**son**), that had infected so many (**rebellious Jews**) with a demonic spirit, into one that had the power to remove demons. The parallels also show that the individual who survived his crucifixion at **Thecoa** was the Messiah. This individual would have been a "Christ" because 'Christ' means 'Messiah', and like his "character type" in the New Testament, he was the sole survivor among three crucified men. This means that these two individuals must be among the few individuals in history to have survived the crucifixion.

We also have the individual named "**Joseph of Arimathea**" who arranged for both survivors to be taken down from the cross. I cannot continue without saying that I agree with Joseph Atwill, who stated that the last names of the two Josephs, "**Josephus Bar Matthias**" and "**Joseph of Arimathea**", are **homophonically** similar, meaning they have the same sound. At this point in the investigation, I agreed with Joseph when he said "**Arimathea**" seems to be an obvious play on **Josephus' last name, "Bar Matthias**", because archaeology has produced no city called **Arimathea**. However, this name appears to reveal more information about the Calpurnius Piso family, again, that information will be examined later. The individual who survived his crucifixion at **Thecoa** is also linked to the **Eleazar** captured on the **Mount of Olives** by Pedanius. Josephus states that it was a *physician* who restored him to life, and because Pedanius accompanied Titus to Judea, he, therefore, would have been the physician at Thecoa. Finally, the **Eleazar**, who committed suicide at the fortress **Herodian**, had pitched camp at **Thecoa** previously and had then answered the question Josephus asked about whether Thecoe was a "**fit place to camp**". The name of the place where the crucifixion occurred, **Thecoa**, is also part of the satirical system. **Thecoa**, or **Theo Coeus**, is the name of the Roman God of the questioning intellect/mind (Place of Skulls **Matthew 27:33**). So the irrational Jewish Messiah was taken to the place of a discerning or questioning intellect, and there he was, as Titus ordered, "**pruned**", and as **Paul** described, "**grafted onto**" (**Romans 11:11-24**) with a new "**root**" and was transformed into a Messiah deemed rational by the Romans. Knowing that the "**magic root**" was named **Eleazar**, as was the man who survived his crucifixion at **Thecoa**, and knowing the **time sequence** in which these events took place, it allows us to see the literary satire created by all the passages working together.

The **Eleazar** captured by Pedanius on the Mount of Olives is taken to **Thecoa**, where he is '**hung on a tree**', so he is crucified, and, as Titus has ordered, "**pruned**". The botanist and physician Pedanius then **grafts** the **magic root of Baaras (son)** onto him. This process then transforms **Eleazar** from a "root" that causes the Jews to be "**possessed**" by a "**demonic spirit**", into a new "**root**" (**son**) that **dispels demons** and cures them of **rebelling** against Rome, thereby attempting to pacify them, so **Eleazar** becomes **Jesus**. Once this **Eleazar** has been satirically "**pruned**" and grafted onto at **Thecoa**, he is "**given back**" to the Jews at **Macherus**. Doing this allows the Romans to introduce a "**tame**" or "**domesticated plant**" (**Messiah**) into a field of "**wild ones**" (**rebellious Jews**), to decrease the wildness of later generations.

It is important to note at this point, that the satire takes the story of Jesus beyond the storyline of the Gospels and begins to describe the implementation of Christianity by the Romans. This satirical introduction of the domesticated '**Jesus**' takes place in the passage that *immediately follows* the description of the "**magic root**". In that passage, the Roman general **Bassus** seeks to make the Jews inside the Herodian fortress, Machaerus, surrender by threatening to crucify **Eleazar** in front of them. Those Jews who "accept these terms" are permitted to survive, and **Bassus** then restores **Eleazar** to them, obviously that **Eleazar** is the one that was "**carried away**" at the **Mount of Olives** and "**treated**" ("**pruned**") by the physician at **Thecoa**. In other words, those Jews who **accept** the "tamed" Messiah, deemed acceptable by the Romans, are allowed to live. At **Masada**, however, another **Eleazar**, a parallel to the **Eleazar** at **Herodian**, refuses to surrender and commits suicide. The point is, that refusal to surrender and accept the new Judaism is virtually the same as suicide. With this Eleazar's death, Josephus is also terminating the "**Root**" and "**Branch**" of the **Maccabean** lineage, so that it will not compete against the newly created "**domesticated**" messianic lineage created by Rome. Josephus concludes the "**Root and Branch**" satire with the description of yet another **Eleazar**, one who performs exorcisms in Rome. This **Eleazar** uses the "**magic root**" to **pull demons out of captives**, clearly indicating **captured messianic Jews**. This image represents a complete victory for the Roman "homeopathic" approach towards the problem of the messianic "**root**", that caused Jews to be "**possessed**" by "**Demons**".

The "**root**" ("**Messiah**") that caused the Jewish rebels to be "**infected**" ("**rebellious**"), has been "**domesticated**" by Pedanius, and can therefore now be used to cure them of the disease it brought about. This creates the fulfillment of the prophecy of **Malachi**, which foresees that the wicked will be left with **no** "**Branch** or **Root**", but the opposite happens and the Romans take over the Messianic trees. Also, the passage concludes the dark comedy theme regarding the inability of "**Demons**" **to pass through water**, which began in the '**Demons of Gadara**' passage examined earlier, and ends here with the demonic spirit knocking over the basin full of water as it leaves the prisoners. These prisoners were the **2,000** rebels who were captured at **Gadara** and thrown into the water. (**Josephus Wars of The Jews, Book 4, Chapter 7**) This is the same as the **2,000** pigs (swine) who are infected with "**demons**", rushed over the cliff, and thrown into the water (**Mark 5:1-20** and **Luke 8:26-39**). These prisoners symbolize the **2,000** rebels who were captured at **Gadara**, and being "**demonically**" possessed, they could not pass through the water and therefore did not drown. As the demon leaves them, it concludes the joke by knocking over the water basin and is the last depiction of the "domesticated Christ/Messiah" by Josephus.

Now one argument for these parallels could be that Titus' campaign was based on Jesus' ministry. However, if that was the case, then the only reason would be to try and make the Jews worship Titus as the Messiah. But Titus encircled the wall of Jerusalem in 70 CE, and Jesus' story did not appear until 73 CE and was barely known. That means there was not enough time between 73 CE and 75 CE., when the *Wars of the Jews* was written, for the Jesus story to have had enough impact on Rome. We also don't read about Jesus' *'life in the flesh'* until after the *Wars of the Jews* was written. But now that we have investigated the above parallels, the next step in this investigation is to delve deeper into what is known about the individual known as Flavius Josephus, including what was said about him, and what he says about himself, including his ancestry, and carefully examining the relationship between the Calpurnius Pisos, the Flavians, and the Herodians.

4. FLAVIUS JOSEPHUS NEVER EXISTED

To find out who Josephus was, we need to investigate whether or not he is mentioned in any historical documents of the time, and we need to see if we can find any more information regarding his background. With the parallels that have just been examined, the next step is to ask two important questions:

First

Even if the parallels can somehow be considered a coincidence, how is it possible to have so many occur in the same place in both books, using the exact words and concepts?

Second

Did Josephus take part in the writing of the New Testament?

We need to ask these questions because, again, it is important to either verify or debunk all angles. Remembering what we have examined in the previous chapter, Josephus becomes an incredibly suspicious individual, especially due to 1) the known fact that the message of the New Testament emerged after the war, 2) because when this man surrendered to the future Emperor Vespasian, he was treated exceptionally well thereafter, which is in contrast to the fate of other Jewish leaders, such as *Jesus ben Ananias* (Josephus, *The Jewish War*, 6.5.3) and *Simon bar Giora* (Josephus, *The Jewish War*, 7.2.1) and 3) because Roman generals routinely took enemy generals to Rome to be publicly executed, Josephus, however, escaped this fate. He was treated immensely well, even living in Vespasian's house and, as we read, receiving the Flavian name through adoption. I find it very difficult to believe this, especially considering he tells us that during the siege of *Jotapata* (Yodefat) he had his men pour boiling oil down upon the Romans and boiling fenugreek over the Roman assault planks in 67 CE (Josephus, *The Jewish War*, 3.271-279).

If there were only a few parallels that contained the same concepts, we could speculate that these events were common occurrences at that time, however, that is not what has been presented, so we must investigate further. The first important detail to mention is that no Jewish historical commentary mentions Josephus, not even in the Talmud, which is suspicious, considering the background he has as a high priest. As Historian and Biblical scholar Steve Mason states:

"Although Josephus most often refers to himself as a general (στρατηγος), he is plainly much more than that: governor, chief magistrate, teacher, and supreme patron (ευεργετης, § 244; προστατης, § 250). He quickly evolves from membership in a triumvirate (§ 29) to sole mastery of the region (§§ 244, 259). Essentially, he is "the man," whose position is legitimized not by an office, but by the populace's overwhelming affirmation of his virtue, prestige, and authority (auctoritas, on which see Galinsky 1996: 10-41)." **(ref** – Flavius Josephus, Translation and Commentary, Volume 9, Introduction, XXXV)

Now one reason they may not mention him could be because they saw him as a traitor, but it could be logically assumed that he was important enough to at least have been mentioned as being a traitor to his people. Given we find nothing in the Talmud or other Jewish commentary relating to Josephus, we must investigate other sources.

His genealogy can only be traced back through two individuals – a) **King Herod 'The Great'**, and b) his first wife, **Mariamne I**, who was the daughter of Alexander and Alexandra Regent. But the way Josephus presents his genealogy makes no reasonable sense. Whiston's translation of *'The Life Of Josephus'* states Josephus wrote that his grandfather's father [great-grandfather] was named Simon, with the *addition* of 'Psellus'. But as the Loeb Classical Library translation is considered the standard for scholarly study, our investigation here will be based on that translation. In the Loeb translation of *'Life Of Josephus'*, it reads *'My great-grandfather's grandfather was named Simon surnamed 'Psellus'* (which means 'stutterer'). This makes a man named Matthias Curtus (born 135 BCE) his great-grandfather; Matthias was a contemporary to the last rulers of the Hasmonean dynasty, particularly Hyrcanus II, who served as high priest from 76–67 BCE and 63–40 BCE. Matthias married an unnamed Jewish woman through whom he had a son called Josephus (Yosef), which *should* make this son the paternal grandfather of Flavius Josephus *if* Josephus is correct in claiming Matthias was born the first year that a man named Johanan Hyrcanus was a high priest (134 BCE) However, the genealogy Josephus gives raises questions that are historically unanswerable when the information is studied literally, as the males of

Josephus' family would have had to have married late or often. Regarding this, Steve Mason, states:

"*It remains unclear why Josephus should have chosen Simon as the patriarch of his family, rather than one of Simon's ancestors or Simon's son Matthias, who actually married into the Hasmonean line. Perhaps the coincidence in name with the contemporary Hasmonean Simon provided a motive. If Simon Psellus was already a priest, then Josephus has spoken ambiguously (open to doubt or uncertainty) at Ant. 16.187 in attributing his priestly heritage to the Hasmoneans.*" (**ref** – *Flavius Josephus, Translation and Commentary, Volume 9, Page 8, Life of Josephus*)

Also:

"*If Matthias II (Curtus) was born in 135 BCE and produced a son Josephus I in 68 BCE, he was a father at about the age of 77. This would have been a remarkable feat, especially in view of ancient mortality rates: When Abraham fathered Ishmael at 86 (Gen 16:16) it was a charter miracle of Israel's history. Since Josephus does not draw attention either to this feat or to its counterpart in the next generation, it is unlikely that he notices, or expects his audience to notice, the chronological problem. More likely, he has accidentally omitted a couple of generations or fabricated much of the genealogy. Possibly our text is corrupt.'…'If Josephus I was born in 68 BCE and fathered Matthias III at age 73 or 74 (in 6 CE), we are once again faced with a patriarchal feat unmentioned by Josephus.*"

Given the chronological gaps & Josephus' tendency to defend himself, rejecting his family tree as a fabrication would not be unreasonable. But because he insists that his genealogy is based on public records, (Loeb, *Life Of Josephus*, 4-11) and also states that *priestly* pedigrees were carefully preserved in the major Judean centers, and that after a war the priestly survivors would quickly recreate those records that had been destroyed (*Apion* 1.31.5), it makes this assumption hard to justify when studying the information *literally*.

Priestly lineage was enthusiastically recorded by Jerusalem's conservative ruling aristocracy, and it was the priest's job to regulate the priestly courses (groups). It is highly unlikely that Josephus would have claimed descent from the Hasmonean royal house if he was not of that lineage, especially considering the audience for his works. Therefore, he must have been a descendant of that royal house, surely? When taking a step back, there are only certain facts available to work with, those being that his genealogy can only be traced back through *King Herod 'The Great'* and his first wife, *Mariamne I*, as mentioned above. As a son of *Matthias*, Josephus' descent would be from the Hasmonean royal house, but because of what is known about that royal house, his genealogy makes no sense. Therefore, if we note the reasoning of Steve Mason above regarding a possible genealogical fabrication, and follow the advice of Sir Ronald Syme: '*When the attempt is made to expose a fraud, attack on all fronts is to be commended...*' (*Emperors and Biography: Studies in the Historia Augusta*) it is logical to examine more deeply other possible ancestral lines for Josephus, and this is where preconceptions need to be put aside.

Josephus, or the man who used this name, gave the necessary information to discover his actual genealogy via his writings, but vital information needed to confirm it was not given in a straightforward way, it was, it appears, very much scattered into little pieces of information here and there, the question to ask is, why? The individual who appears to have used the name *Flavius Josephus* used what I can only describe as naming techniques to disguise his genealogy, and those naming techniques incorporated literary 'rules' already used by the Roman aristocracy, for example, nomenclature, a combination of personal and family names used to create a new name.

Leaving behind the Sadducean believers and other 'Jews', the Herodians look to have been evacuated to Rome just before the siege. Berenice and King Agrippa II seem to have been treated very well by the Flavians, the reason could logically be that, as is written, Agrippa tried to convince the people that they could not win against the might of Rome. When this failed, he supported Rome in the war and fought in Vespasian's campaign. But when researching Flavius Josephus' genealogy, and data concerning the Herodians and Flavians, including the New Testament statement "*Greet Herodian, my kinsman*", the scholar who discovered this information, who goes by the name of '*Roman Piso*' (although it appears much of his research was destroyed) found that certain individuals kept reemerging because of various *dates*, *places*, and other items linked to the connections he was investigating. One important name that re-emerged with certain individuals was the name '**Pollio**', those individuals being **Vespasius Pollio** (I) and **Herod Pollio** (grandson of Herod the Great and Mariamne – Pollio is also recorded as Herod II/III/IV/V and 'Herod King of Chalcis'; he also had the titular rank of praetor (a Roman magistrate). (supporting reference – Sir Anthony Richard Wagner, *'Pedigree and Progress: Essays in the Genealogical Interpretation of History'*, page 174; Professor of Jewish History, Richard A. Freund, *'Digging Through The Bible'*, Chapter 4, page 612-615.)

Both had the *'Pollio'* name and a connection to the *Herodians* and the *Flavians*. In 44 CE, at the age of 16, Julia Berenice (born 28 CE), sister of King Agrippa II and granddaughter of Aristobulus IV, became the second wife of Herod Pollio, her uncle, but he died when she was 20. Also, as mentioned, both Berenice and Agrippa publicly supported the Flavians during the Jewish revolt. Herod Pollio's first wife was a woman called Mariamne IV, whom he married in approximately the late 20's CE, and she was a daughter of Joseph ben Joseph, Herod the Great's nephew, and Olympias the Herodian, daughter of Herod the Great. A son is recorded from this marriage, his name is Aristobulus III (born c. 30's CE), who later became Aristobulus of Chalcis in 57 CE. (**ref** – Josephus, *Bellum Judaicum*, 7; William Smith, *'Dictionary of Greek and Roman Biography and Mythology'*, pages 301-302.) This son is also recorded as joining a proconsul of Syria, a Caesennius Paetus (*Lucius Junius Caesennius Paetus*) in the war against Antiochus, king of Commagene, in 73 CE. (**ref** – Josephus, *Bellum Judaicum*, Book 7, 7, 1-3 1-3. F. Millar, *'The Roman Near East 31 BC-AD 337*, 1993, esp. 80-3.)

'Pollio' is a common extra personal name given to ancient Roman citizens, which the family of Herod the Great became. However, when dates and family trees for these individuals are compared, using the gathering of scattered data, they are alike, only with different names having been used, essentially indicating they were the *same person*. Herod Pollio (born 10-9 BCE – died 48-49 CE), son of Aristobulus IV and brother of Herod Agrippa I and Herodias, was granted the kingdom of Chalcis in 41 CE by Emperor Tiberius Claudius Caesar Augustus Germanicus. The birth date for Herod Pollio is concluded from information provided in Antiquities 19.350. There we read that Agrippa I was in his fifty-fourth year when he died in the summer of 44 CE. If his fifty-fourth year began in late 43 CE, his birth can be concluded as being in the late 11 BCE; his father, Aristobulus I/IV, had returned from Rome in late 12 BCE.

Vespasius Pollio, whose wife is unnamed in history, is recorded as an equestrian from Nursia (Italy), equestrians being above ordinary citizens. He became a *tribunus Militum* ('tribune of the soldiers') three times; those of equestrian rank who served as military tribunes often became senators. He is also recorded as becoming a *praefectus castrorum* no earlier than the time of Augustus (63 BCE-14 CE – reigned 27 BCE-14 CE) (**ref** – Suetonius, *Life of Vespasian* – see also *Epigraphische Notizen aus Italien III. Inschriften aus Nursia*, by G. Alfoldy – source: *Zeitschrift fur Papyrologie und Epigraphik*, Bd. 77 (1989) pp. 155-180.) Vespasius is recorded as having a son and daughter, the daughter's name is recorded as Vespasia Polla/Pollia and we can logically conclude the son was recorded as Vespasius Pollio (II) (**ref** – James Anderson D.D. 'Royal Genealogies', page 362). Suetonius records that this son *'became a senator with the rank of praetor'*, a praetor of which exercised extensive authority in the government. Polla is described as being superior to her husband in social position, of her husband, Titus Flavius Sabinus I, Suetonius states he *'farmed the public tax of a fortieth in Asia.'* and *'...there existed for some time statues erected in his honor* *by the cities of Asia...*' Suetonius states that many monuments of the family of the Vespasii were still to be seen in his time at a village called '*Vespasiae*' between Nursia and Spoletum, therefore, in the Sabine country, '*affording strong proof of the renown and antiquity of the house.*' (**ref** – Suetonius, Loeb, *Life of Vespasian*, pages 281-282)

When investigating the historical documentation further, we can find that a King Julius Tigranes VI of Armenia (born before 25 CE) (Tacitus, *Annals*, Book 14, Volume 5, page 151), an apostate to Judaism, and a Herodian Prince who served as a Roman Client King of Armenia in the first century (first reign 58-61 CE – second reign 66/7 CE) married a noblewoman of *Phrygia* (near Chalcis) called '**Opgalli**', her royal title being ΒΑΣ ΟΠΓΑΛΛΥ. Her existence is known only through numismatic evidence of Tigranes' second kingship; in a paper called '*Tigranes IV, V, and VI: New Attributions*', found on page 347 in the American Journal of Numismatics Vol. 2, Frank L. Kovacs suggests her inclusion on the coinage of Tigranes' second-reign suggests a recent marriage or at least an enhanced importance. (further ref – Classical Numistic Group, Inc., Kings of Armenia. Tigranes VI). Tigranes' father was Alexander (Gaius Julius Alexander), according to Josephus (*Jewish Antiquities* 18.140) the second-born son of Alexander and Glaphyra, making Tigranes' grandfather **Alexander**, son of Herod the Great and Mariamne I, Tigranes grandfather, therefore, is the brother of **Aristobulus IV**:

"Alexander had a son of the same name with his brother Tigranes, and was sent to take possession of the kingdom of Armenia by Nero" (Josephus, Ant, 18.140)

Tigranes, who was raised in Rome (**ref** – Tacitus, *Annals* 14.26), is recorded as having a daughter called Julia, a Herodian Princess who married a Roman senator called M. *Plancius Varus of Perge*, the governor of Bithynia-Pontus under Emperor Vespasian. This daughter's name was deciphered through the finding of a modest stone of the early second century that records an offering by a Julia Ammia to an unnamed deity in the town of Falerii in Etruria – [I]*ulia Tigranes regis f(ilia) Ammia*. (**ref** – CIL 11.380 = ILS 850; Tacitus, *Histories*, 2.63; George W. Houston, M. *Plancius Varus and the Events of A.D. 69-70*, Transactions and Proceedings of the American Philological Association, Vol. 103.) Tigrane's son, Julia's brother, Julius Alexander, entered mainstream Roman politics between 90 and 110 CE by becoming a *consul suffectus*. Julia's and Julius' paternal great-great-grandparents were Herod the Great and Mariamne. This Julia looks to have the feminine form of her father's name, Julius; it is also the same name as Herod Pollio's wife, *Julia Berenice*, also spelled *Berenike*. If we now look again at the name of Tigranes' wife, 'Op**galli**', an important point must be noted. 'Galli' can be '*galla*', just as *Mariamme* can be *Miriam*, and 'galla' means the same as '*polla*', the feminine form of **Pollio** (Cock, Chicken, Rooster), i.e. the same as Herod Pollio. If Tigranes' wife was the daughter of Herod Pollio, then the great-great-grandparents of Tigranes' daughter would be Herod and Mariamne on *both* her father and mother's side; interestingly, Julia's brother, C. Julius Alexander, King in Cilicia, named his son C. *Julius Alexander Berenicianus*. (**ref** – Seth Schwartz, '*Josephus and Judean politics*'. Columbia studies in the classical tradition.) Scholar Edmund Groag, also suggested in '*Pauly-Wissowa*' (Stuttgart, 1917), 19:157-158), that Gaius Julius Alexander Berenicianus, presented on inscriptions of

Ephesus and Laodicea, (a three-hour walk from *Phrygia* and near *Chalcis*) was a descendant of the Herodian house of Chalcis, i.e., the family of Queen Berenice – the question to answer now is, who was the mother of 'Opgalli'?

We appear to have identified a son and daughter for both Vespasius Pollio *and* Herod Pollio, all of which were active within elite circles in the same period. *If* Vespasius Pollio was Herod Pollio, then some blanks in the historical data would be filled in, for example, it would provide details about the children of Vespasius Pollio and give the name/s of his wife or wives. It would also show his brother to have been **King Agrippa I**, and that would explain why both *King Agrippa II* and *Emperor Vespasian* (born 9 CE, according to Suetonius, *Life of Vespasian*, whose identity is examined in the chapter 'Origin of the Popes') would have a physical family resemblance, as seen on the royal coinage, because of the sharing of the same common ancestry, which is their descent from King Herod the Great; King Agrippa II would be Vespasian's first cousin, once removed, and great uncle on Vespasian's mother's side.

Emperor Vespasian and King Agrippa II

It is necessary to note, as has just been demonstrated, that public genealogies of ancient royals usually began at a certain point, with a certain person, making the genealogy virtually impossible to be traced back any further via *superficial* readings of the histories that were left to us. Also, important dates and details are often omitted, adding frustration for a historian. But the reason critical information was not given seems to be because revealing those genealogies would reveal the connection to other royals (i.e., their royal lineage), but why would they want to hide their lineage? We must understand that the nobility was in control of everything, including the writing of religious literature, histories, stories, and who would rule. If the common people, who vastly outnumbered the royals, had discovered what was happening, in terms of manipulation, and being lied to, royalty would have been killed and their whole system overturned through a mass revolution, which is what was happening in Judea.

The people were given the hope that anyone could advance in life and perhaps even become emperor, as the illusion of different royal family dynasties had been created. In reality, that was not the case, as it appears the same royal family circles kept their rule by only providing certain information to the public. To maintain their very comfortable lifestyle and keep control, royalty had to hide the fact that they were the only ones creating published writing, as they were the only ones educated to a standard high enough to create the kind of prose seen in the histories and religious text that were produced. Essentially, the majority of the people of the Roman Empire only knew what the aristocracy allowed them to know.

Exposing '*Vespasius Pollio*' as a pseudonym of *Herod Pollio* would show 'Vespasius' as a King, and therefore, his and his descendant's right to rule. If the name 'Vespasius' was a pseudonym, understanding a possible reason as to why it was chosen is a good idea. It is known that ancient royals used titles as part of names, for example, '*Ptolemy Soter*', a title bestowed upon many monarchs, is a Greek form of the Egyptian God-title, '*Ptah-Mes Soter*', meaning 'son of God the Saviour', '*Mes*' meaning 'son of', and '*Soter*' meaning 'Saviour'.

In the Acts of the Apostles 12.20, we read:

"*And Herod was highly displeased with them of Tyre and Sidon:*

but they came with one accord to him, and, having made Blastus the king's chamberlain their friend, desired **peace**; because their country was nourished by the king's country."

Acts is stating that the people of these cities asked the **king for peace** because they received food supplies from his country. So Acts is informing us of special relations between King Herod Pollio of Chalcis and the population of two Lebanese cities, Tyre and Sidon; Chalcis was situated exactly 'under Mount Libanus' (modern Mount Lebanon):

"But Ptolemy, the son of Menneus, who was the ruler of Chalcis, under **Mount Libanus**, took his brethren to him; and sent his son Philippion to Askelon, to Aristobulus's wife..." (Josephus, Ant 14.7.4).

The name 'Vespasian' then, from the information found, looks to be a created title. The origin of this name has confused some, but it appears to have been created using two components: '**Vas**' becomes '**Bas**' (V and B are interchangeable) and '**Pasius**' becomes '**Pacius**' (C and S are interchangeable). 'Vas/Bas' ΒΑΣ is the royal abbreviation for the Greek word '**Basilius**' βασιλεύς ('King') and '**Basilissa**' (Queen), just as '*Imp*' is short for *Imperatori* (Emperor) or '*Caes*' short for *Caesari* (Caesar), and '**Pasius**' ('Pacius') = *Peace*. Therefore, this "*peace*" word used in the name **Ves-pasius** can logically mean '**King-Peace**', or "*Roman Peace*", because in the minds of the aristocracy, "peace" was guaranteed by destroying the opposition; Vespasian's reign is recorded as a time of peace and he even had a '*Forum of Peace*' constructed to celebrate the pacification of the east.

For the nobility, war was necessary to obtain a measure of peace, at least for them, even if that peace was only temporary. It must be remembered that the Herodians were schooled in Rome, in the Roman ways. For example, Aristobulus IV, the eldest son of Herod the Great and Mariamne, was sent to Rome at the age of 12, along with his brother Alexander, to be schooled in the household of Augustus (20-28 BCE), staying in the household of Gaius Asinius Pollio, a politician, literary critic, Roman soldier, and historian; Aristobulus and Alexander were later executed by Herod in 7 BCE. Agrippa II was raised and educated at the imperial court in Rome, and, according to Josephus, Herod Antipas the Tetrarch, his full brother Archelaus and his half-brother Philip were also raised and educated in Rome. (Josephus, *Antiquities*, Book 17)

Regarding Herod Pollio as 'Vespasius Pollio', we have learned he must have had a son *and* daughter, recorded as *Vespasia Polla* and *Vespasius Pollio II* (Aristobulus?) in the writings of Suetonius. **Vespasia Polla**/Opgalli/Julia Polla/Julia of Chalcis married **T. Flavius Sabinus I**, a tax-gatherer in Asia, who had two sons, **T. Flavius Sabinus II**, and the future **Emperor Vespasian**. This marriage must have been before the marriage of 'Vespasia'/Opgalli to Tigranes, and she has to be the daughter of Herod Pollio and Mariamne IV (born possibly just before or just after the beginning of the Christian era, *if* her mother, Olympias, was born 22 BCE.) This would mean Emperor Vespasianan would be of royal blood and anyone descended from either Vespasian or his brother could then trace their ancestry back to King Herod the Great, and then also to his ancestry and/or that of his wives, including Mariamne I. This also means the Roman historians presenting Vespasian as a military man of very humble origins, who had *"risen"* to become Emperor, is also an illusion – Vespasian's date of birth of 17 November, 9 CE, as given by Suetonius, may also need to be reconsidered. The Synoptic Gospels state Jesus died on the *ninth hour* and in the Bible the number 17 symbolizes *"overcoming the enemy"* and *"complete victory"*, given this parallel, Vespasian's birth date becomes suspect – could he have actually been born around the same time as Agrippa II? The illusion, based on what is written and what we have discovered so far, was that presenting Vespasian as a commoner during his time in Judea would give the ordinary soldiers the hope that they too could perhaps one day become emperor, leading to their supporting of his bid for the throne. The reality, however, behind the scenes, was that Vespasian was a royal.

The question now is where does the individual named 'Flavius Josephus' fit into this family? Well, that name *does not* fit in, anywhere, as detailed earlier, there is <u>no connection</u> to the Hasmonean royal house under that name or using the genealogy presented under that name. Flavius Josephus was a *pen-name* that belonged to a particular individual who was a member of a powerful and distinguished senatorial family the ancestry he presents belongs to, the family in question is a Roman-Jewish family called the **Calpurnius Pisos**, of the noble ancient house of Calpurnii. The house of the Calpurnii claimed descent from *Calpus*, the son of *Numa Pompilius*, the second legendary king of Rome, succeeding *Romulus*. But to understand the Calpurnius Pisos' connection to the Flavian family, we need to look within the historical writings that document Emperor **Vespasian** and his son **Titus Flavius**, and *their* descent from Herod Pollio. If Josephus was apparently 'adopted' and given a wife and house by Vespasian, we could expect to find contemporary records mentioning and confirming this. But again, we find none, only quotes from historians of the time, and any mentions are brief, Suetonius mentions him, but even what he says is slightly suspicious.

Suetonius says:

"*...Also, a distinguished Jewish prisoner of Vespasian's, **Josephus by name**, insisted that he would soon be released by the very man who had now put him in fetters and who would then be emperor...*" (Suetonius, The Twelve Caesars, Vespasian)

Notice that Suetonius says '*Josephus **by name***', why would he say *by name*? To me, this implies 'Josephus by name and not by birth.'

From the family of Emperor Vespasian to the family of the Pisos

Researching historical documents related to the Flavian's, and taking into consideration the parallels already investigated, 'Flavius Josephus' is revealed as being an alias name for a man called **Arrius Calpurnius Piso**. This name has been found within the original Koine Greek writings of the New Testament, particularly the *Gospel of Mark* and the *Book of Revelation*, and those writings present the words 'Arrius', 'Calpurnius', and 'Piso' using the *languages* and *numbers* of the time. Through prior research done regarding the Flavian and Piso family history, most notably by *Sir Ronald Syme*, the connection between the two families is revealed. It begins with a lady called **Arria Clementina** (Arrecina Clementina/Arria the Elder/Sr./Major) of royal Jewish descent marrying Emperor Vespasian's brother before Vespasian became emperor. Vespasian's brother was called **T. Flavius Sabinus II** (Caecina Paetus) the same as his father *Titus Flavius Sabinus I*. In historical documentation connected with T. Flavius Sabinus II, and inscription, the name '**Paetus**' in regards to the marriage of Flavia Sabina (Arria the Younger) is shown as being a name used by the **Pisos**; although the name on the inscription looks to have been connected with the wrong Piso family member. (**ref** – *'Doctors and Other Health Professionals In the Latin Epigraphy of Rome and the Italicae Augustae Regions,'* page 239 – *Flaviae T(iti) [f(iliae)] / Sabinae / Caesenni Paeti* (uxori) (CIL XIV, 2830)).

The marriage of *T. Flavius Sabinus II* to *Arria Clementina* (Arrecina Clementina/Arria the Elder/Sr./Major), shows that the man who will be shown to have been called *Arrius Calpurnius Piso* was also of **Flavian** descent. In Sir Ronald Syme's paper, *'People in Pliny'* JRS, pages 144, 146, and 148, quite a bit of information is provided for this family. In that paper, he states that an A. Caecina Paetus is a Roman consul in 37 CE in Patavium, with the Patavine **P. Clodius Thrasea Paetus** taking his daughter for a wife. The late professor Gavin Townend also provided much information in his *'Some Flavian Connections'* JRS 51, Parts I and II, where a Caesennius Paetus, a consul in 61 CE, is shown as a son of the former Paetus. Also mentioned here, as well as being found in the work of Tacitus, and researched by Syme (*Tacitus* 595, n.5), is the fact the Caesennius Paetus (son of the former Paetus) is married to Vespasian's niece, *Flavia Sabina*, in the early 70's and governs Syria.

Emperor Nero executed Arrius Calpurnius Piso's father, a very wealthy politician called **Gaius Calpurnius Piso**, in 65/67 CE, as a result of the failed '*Pisonian Conspiracy*'. This is recorded under the name **Thrasea Paetus**, Stoic philosopher (Tacitus, *Annals*, 16), whose wife was Arria the Younger (Tacitus, *Annals*, XVI.34) and a few pages previously in the *Annals*, the leader of the group of conspirators against Nero is named as **Calpurnius Piso** (Tacitus, *Annals*, 15.59); here Gaius' wife is presented as '*Satria Galla*', which can be viewed as T.S. Aria Galla, **Titia** (the feminine form of Titus) **Sabina** (the feminine form of Sabinus) Aria Galla (the feminine form of *Gallus*, which has the same meaning as *Pollio*, 'rooster'/'cock'/male chicken). That record of the execution led to the later discovery that **Arrius** was the son of **Gaius**, as Arrius is recorded under the name of **Caesennius Paetus**, governor of Syria (*Jewish War*, Book 7, 56-64) as well as 'Montanus' (Tacitus, *Annals*, 16.33); it seems he used many created names through the use of nomenclature, which will be shown, including *L. Caesoninus Junius Paetus*, discussed in Gavin Townend's paper above. It appears Arrius was given a masculine form of his mother's name **Arria**, who was the daughter of Arria Clementina (Arria the Elder/Sr./Major). I must say here that Gaius Calpurnius Piso's mother, Arrius' paternal grandmother, was called **Plancia Munatia**, who was the wife of *Gnaeus Calpurnius Piso*, consul in 7 BC. Plancia's father, Arrius' great-grandfather, was **Plancius Munatius**, the namesake of his *father, grandfather,* and *great-grandfather*. The name '*Mun-atia*' becomes '**Nun-atia**', as N is often used as a feminine ending in place of the female M in ancient languages. In Hebrew, M and N can be seen as equivalent, for example, the root of the word *Massekah* is 'Nesek'. '**Nun**' becomes '**non**', phonetically, producing the name '**Nonia**', and Nonia is a known name of the Balbii family, and '*Atia*' infers '*Balbii*' and '*Balbii*' means '**stutterer**', just as the name 'Psellus' does. (**ref** – Josephus, *Life*, Loeb, 1)

The information presented within the text of the New Testament, as will be examined later, indicates that **Arrius Calpurnius Piso** used the literary pen-name/pseudonym of 'Flavius Josephus'. It appears this name was created to not only provide a historical appearance of authenticity regarding the new religion of Christianity but also provide a 'role model' of sorts for later generations of Jews turning away from Judaism. The information above shows Arrius was already a Flavian through his inherited name usage, and *not* because Emperor Flavius Vespasian adopted him, as the ancient writers have told us. Essentially what we have is information leading us to understand that *T. Flavius Sabinus II* (Flavius Vespasian's brother) and *Arrecina (Arr(ia) (Ca)ecina) Clementina* (Arria the Elder/Sr./Major) had a daughter called *Aria/Arria*, who married *Gaius Calpurnius Piso*, and this is where the alliance of the **Flavian's** and the **Piso's** would begin.

Following The Trail From One Alias Name To The Next

To confirm the facts from this information, the family of 'Thrasea Paetus' (Gaius Calpurnius Piso) and *Arria the Younger* needs to be examined closely. To begin, they had a daughter, also named **Arria**, but we find the daughter being called '**Fannia**' in historical documents, which is also a name created using her Arria name. Information about a 'C. Fannius' (most likely Arrius Piso) as a barrister, who wrote the biographies of Nero's victims, is given in the '*Prosopographia Imperii Romani*' (Edmund Groag in PIR-2, F116). In there it reads:

> "C. Fannius (v, 5). *Barrister who wrote biographies of Nero's victims. Supposed a relative of Fannia, the daughter of the Patavine (P. [Publius] Clodius) Thrasea Paetus by his marriage with Arria, the daughter of A. [Aulus] Caecina Paetus (suff. 37) [T. Flavius Sabinus I].*"

Sir Ronald Syme, who researched this information, said:

> "Why she should be called '**Fannia**', no clue."

(**ref** – 'People in Pliny', *Journal of Roman Studies* 58)

I agree with Sir Ronald, it would be safe to think that a daughter of an **Arria** would use the name of her mother, somewhere. A closer look at this name reveals the **Arria** name *is* there: Her actual name would be **Flavia Arria**, which are the feminine forms of the names **Flavius** and **Arrius** combined. They used the '**F**' in '**Flavia**' as an initial and left it in front of her **Arria** name and changed the '**r**'s in her name to '**n**'s, which created the name '**Fannia**' (F. Annia.) But why are the r's replaced with n's? A definitive answer cannot be given, however, l, n, and r can be interchanged in Hebrew and in Semitic languages (**ref** – Aloysius Fitzgerald, 'The Interchange of L, N, and R in Biblical Hebrew', JBL, Vol. 97). Other possibilities include the letter 'n' being used as a link to Christianity, as the Phoenician letter was named 'nun', meaning '*fish*', and the fish and anchor symbols were used on the Flavian coins and other artifacts of that period, and the first symbol of Christianity was a fish. And let us not forget that one of the letters that make up the number '666' in the Book of Revelation, is Phoenician. (**ref** – **Thrasea Paetus** and **C. Caecina Paetus**; '*Domitius Corbulo*', by Sir Ronald Syme, *Journal of Roman Studies*, (post-1969). His source was **Pliny the Younger**, Epp. III, 16. 7 ff.)

Supporting information to confirm the above can be found by reading Tacitus. (**ref** – Tacitus, *Annals*, XVI. 33., Loeb Classical Library edition. See also the Bibliographical Index in *the Letters of Pliny the Younger* (Letters and Panegyricus), Loeb Classical Library edition.) In these supporting references, he is mentioned as '**Arrius Antoninus**', which, as will be explained later in the book, is just one of many alias names used by him or for him. When reading the above reference documents, we find out that a '**Montanus**', meaning '**mountain**' in **Latin**, was also '*spared out of consideration for his father*' Thrasea Paetus (Gaius Calpurnius Piso). This 'Montanus' must be *another* alias name for Arrius, and this and other alias names, and the forced suicide of his father, will be examined. (**ref** – Tacitus, *Annals*, Book XVI, XXXIII, pg. 387, Loeb). The references provided above give data for **Thrasea Paetus**; **Arria the Elder**; **Atria the Younger**; **Fannia**; **Montanus** and **Arrius Antoninus**. Please Note that Atria the Younger is also called '**Caecina ANNIA**' in history. (**ref** – Tacitus, *The Annals*, Book XVI, XXXIV, pg. 387, Loeb edition).

EVIDENCE

This next section will explain the discoveries that support the evidence that the Roman-Jewish royal man **Arrius Calpurnius Piso** ('Flavius Josephus') existed. But it is important to understand and keep in mind that the discoveries which have been made regarding this, mean that the current understandings related to this period in history are not accurate.

> The following information will present how it can be shown that:
>
> **1)** 'Flavius Josephus' was indeed a royal man named
>
> Arrius Calpurnius Piso
>
> and
>
> **2)** That the activities of 'Jesus' are based on the activities of Arrius Piso

Arrius Piso's name does not appear in *full* in historical documents, which means he must have made certain, with help from close friends and family members, that his real name was never to be found anywhere *obvious* or straightforward in history. That means his identity was hidden from everyone but a limited few, and it is only by connecting his name to his father's alias name of 'Thrasea Paetus', and by finding his mother's name as Arria, and finding his names *Arrius*, *Calpurnius*, and *Piso* presented in the New Testament, that Arrius' name is revealed. His name was discovered and put back together because it is found in parts *'chopped up'* here and there, mainly being used as part of his alias names, but also by being found within key statements made by the character 'Jesus'. As far as I can tell, one of the biggest challenges for the original researchers, in this case, must have been the process of putting all of those 'pieces' together to reveal his full name. The Jewish historical literature of the time also appears to try to point to Arrius Piso being the creator of the 'Jesus' or *Yeshu* character in the Gospels, and this was done with the use of the '**Pantera**' riddle, which again will also be explained in more detail later on. But to prove that **Arrius Calpurnius Piso** was the *main* author of the Gospels, we need to **1)** remember the parallels we have just investigated in the previous chapter, and **2)** understand the *words* and important phrases in the New Testament that reveal Arrius' name and alias names.

Regarding the historical documents we have available to research, we can learn about what actually happened, because the Romans were not the only ones who left records behind for us to discover. The Jews (**Pharisees**), who Rome was at war with, likewise left us what information they could, but because of the situation they found themselves in, they too used what has been referred to, by 'Roman Piso', as a *'royal language'*. The Jews (**Pharisees**) would **not** have been able to write about these events openly and so would have had no choice but to resort to using hints, riddles, and clues, however *'conspiracy-like'* that may sound.

A little bit about the 'Royal Language'

To understand the information in the next chapters, it is very important to first understand information regarding how Arrius and his family used the various languages of the time within the New Testament. They seem to have created a language *within* a language that incorporated literary techniques already being used by the aristocracy at the time, the original researchers have referred to this as *'the royal language'*. Its purpose was to deliver or present information that only *they* understood and knew about, similar, in a way, to the code system Julius Caesar and Spanish king Ferdinand II of Aragon used. This 'literary code' was used because many things could be said or presented to other royals and members of the aristocracy, within the texts, in such a way that those who were not involved, i.e. – those classed as commoners, could not discover. These discoveries were made when reading the primary source or *Prima Facie* documents, a term used in academic philosophy, which is defined as something that has been proven or assumed to be true unless there is evidence presented to the contrary. Like the 'Josephus' discoveries, these discoveries have been ridiculed, which, of course, can only be expected. In certain places in the New Testament, there were different meanings behind words, and whilst reading the texts in **Koine Greek**, there would be alternate or different meanings presented if the same text was read as if it was in **Latin**, the language of the Roman aristocracy. This means the words and letters used to present something thing in **Greek**, would mean something different if someone knew what the word/s meant in **Latin**. The importance of this discovery may not be clear at this stage, but when the words are examined, and their meanings understood, it will hopefully bring clarity to the confusion the Bible texts have presented. The examination will also hopefully show that the grammar "mistakes" within the scriptures were written on purpose.

A little example of this 'royal language' would be the use of the Latin letter '**P**', which has the **same sound** as the **Greek letter** '**Pi**' (π) which is pronounced '**Pay**', but the Latin letter '**P**'s *glyph* (symbol) looks like the **glyph** for the **Greek** letter '**Rho**' (ρ) which is pronounced like '**row** a boat'. That means letters would be written the *same way* but would be *pronounced* differently. This use of letters is a tiny part of what has been discovered, and, as stated above, these subtle differences in appearance and pronunciation were used by the ancient authors. They also used small literary techniques, regularly, and these techniques also made up a tiny part of what this *'royal language'* was, essentially, an entire language in itself. What has also been discovered is that patterns of words in texts ran repeatedly. For a skilled reader in the know, they presented what can be referred to as '**keywords**', and two types were discovered. One type is referred to by 'Roman Piso' as a '*circle*' and the other as a '*string*', and that is because of the way the 'keywords' were used. These 'keywords' could have been seen as a subtle 'signature' by the authors of these texts.

An example of a 'circle' of words that link the names '**Flavius Josephus**' and **Arrius Calpurnius Piso** together, are as follows –

'**Vita**' is the Latin word for 'Life' or 'Bio', so Flavius Josephus'

Vita (*life*) means '**Bio**'. In **Latin** the word '**Vios**' also means '**life**', but '**V**' is also seen as a '**U**', which gives us the word '**uios**', which means '**son**', as in 'Jesus' as the '**son**' of God.

But '**Vita**'/'**Vios**' in Latin, which is '**Bios**' in Greek, can also become '**Piso**' because the '**V**' sound changes to an '**F**' sound by becoming '**PH**' and '**PH**' is the same as '**P**', so we get '**Pios**' (Pius/Piso) instead of '**Bios**'. '**Pio**' is also '**Piso**' because '**Pia**' or '**Pisa**' can be the feminine versions of '**Piso**' and the male form as we have seen can be '**Piso**' or '**Pio**'.

So not only does the word '**Vita**' become the word '**Son**', but it can also become the word '**Piso**', which is connected to the word for 'Life', as in "the **Life**" (Jesus) or '**Bios**' or the '**Vita**'. That means the word '**Vita**' circles from '**Flavius Josephus**', through Arrius **Piso**, through to '**Jesus**' (Life), and then back to '**Flavius Josephus**'. What we have then is **Vita/Vios** changing to **Uios** (Son) – and then the **V** in Vita/Vios also becoming an **F sound** by becoming **PH** (P), creating **Pios** (Piso)

In **John 10:17**, 'Jesus' says, "*I lay down my Life* (**Vita/Vios**)", now, *Pliny the Younger* says, in his Epistles in Book II of II, the Loeb Classical Library edition, page 267, "*the Law laid down*" ("laid down the Law"), but when Pliny says '*laid down*', he means "*written down*". So we have two ways of looking at this statement –

1) Is with 'Jesus' in terms of the story saying he is sacrificing his life (Vita/Vios/Piso).

2) The other way to look at this statement is by realizing that

Arrius Piso (as 'Jesus'), is saying he has **'written down his Vita (Life)'**. But 'Jesus' never writes his 'Vita' or 'Life' or 'Bio'. The only 'Vita' in this case, is the 'Vita' of **Arrius Piso** writing as **'Flavius Josephus'**, which would also be the 'Vita' or 'Life' of 'Jesus' when the parallels between 'Josephus' and the Gospels are compared.

'**Jesus**' says he is 'the **Life**' in **John 14:6** by saying "*I am the way, the truth, and the Life*" ('Vita'). **John 1:4**, says "*the Life was the Light*", i.e. 'Jesus' was the 'Life' (Vita). In **John 14:6**, 'Jesus' also says "**no one comes to the 'Father' but by me**", which in the Bible story means 'God', but the Bible says 'Jesus' and 'God' are the same person. In reality, that would mean that the 'Father' being referred to is the 'Pater' (Peter) of the Church. This statement should then be understood in the following way – it means that for someone to discover, or '*come to*', the 'Father' or 'Pater' of the Church, these discoveries regarding Arrius Piso have to be made.

It also appears that this 'royal language' was used universally, which is quite fitting considering 'Catholic' means 'universal'. The Pisos and members of the aristocracy used this language in such a way that it would be able to "crossover" in usage within various languages. The royals knew many languages, *Latin*, *Greek*, and *Hebrew*, for example, and how those languages worked. They then used the 'rules' in those languages when writing in different languages, for instance, using the *vowel switching* of the **Hebrew** language (a,e,i,o,u) when writing in **Latin**, to give information. That means the way they used this language *within* a language, incorporated more than one language in several ways. One of those ways included the use of **syntax**, the arrangement of *words* and *phrases* used to create well-formed sentences in a language. In effect, those who only knew **one** language in use at that time, for example, Greek, could not read and therefore understand what was being said within those texts. Understanding the above information within the context of the history of the time in which it was used is vital in understanding why a 'royal language' would have been used in the first place, and it allows us to read it just as it would have been read and understood by those who knew about it. Because this information is found within the New Testament texts, it shows that 1) the authors most likely knew at some point it would be found by those who knew the language, and 2) that the way the names/words were presented was deliberate. The ancient royal authors were highly educated people and were in complete control of what kind of evidence, facts, and various information they would decide to leave us through their literary work, meaning *nothing* was written by accident. Another very important fact to know is that these ancient royal authors appear to have only written about their relatives and close acquaintances. This was accomplished by either using an alias/psuedonym, real name or a combination, as discussed above. This means that if royals and other members of the nobility were the only ones who had the means and freedom to create this kind of literature, identifying who wrote what is narrowed down to certain historical individuals of the time.

ONTO THE EVIDENCE

Before we move on and look at the proof within the scriptures themselves, I feel it is a good idea to first inspect the alias names that Arrius Calpurnius Piso used, and how they link to the events he took part in. The reason is that the information presented later may not otherwise be understood. To begin, as mentioned before, we find nothing relating to the name 'Flavius Josephus' in the Jewish literature, and the Hebrew version of this name, **Yosef Ben Matityahu**, does not appear either. We must also be mindful that alias names are an annoying problem and create a gap in establishing convincing proof. That said, other areas can be pursued to expose what really happened, for example, building genealogies for the main suspects is a good starting point, as that can indicate which ancestral names were used for certain alias names, and we do know that aliases were used in those times and names were much more flexible. We also need to remember that the authors of that time would have known who they were writing about and why they were using and referencing these various names to refer to Arrius Piso. The first clue, albeit not much of a clue, that **Arrius Calpurnius Piso** was 'Josephus' is that the birth dates are the same, 'Josephus' says he was born in **37 CE** and **Arrius Calpurnius Piso** was born in **37 CE**. It looks like Arrius died in the year **119 CE**, his death appears to have been recorded under the name (G)C. *Antius Julius Quadratus Bassus*. This name is used for an individual who had governed several provinces and commanded a corps of several legions in the second Dacian war under the Roman Emperor Trajan. The name Arrius seems to have been disguised as 'Antius', with the double 'r' of Arrius being changed to 'nt', using both the Greek and Hebrew language rules. 'Quadratus' is Latin for '*square*', of which 36 is a square number and *Pythagoras*' most famous theorem was his 47th, which said the square of the *hypotenuse* equaled the sum of the squares of the other two sides (the significance of this will be explained later). The name 'Bassus' may have been used because he saw himself as 'Bacchus' or 'Dionysios', the god of the vine, as in **Acts** Jesus says he is the *true vine* and his "father" (creator) is the vinedresser. As C. Antius Julius Quadratus Bassus, Arrius died whilst campaigning when he was sent to Dacia as the final consular governor; at that time he would have been approximately 80-years old. (**ref** – *Syme, Sir Ronald, The Roman Papers, Vol. III, pp.* 1286, 1392). Apparently 'Josephus' died in approximately **100 CE**, which is concluded because no publications under that name appear after the death of Emperor Domitian.

Next, we learn that 'Josephus' gives details of his sons who were born during the reign of Emperor Vespasian, they are called **Hyrcanus**, born in the fourth year of the reign, **Justus**, born in the seventh year of the reign, and **Agrippa**, also called *Simonides*, (for reasons unknown at this point, but possibly used as a connection to the Herodian family,) born in the ninth. I must note here that the actual names of Arrius sons have been concluded by the information that will be explained later, but, to continue, 'Josephus' writes about the Maccabees, including *John Hyrcanus* who is a high priest and is first mentioned in the background portion of the *Jewish War*, 'Josephus' calls him "*John, also called Hyrcanus*". Next, we have **Justus**, who appears as '*James*' in Josephus' *Vita* as a bodyguard, and on one occasion that bodyguard is named *Justus*, and lastly, we have **Agrippa** (*Simonides*), which is simply a longer form of the name '*Simon*'. In the *Vita* ('Bio') of 'Josephus', we learn that Arrius was ***first*** married to a virgin of Jotapata and that he divorced her, he does not mention any children from this marriage. His **second** wife was of Alexandria, Egypt, and was apparently of the line of the 'Alexanders'. She may also have been Boionia Priscilla/Procilla, as in history, an individual named Arrius Antoninus is recorded as marrying a Boionia, however, more research needs to be done regarding this wife. But Arrius writes, as Josephus, that she was with *Titus* at the siege of Jerusalem. Arrius Piso had divorced her as well, but he had three children with her before doing so. He says that *two* of those children are 'dead' (at the time of writing his *Vita*).

According to the researchers, one of the sons of this second wife was named '*Alexander*', the eldest, but he was dead at the time the *Vita* was written, which would have been during the end of the reign of Emperor Domitian. The remaining children from that marriage were a daughter called Claudia Phoebe (*Arria Fadilla, Pompeia Plotina*), and a son, who was still alive, called *Julius Calpurnius Piso*. Arrius' **third** wife had lived in Crete and was a Jewess by birth, but because of what he says about his third wife, she *appears* to be *Queen Berenice*, sister of *King Agrippa II*, he does not say that he divorced his last wife, and tells us that she gave him two children. Those children are known to us in history as (*Fabius*) *Justus Calpurnius Piso*, and *Proculus (Calpurnius Piso)*, Pliny the Younger even writes a letter to Proculus, using the name *Silius Proculus*, in book 3, letter 15, where he replies to Silius Proculus who had asked him to comment on his '*poetry*'. Also in the *Vita*, as mentioned above, Arrius gives the year of birth for his three living sons, and he does this by saying they were born during *certain years of the reign of Emperor Vespasian*. That means by deduction we find out that **Julius Piso** was born in 73-74 CE and died in 138 CE;

Arrius would be about 35 or 36 at the time writing, Julius would be about 21; **Claudia Phoebe** was born before 77 CE and died 129 CE as *Pompeia Plotina*; **Justus Piso** was born in 76-77 CE and died after 140 CE; he would be about 17, Arrius would be about 39 or 40, and **Proculus** (*Agrippa*) was born in 78-79 CE and died after 115 CE; he would be about 16, and Arrius, 40 or 41. This is information that tells us much more than just the birth dates of these sons, it also tells us Arrius was still with his second wife up until at least 74 CE and that he married his third, and final wife, sometime before 77 CE.

To clarify, Arrius says, "*I have three (living) sons...*" Arrius Piso had divorced his first and second wives, and his sons *Alexander* and *Julius* were of the same mother-his second wife. According to scholar '*Abelard Reuchlin*', Alexander seems to have been placed in the New Testament as '*Andrew*' and is found in Matt. 4:18; 10:2; Mark 1:16, 1:29; 3:18; 13:3; Luke 6:14; John 1:40, 1:44; 6:8; 12:22; and Acts 1:13. He may have been the person mentioned as a kinsman of '*Paul*' who is called '*Andronicus*' in Romans 16:7. Alexander also seems to appear as a disciple named Andrew-who is the/a 'brother' of *Simon Peter*. (**ref** – Abelard Reuchlin, *The True Authorship of the New Testament*, page 12). In Romans 16:7 '**Junias**' is mentioned, and the current understanding is that this individual was a female, but when the information indicates that Alexander and Julius Piso had the same mother, and you know that letters such as '**l**' and '**n**' were interchangeable, in *Biblical Hebrew*, which is information given by the use of phonetics, you can see that passage read; "*Salute Andronicus and JULIUS, my kinsmen...*" Scholar '*Roman Piso*' has stated that "*putting Andrew/Alexander (as Andronicus) together with Julius, confirms what we had found in the Vita-that these two* *brothers belonged together as they both shared the same mother."* Alexander appears to have been killed by Domitian, which then led to Domitian, in turn, being killed, that means we find out, by deduction, that Alexander was born between 71-73 CE and died around 95 CE, Justus and Proculus Piso's mother was a Jewess who had lived in Crete. In regards to the son called 'Alexander', I must note that the third Pope of Rome was called St. Anacletus, who was martyred under Emperor Domitian. The name 'Anacletus' is interesting, as it appears to be the two names An(drew) and Alex combined, as the 'c' in the 'acletus' part sounds like 'ch', as in 'loch', but its glyph is X, which renders Alex(c) when the letters are rearranged. That gives us the names An(drew)Alex(ander), and the 'tus' on the end is theos, which in Greek means God, as *tus* can be *thus*, which comes from the Ancient Greek *thuos*, which becomes *theos*.

If Arrius was the '*creator*' of 'Jesus', then he may have considered his created/invented character Jesus as a "son" as well, possibly. With that being the case, it may give us a clue as to why **Matt. 13:55** says that Jesus has *four* brothers. Since the 'core' or prototype of the Gospel of 'Matthew' was written around the year 75, (which I will explain later), we can deduce that either these sons of Arrius Piso were added to it after they were born or it was not truly finished until all of his sons were born. Meaning that 'Matthew' was not finished until sometime *after* 79 CE (the year of birth of his last son, *Proculus* (Agrippa) C. Piso. To again clarify the above information, what we seem to have is Arrius writing in his *Vita* that he has three sons (five, but two are 'dead'). One son, 'Alexander' was dead when Arrius wrote his Bio/Vita, the other 'son' he says was '*dead*', may have been his daughter, or he could have been hinting at his "dead son" Jesus. The **Hasmonean** names of his fictional sons are: *John Hyrcanus, Justus,* (remember, they are Flavians), and *Agrippa Simon,* but what would their Roman names be? The son John Hyrcanus would have been the same age as Julius Calpurnius Piso, the next son would be Fabius Justus, and the third son, known in history as S. Proculus in the works of *Pliny The Younger,* may have been named after the Pisos' relative 'Proculus Vitellius', the brother of Emperor Aulus Vitellius, who appears in Arrius' *Antiquities of the Jews,* book 19, chapter 6.

Regarding Arrius' genealogy, as 'Josephus', he claims to be from the Royal Family, on his ***mother's side***. She is descended from the **Royal Hasmonean** priest's family (the family of **Herod the Great**). This family was running the Maccabean Kingdom at that time, and 'Josephus' introduces himself as **Iosepos** son of **Matthias**, and this is the exact ancestry of Arrius Piso. His mother was a great-granddaughter of Herod the Great, which would be the family of **Matthias**. Next, we look at the military campaign of **'Titus'** (Titus Flavius), the son of Emperor Vespasian. This is the man who is said to be the individual whom 'Josephus' is talking about regarding the military campaign in Judea. But because of the events described in the *Wars of the Jews,* the *'Titus'* individual cannot be Emperor Vespasian's son, during parts of the historical account. That means that 'Josephus' is writing about Arrius Calpurnius Piso, that is to say, Arrius is writing about himself, or again writing his *Vita* or *Bio* for the majority of the activities described. Arrius is using the name *'Titus'* and is only referring to Titus Flavius in certain parts of the books. Most of the information regarding Vespasian's son, Titus, was explicitly stated by making it clear that the individual being discussed was either Vespasian's son or Domitian's brother.

Arrius Calpurnius Piso In The Writings Of 'Josephus'

Emperor Nero exiled Arrius Piso to Syria to act as governor, which also gave him command of the legions controlling **Judaea**. When writing as **'Josephus'**, he records his service in Judaea in the year 65 CE under the name of **'Gessius Florus'** and then in 66 CE with the alias name **'Cestius Gallus'**. The historical records state that **Nero** exiles a **'Caesennius Paetus'** to **Syria** after executing Gaius Calpurnius Piso, and if we remember who 'Caesennius Paetus' was, it means the records are referring to **Arrius**. So it was **Arrius Piso** who Nero exiled to **Syria** to act as governor. To understand the entire reason why Gaius Calpurnius Piso was executed, it is important to first understand the events *after* the execution, and how they relate to Arrius Piso. To do that, Arrius' alias names must be examined to make sure they do indeed link to him, so you can recognize them within the context and events in which he used them.

To recap, so far, the above information leads us to find the full name of the unnamed son of Thrasea Paetus/Gaius Calpurnius Piso. It then leads us to Flavius Josephus and then to 'Montanus' as a supposed alias name of Arrius. What appears to be the case, is that the following names were created using either the family names of the Pisos, words which refer to phallic god symbolism, words that relate to themes within the New Testament, or a combination of these. An important point to note is that in ancient languages vowels were interchangeable, for example in the Egyptian language they were seen as not being there, i.e. *'invisible'*, and how they were used in the examples below, means the interchanging of vowels were used to make names appear to be different to readers. What will hopefully become clear is that Arrius only pretended to be a *'Jewish'* General, when writing as 'Josephus', which is technically not a lie. He *was* of Jewish descent on his mother's side, but what he *should* have said was that he was a *Roman General* of Jewish descent, because of his descent from King Herod.

Arrius Calpurnius Piso's alias names

|

CAESENNIUS PAETUS

As we have examined leads us to discover **Arrius Calpurnius Piso**.

|

ARRIUS CALPURNIUS PISO

This name leads us to the alias name '**Montanus**'. '**Montanus**', which means '**mountain**' in **Latin**, is spared out of consideration for his father when killed by forced suicide on the order of **Nero**, his father being Gaius Piso ('**Thrasea Paetus**'). One of the reasons for this alias name of Arrius could be because he saw himself, in human form, as the god Mars, who was the God of War. It seems he may have joked about this in the New Testament, where "**Mar's Hill**" is mentioned, because "*Mar's Hill*" in Greek is "**Areios Pagos**". A 'mountain', or large hill, in Greek, is "*Pagos*", which means we have "**Areios** (*Arrius*) Mountain/Montanus", and "***pagos***" can also be "*opus*" ("**ippos**" phonetically in Greek) and "ip(p)os" is "horse" or "beast" which is also what Arrius seems to be referred to. Out of the word "**Ippos**" we can see the name **Piso** rearranged, and in the Book of Revelation, Arrius is referred to as "the Beast", which we shall see. So, "*Mar's Hill*" in Greek means **Arrius Ippos/Piso**. (**ref** – Acts 17:19 and 17:22). *Pliny The Younger* also makes mention of a 'Montanus' around this time. (**ref** – Pliny The Younger, Loeb Classical Library Edition, VII. 29; VIII. 6)

|

MONTANUS

leads us to the alias name **Arrius Antoninus**, but why?

In ancient Rome, alias names incorporated the parts of other names and/or **initials** or **abbreviations**. The Piso family, and therefore Arrius Calpurnius Piso, was descended from the **Antonii** family line, which means they were descendants of **Marc Antony**. That means Arrius would have been able to use this inherited name to form part of this name, which explains the '**Anto(ni)**' part of this alias name. The '**Ninus**' part of this name appears to be a title or nickname, that Arrius added on. It is the **Greek** '**nini**', which means '**baby**' or '**infant**'. In the **Book of Revelation**, the word *dragon* is mentioned, the word **dragon** in **Greek** is '**Draco**' and means '**baby boy**', and can also be a name for a boy. So here we have Arrius using an alias name that incorporates the word '**nini**' meaning '**baby**'.

|

ARRIUS ANTONINUS

leads us to the alias name **Arrius Varus,** why?

The name '**Varus**' is the Roman form of the Egyptian word '**Veru**', meaning '**great men**'. But if someone uses it as part of the name of an individual, then it means the man who used it would have considered himself a '**great** man'.

As '**Arrius Verus**', Arrius is discovered as being the founding ancestor of the later great Roman family the '**Annii Anicii**', who were prominent Romans in the later Roman Empire (**ref** - Piso Christ, THE ANNI ANICI, pg. 37). '**Annius**' and '**Arrius**' are the same, as we have seen with the example regarding his sister '**Fannia**', where the letters '**n**' and '**r**' have been switched. So Arrius Piso is the founder of the '**Annii Anicii**', a family that came from a great-grandfather of Emperor Marcus Aurelius, founder of the **Annii Verii**. This great-grandfather of Marcus Aurelius was also the grandfather of **Annia Galeria Faustina I**, who was the wife of Emperor **Antoninus Pius**. In 'Marcus Aurelius, a Biography', by Birley, published at Yale, circa 1986, there is a genealogy chart for the **Annii Veri**(i). This chart mentions '**Annius** (Arrius) **Verus**' of Ucubi as the common ancestor of the **Annii Verii**. To fully understand this, you would need to understand the use of alias names in antiquity. The term "Annii Anicii" is very telling because one of Arrius' main alias names was "**Nicomachus**" (as will be examined). "Annii" refers to "**Arrii**(us)" and "Anicii" refers to '**Anico**(machus)', with '**A**' as an initial for "Antonius/Antoninus". The reason being is because Arrius Piso seems to have also been known as/used the name "**Antonius (Primus)**". Again, the "**A**" in "Anicii" is an initial that is in front of "Nicii". "**Nico**(n)" means winner or 'victor', and as a Roman general at the battle of Garaza, that is what Arrius was, the 'victor'. This must be the origin of his 'nickname' "**Nicomachus**", which is found in his works of Flavius Josephus, as some of the Annii Anicii family boldly joke about this by naming their offspring "Nicomachus". Examples of which are: *Amnius Manlius Nicomachus Anicius Paulinus*, and *Marcus Junius Caesonius Nicomachus Anicius Faustus*.

Regarding **Antonius Primus**, **Tacitus** says – "As **Antonius** ('**Antonius Primus**') *hurried forward some dispatchments from the cohorts and part of the cavalry to invade Italy, he was accompanied by* "**Arrius Varus**" ... Arrius Piso was both 'Arrius Varus' and 'Antoninus Primus'. So the word '**accompanied by**' in this case, means that he was the same person, wherever '**Antonius Primus**' went, '**Arrius Varus**' went. In the same passage, **Tacitus** says – "However, **Antonius** (Primus) and **Varus** (of course) occupied **Aquileia**...", this is because it was the same person. **Tacitus** also calls "**Antonius Primus**" – "**Primus Antonius**", which is interesting. It can be speculated that the purpose Tacitus had in mind, was to confuse the reader into thinking he was speaking about two different people, just as he does in calling **Arrius Piso** several (alias) names. (**ref** – Tacitus, II, *Histories*, Book III, V1, pg. 337. Loeb Classical Library edition).

|

ARRIUS VERUS

leads us to the alias name **Annius Gallus**, why?

'**Annius**' is just another way of spelling '**Arrius**', because as before, '**r**' and '**n**' could be switched, so now we have **Arrius** we look for '**Gallus**'. When the writings of **Suetonius** are investigated, it is discovered that the person who killed the emperor **Vitellius** was '**Antonius Primus**', who had the nickname '**Becco**', which is Latin for '*cock*'. But 'cock' is also a word for a male chicken, or a '**rooster**', and '**Gallus**' means the same thing *and* refers to a person from the province of **Gaul**. But '*Gallus*' is also another way of using the word '**Pollio**' (Pollo), which is a name that Arrius had inherited from his great-grandmother **Vespasia Polla**, and these two words mean the same thing. They refer to the '*rooster*', and the '**rooster**' is connected to the **Phoenix** which is found to be associated with the phallic symbol which is used to symbolize '**God**'. So, in a hidden way, calling Arrius '**Gallus**' means that when this word is used as a name, it can be seen as referring to him as a 'phallus symbol' which represents '**gods**'. If you search for the term '*Phallic God*', you will find information referring to the Phallus as symbolizing Roman Gods. So **Suetonius** was an author who used the alias name '**Annius** (Arrius) **Gallus**', but we also find the name used in **Plutarch's** *Lives under* Otho and **Juvenal** also mentions '**Gallus**' in his works. (**ref** – Juvenal, VII. 144, Loeb) **Tacitus** also used this name, see- Tacitus, II, *Histories*, Book II, XLIV, pg. 233 and Tacitus, II, *Histories*, Book II, XXXIII, pg. 215, and Tacitus, *Histories*, Book II, XI and *Tacitus*, II, *Histories*, Book I, LXXXVII, pg.151).

|

ANNIUS GALLUS

leads us to the alias names **Gessius Florus** and **Cestius Gallus**, why?

'**Gessius** *Florus*' looks to be the ancestral name '**Cassius**' disguised, that ancestral name could be *Gaius Cassius Longinus*, who was expelled from Rome by Nero for being a part of the Pisonian Conspiracy, only to return when Vespasian took the throne. The '**FL**' from '**Flavius**' is attached to the '**orus**' part of '**Florus**', '**Orus**' possibly being a part of the name '**Horus**', who was the '**Egyptian God**' and who has been likened to Jesus, although there is no agreement on that. But from what has been discovered, and from what we know about ancient Roman leaders in general, Arrius now appears to see himself in the role of '**God**', as the words used to create these names suggest. As '**Gessius Florus**', Arrius is a Roman procurator in **Judea** and causes the Jewish revolt. Writing as 'Josephus', Arrius tries to make it appear that '**Gessius Florus**' and '**Cestius Gallus**' are two different people, but that doesn't seem to be the case. The name '**Cestius**' is the same as the name '**Gessius**', as seen in the *'royal language'*, because in Latin '**C**' and '**G**' is switch-able to the point of being the same, and '**S**' and '**T**' are used in the same way, for example, in the Biblical name *Zur* and *Tzur-Tsur*, which means '**stone**' or '**rock**'.

Steve Mason stated in the book '*Flavius Josephus Judean War 2*', page 226, that:

"*When abbreviating the tria nomima, Romans usually referred to their peers by the nomen gentilicium, the middle of the 3 principal names—as Josephus does here, and he will similarly call Cestius Gallus "Cestius." Normally, however, he uses the governor's cognomen, Florus (e.g., 32 times from 2.280 to 343).*"

While we are looking at Arrius Piso and his use of the name '**Gallus**' as being another way of using his inherited name of '**Pollio**', and another way of saying **chicken** or **fowl**, which relates to the winged-phallus that 'Jesus' was synonymous with, *another* name by which Arrius was known was that of **'Annius Pollio'**. Again, the **'Annius'** name is **'Arrius'** because the **'r'** and **'n'** are switched. This name was incriminated in the **Pisonian Conspiracy** (plot) against **Nero** and was sent into exile. Of course, this is what happened to Arrius under other alias names if we remember the names 'Montanus' and 'Caesennius Paetus'. Arrius Piso as a Roman General **'Cestius Gallus'** had fallen while on his horse and must have had his leg crushed under the weight of that horse, he could have died. But the Jews (**Pharisees**) captured him and put him in prison. It seems they had compassion upon him and wanted him to recover (perhaps so they could question him), and they most likely removed his leg and assisted in his recovery. Arrius writing as 'Flavius Josephus' tells us a little about what had happened, he says that the Jews (**Pharisees**) had even allowed his mother (Arria) to visit him while they imprisoned him. (**ref** – *'**Domitius Corbulo**'* by Sir Ronald Syme in the *Journal of Roman Studies*, post-1969; and also **Tacitus**, *Annals*, XVI, 30, 3, and **Tacitus**, *Annals*, XVI, 21, I. Arrius Piso as **'Annius Pollio'** was sentenced to exile – in **Tacitus**, *Annals*, Book XV, LXXI, pg. 329, Loeb Classical Library Edition). Also, the Roman writer **Martial** (Marcus Valerius Martialis) mentions **'Cestius Callus'** in his works (**ref** – Martial, XLII, 2., Loeb Classical Library), so we discover that Martial must have been aware of who Arrius was and why he used this name.

|

GESSIUS FLORUS AND CESTIUS GALLUS

lead us to the alias name **Antonius Primus**, why?

Arrius as '**Antonius Primus**' is supposed to have been born in **Gaul**, so, he can be referred to as '**Gallus**', according to **Suetonius**. Also, as seen above, he adds that as a boy '**Antonius Primus**' had the '**nickname**' (alias name) of '**becco**', which means **rooster's beak**. '*Primus*' in **Latin** means '*the first*'/'*foremost*' and '**St. Peter**' is considered the first '**Bishop**' of Rome, which later became known as '*Pope*' or '*pater*' (Peter), '*Pater*' meaning 'father'. So if Arrius was the creator of Christianity, then he would be the first '*father*' ('*pater*') of Rome. Also, the name '**Antonius Primus**' was used by Arrius himself in the works that he wrote as '**Flavius Josephus**' and as shown above, that name is also found used about him in the works of **Suetonius**, and **Tacitus**. (**ref** – Tacitus, ll, Histories, Book 11, LXXXVI, pg. 131, Loeb Classical Library Edition).

The following information supports the realization that '**Marcus Antonius Primus**' was indeed a pseudonym/alias name of Arrius Piso.

– From (n) (Tacitus, *Histories* III.6)

1) Pliny the Younger married Arrius Piso's granddaughter, who was the daughter of Arrius' son Alexander, and so Pliny the Younger became a '*new son*' with the name '*Alexander*', as the masculine form of '*Calpurnia Alexandra*'.

2) Suetonius wrote in his *Lives of the Caesars*, Book IV. XXXV, that Emperor (G)*Caius Caligula* 'appropriated' (took) Gaius' wife at their wedding, which would have been before Arrius was born, about the year 36 CE. Caligula fancied Gaius Piso's wife Arria (recorded as *Livia Cornelia Orestilla*) and so banished Gaius Piso from Rome, but he would return a year later.

Caligula was also a descendant of Marcus Antonius (Mark Anthony); Arria the Younger's name of *Livia* is another form of *Julia*. So her name is seen as **L** (for Lucia) which becomes **Iul**(i)**a** [Julia] – ('*ivia*' becomes **Julia**-I and J were identical as were V and U) **Ari**(a) ('Ore' in *Orestilla* becomes **Ari** using the Hebrew vowel switching rule) **S** (Sabina-the s in Ore**s**tilla), and Tull(i)a (from the *Tilla* part of Orestilla). Her 'Julia' name connects her to the Julian ancestry, her Cornelia name connects her with others who used the female and male forms of the name, for example, the historian Tacitus. The Tull(i)a portion of her name comes from her Flavian ancestry, that of Titus Flavius Petro's wife, Tertullia.

Reference for the above is in '**Lucian**', written by **Marcus Aurelius**. Also in **Pliny's letters**, **Arrius** is mentioned under the name '**Arius Antoninus**' as the Grandfather of Pliny's wife (Calpurnia Alexandra).

– The above information from Suetonius is quite interesting in terms of the birth story of 'Jesus'. Please see the notes section at the back of the book.

3) Tacitus' description of **Marcus Antonius Primus** would certainly fit a description of someone who deliberately caused people to rebel, such as **Arrius Piso**:

Tacitus describes him as: "*being brave in action, ready of speech, clever at bringing* **others** *into odium (which means general or widespread hatred or disgust created by someone as a result of their actions), powerful in times of* **civil war** *and* **rebellion**, *greedy, extravagant, in peace a bad citizen, in war an ally not to be despised*".

4) Arrius Piso used his '**Antonius**' name in the creation of his '**Antonius Primus**' name, which is mentioned by **Tacitus** & **Pliny The Younger**. He further hints at his ancestry from **Marc Antony** using this name by letting us know that this '**Antonius Primus**' was '**Marcus Antonius Primus**' in his fuller name, by providing the '**M**' at the start of the name. Arrius uses his name in the alias name he used in history as '*Arrius Antoninus*', the founder of the '**Antonine**' dynasty, and it was Arrius himself in his *Jewish War* IV.495 who was the first to give details of the campaign conducted by 'Antonius Primus' for Vespasian against Emperor **Vitellius**. Also, Arrius ('Josephus') inserts 'Antonius' (himself) as a centurion who dies at the capture of Jotapata (*Jewish War* III.333).

5) Marcus Antonius Primus' colleague in the campaign against **Vitellius** is named '**Arrius Varus**' (Tacitus, *Histories* III.6), but as we have found out above, this is another alias name of **Arrius**. In the mid-'50sCE, while in his late teens, young Arrius was a prefect of a cohort (an ancient Roman military unit) of legionnaires in the campaign against **Vologeses, King of Armenia** – serving there in **Tacitus**, *Annals* XIII.9, under the name of '**Arrius Varus**'.

6) His exploits as General '**Marcus Antonius Primus**' clearly explain his absence from **Judaea** in the years **67-69** CE, between his defeat as '**Cestius Gallus**' at **Beth-Horon** (mentioned earlier in regards to 'The Good Samaritan') and his reappearing to assist **Titus Flavius** at the siege of Jerusalem in **70** CE. After the Pisonian Conspiracy, Arrius was exiled to serve in Syria. After he tried to instigate a revolt, Nero then exiled him to Pannonia. (**ref** – Tacitus, *Histories*, III. 82-86)

5. WHY THE NEW TESTAMENT WAS WRITTEN

To understand the evidence presented within the New Testament, we need to understand what those texts are presenting. At this point, we are going to look at how the previous information fits within the context it was used. That involves investigating the details that can tell us why the Calpurnius Piso family, and their relatives, would even want to create a new religion, a new law, in the first place, and why Arrius would want to finish what the members of his family had started. If the New Testament was created because of war, it means the motives and evidence for that being the case remain within it. To begin, we need to investigate the personal motives that led Gaius Calpurnius Piso to initiate a secret conspiracy to replace Emperor Nero, which became known as the Pisonian Conspiracy; Gaius intended to have Nero assassinated, and replace him as emperor through approval by the Praetorian Guard.

The War Behind The Creation Of Christianity

The creation of a new religion, that would come to be known as Christianity, was both a political and personal response that resulted from a long drawn out war that originated as a battle between the factions of the Jewish sects, those sects being the

Pharisees, Scribes, Sadducees, Essenes, and *Zealots.* The beginnings have been traced back to the transferring of power over the Jewish people from the **Syrian Seleucean** rulers, a dynasty that existed from 312 BCE to 63 BCE, to the dynasty known as the **Hasmonean** rulers of Judaea (the Maccabees). The Hasmonean rulers were a group of Jewish rebel warriors who took control of Judea, which at the time was part of the Seleucid Empire, and that transfer of power would have happened in 135 BCE. The Hasmonean rule lasted until 63 BCE when the Roman general *Gnaeus Pompeius Magnus* intervened in the Hasmonean civil war, turning Judea into a client kingdom of Rome. The Hasmonean dynasty then ended when the Idumean, *Herod the Great,* became king of Israel. The main battle between the Jewish sects that will be examined in this book is the battle between the **Pharisees** and the **Sadducees**, and how that battle caused great concern for the aristocracy of Rome.

The **Pharisees** were battling with the **Saducean sect** over three main issues –

1) **Basic human rights for all people.**

2) **An end to slavery.**

3) **A new honest form of a democratic governmental system.**

Problems arose for the **Saducean sect**, which consisted of high priests, aristocratic families, and merchants, because the people (*commoners*) and the **Hasmonean Jewish leaders** showed support for the **Pharisees**, to where the Pharisees had gained power over the Hasmonean rulers (the Maccabees).

That is the reason the Sadducees had called upon Rome to help restore their power and control of Judea, and at that point, some major changes had taken place. When the Sadducees asked Rome to intervene, it was when the **Roman Republic** was ending, just before *Gaius Julius Caesar*, became Dictator. Julius Caesar was a politician and general and was one of the main reasons for the demise of the Roman Republic and the rise of the Empire. In Rome, there was a revolt taking place, but it was not just a revolt, it was an actual war within the Roman provinces, and once Julius Caesar had become ruler, establishing a Roman Empire, as opposed to the Republic, he also established the **Julio-Claudian dynasty**.

However, right before Julius Caesar became ruler, the Roman Empire (or still the Republic) had agreed to a change of power in Judea, and the reason was that the power that the Hasmonean rulership once had there was gone, and now the *Pharisees* were in power. But Rome wanted the *Sadducees* back in power in Judea, as they wanted to gain back and maintain their control. So they "installed" **Herod** as King of Judea and the Jewish people, which included the Jewish sects and the Temple. Herod would publicly be seen as an **Idumean**, who would marry **Mariamne I** and receive rightful power over Judea. In actuality, Herod was of royal Hasmonean blood and a cousin of Mariamne I, who was a Hasmonean princess and daughter of *Alexander of Judaea* and *Alexandra Regent*. The Maccabees founded the Hasmonean dynasty, and King Herod was a descendant of **Eleazar Maccabeus** (Eleazer Auran) of the Hasmoneans. The following is found within the Loeb *Jewish Antiquities* and also *Whiston's* translation: **Jason, son of Eleazar** (Auran), found in two places in Whiston: pg. 256; Ant. 12.10.6

– '*Eleazar, who was called Auran*' (of the Maccabees), Whiston: pg. 258; Ant. 12.6.1 – **Eleazar** (Auran), **brother of Judas of the Maccabees** (Hasmoneans), Whiston: pg. 263; Ant. 12.9.4 – **Antipater** (I), **son of Jason**, Whiston: pg. 274; Ant. 13.5.8 – **Antipater II** (Antipas son of Antipater), Whiston: pg. 289; Ant. 14.1.3. – **Herod son of Antipater II**, Whiston: pg. 289, 293, 295, 296, 297, 303, 434, 439, 441; Ant. 14.1.3, 7.3, 9.2-3, 11.4, 13.1, 14.4, 16.4, etc.; Jewish War, 1, Preface; 8.9, 10.4, 11.4, etc.

What this means, is that the **Herodians** were secretly just another '*branch*' of the **Hasmoneans**. This enabled the power over Judea to be given back to the Hasmoneans, through this "*new*" line and renaming of the leadership, which became known as the Herodians, even though it was the same as it had been. They did this to take the power back from the Pharisees, so the power the Pharisees had gained was given back to a new or revised version of the Hasmonean line. This meant that the Sadducees would have power over the entire Jewish sects once more because of the combining of the two powers. This installation of Herod by Rome meant that Julius Caesar's *main alliance* within Judea was with the *Herodians*, who were now the representatives of the *Sadducean leadership*. When Julius Caesar died and *Augustus Caesar* became ruler of the Roman Empire, that alliance carried over and it remained in place when *Tiberius* became emperor. But as the years passed after the death of Tiberius, some of that alliance broke down by the time of Nero, and he and several other royal Romans had become sympathetic to the cause of the Pharisees, which meant that Nero was not open to the creation of a new Roman religion, as will be discussed.

Beginning in the middle of the first century, the aristocracy of Rome was trying to deal with a growing problem. Judaism was continuing to grow and convert more people, with over **8,000,000** Jews making up **10%** of the population of the empire, **20%** of that portion was living in Judea, Israel; **Judea** is a Greek and Roman adaption of the name "**Judah**". Approximately half or more of the Jews lived outside Palestine, many descendants of proselytes, both male and female. (**ref** – Baron, Salo, A *Social and Religious History of the Jews*, Columbia Univ. Press, N.Y., and Jewish Publication Society, Philadelphia, 1952, vol. 1, p. 170-171. (**Salo Wittmayer Baron** was described as "*the greatest Jewish historian of the 20th century*"). The ethics being taught through Judaism did not match the Roman institution of slavery, which is how the Roman aristocracy fed, lived, and ruled. These ethics were so different, Judaism could not coexist with how Rome operated, eventually leading to fear among the aristocracy of Rome. The problem, in Rome's eyes, was that Judaism, with its different principles and ethics, would become the main religion of the empire. *Annaeus Seneca*, the Roman author who was a tutor and confidant of Emperor Nero, suggested banning the lighting of Sabbath candles in a letter to his friend *Lucilius*, a synonym of **Lucius Calpurnius Piso**, brother of Gaius Calpurnius Piso. This tradition is a rabbinically mandated law, with the candle lighting traditionally done by the woman of the household and is an act of 'bringing in' or 'guiding in' the Sabbath.

Seneca the Younger is later quoted by 'St. Augustine' in his "*City of God*" as stating that:

"*the (Sabbath) customs of that most accursed nation have gained such strength that they have been now received in all lands, the conquered have given laws to the conqueror.*"

Supporting Information-St. Augustine, "*City of God*", Modern Library, Random House, 1950, 6.11, p 202) Seneca, *Ad Lucilium Epistulae Morales*, Vol. III, Epistle XCV.47, pp. 87-89)

The Calpurnius Piso family, headed by **Lucius** and **Gaius Calpurnius Piso**, were confronted with a mutual problem far more personal regarding the spreading of Judaism. Gaius and Lucius had *both* married **Arria the Younger**, (Lucius Piso would marry Arria after Nero killed Gaius). Arria received her name from her grandfather **Aristobulus I**, the first ruler of the Hasmonean Dynasty and the eldest son of John Hyrcanus, the previous leader. Both Gaius and Lucius had concerns, the violent rebellions of the Judaean zealots were against Arria's relations, the **Herodian** rulers of Judaea, meaning the power of the Herodian leadership was being taken away. This would lead Gaius and Lucius Piso, as well as their close supporters, to attempt to find a solution to once again strengthen, and maintain, the control of the Herodian rulers of Judaea over the Judean population. They believed that solution came in the form of the *Jewish holy books*, which were the reason (or '*root*') for both the fast spread of the religion and the zealot's refusal to be governed by Rome's client, the Herodians. Because the Jewish population had refused to accept any Roman as a 'God', the creation of a new "*Jewish book*" was considered to be the perfect method to control the beliefs of the Judaean people. The idea was that this new religion would bring an end to the violent rebellions, which would then cause the Pharisees to lose their power in Judea, therefore giving the power back to the Pisos in-laws, the Herodians.

The Jewish leaders of the Pharisees had been at war with the Hasmonean leadership for many years, and because the Pharisees were so popular with the common people, it meant they had gained both public support and wealth from contributions from the public because they were fighting on *their* behalf, which meant the Pharisees were running things. Once they had gained this authority and position of power, the enemies of the Pharisees called upon Rome's help to overthrow their power and influence. That is when Rome made Herod king of Judea, and so, in that sense, *King of the Jews*. Whereas before, the Hasmonean leadership was also in charge of the Saducean sect, the leadership of that sect then transferred to King Herod and his sons. To make this a more formal and binding transition, *King Herod* was then married to *Mariamne I*, his cousin and daughter of *Alexandra Regent* of the Hasmoneans. The Maccabees founded the Hasmonean dynasty, and King Herod was a descendant of *Eleazar Maccabeus*, nicknamed *Eleazer Auran*, of the Hasmoneans.

It has been stated by the original researchers of this information, that **Lucius Piso** composed '**Ur Marcus**', the *first* version of the **Gospel of Mark**, in about the year 60 CE, that version no longer exists. Both '*Roman Piso*' and *Abelard Ruechlin* have said that he was both *encouraged* and *helped* by his friend *Lucius Annaeus Seneca*, otherwise known as **Seneca the Younger**, the Roman Stoic philosopher, statesman, and dramatist, and possibly assisted by *Persius the Poet*, Arria the Younger's young kinsman. Apart from the personal motive described above, there is a letter from Seneca to his friend Lucius regarding a 'New Book' that Lucius has written:

"*I received the book of yours which you promised me. I opened it hastily with the idea of glancing over it at leisure; for I meant only to taste the volume. But by its own charm the book coaxed me into traversing it more at length. You may understand from this fact how eloquent it was; for it seemed to be written in the smooth style, and yet* **did not resemble your handiwork or mine**, *but at first sight might have been ascribed to* **Titus Livius** *or to* **Epicurus**. *Moreover, I was so impressed and carried along by its charm that I finished it without any postponement. The sunlight called to me, hunger warned, and clouds were lowering; but I absorbed the book from beginning to end. I was not merely pleased; I rejoiced. So full of wit and spirit it was! I should have added "force," had the book contained moments of repose, or had it risen to energy only at intervals. But I found that there was no burst of force, but an even flow, a style that was vigorous and chaste. Nevertheless, I noticed from time to time your sweetness, and here and there that mildness of yours.* **Your style is lofty and noble; I want you to keep to this manner and this direction. Your subject also contributed something; for this reason you should choose productive topics, which will lay hold of the mind and arouse it.** *I shall discuss the book more fully after a* second perusal; meantime, **my judgment is somewhat unsettled, just as if I had heard it read aloud, and had not read it myself.** You must allow me to examine it also. **You need not be afraid; you shall hear the truth.** Lucky fellow, to offer a man no opportunity to tell you lies at such long range! Unless perhaps, even now, **when excuses for lying are taken away, custom serves as an excuse for our telling each other lies!** Farewell.

(**ref** – Seneca, Ad Lucilium Epistulae Morales, Vol. I, Epistle XLVI, pp. 299-300)

In Seneca's letter above, I have highlighted certain words or sentences which stand out to me-

First are the statements '*did not resemble your handiwork or mine*' and '*at first sight might have been ascribed to Titus Livius or to Epicurus.*' **Titus Livius**' education has been described as being based on the study of *rhetoric* and *philosophy*, rhetoric being the *art of effective or persuasive speaking or writing*, especially the **exploitation of figures of speech** and **other compositional techniques**. **Epicurus** was an ancient Greek philosopher who taught that the root of all human neurosis (*mild mental illness*) is death denial and the tendency for human beings to assume that death will be horrific and painful, which he claimed causes unnecessary anxiety, selfish self-protective behaviors, and hypocrisy. According to Epicurus, death is the end of both the body and the soul and therefore should not be feared. The style and beliefs of these two writers very much mimic what is found within the New Testament.

The second statement that stands out to me is, '*Your style is lofty and noble; I want you to keep to this manner and this direction. Your subject also contributed something; for this reason you should choose productive topics, which will lay hold of the mind and arouse it.*' If Lucius Piso was writing the first Gospel of Mark, and the reason, *or subject*, for doing so was to stop the war against the aristocracy, then Seneca advising Lucius to choose productive topics that will '*take hold of the mind*', again resembles what we find in the New Testament.

The last statement that stands out to me is, '*You need not be afraid; you shall hear the truth. Lucky fellow, to offer a man no opportunity to tell you lies at such long-range! Unless perhaps, even now, when excuses for lying are taken away, custom serves as an excuse for our telling each other lies!*' The first part of the statement 'You need not be afraid; you shall hear the truth resembles both the Old Testament and the New Testament. The last part of the statement is also odd, what lies are being told? Again, if Lucius is writing 'Mark', then he is creating a satire based on what happened, and within that satire are *lies* intermixed with some truth.

The Gospel of '**Mark**' was the first gospel to be completed in its finished form. The majority of biblical scholars agree with the view that Mark was the first Gospel written, a view which is based on certain observations, including the fact that Mark's literary style sometimes lacks the *sophistication* and *polish* seen in Matthew and Luke, and in 'Mark', Jesus and the disciples are sometimes portrayed in an undignified way. More often than not, these passages are 'touched up' or omitted altogether by 'Matthew' and 'Luke'. But when thinking about the task of creating a new religion, it is reasonable, and logical, to think that a committee or council must have been formed to decide on the content of the scriptures. Evidence of the compiling of religious documents and temple scriptures from Europe, Egypt, Western Asia, and India before this can be seen in the creation of the Library of Alexandria. With the constant and more or less simultaneous revolts in Europe, Africa, and Asia, the military operations were becoming very expensive, a solution, therefore, was needed.

Considering the Piso family had a greater personal reason for creating a new religion, and the aristocracy of Rome was in charge of the leadership in Jerusalem, it is safe to suspect that the Pisos would have been the ones to organize such a committee, but where would this committee meet? Well, Josephus describes a large building, most likely the main synagogue in Tiberias, as the seat of the boulé, or city council. He goes on to describe the building as being the location of various assemblies held in Tiberias at the beginning of the Great War in 66 C.E. (Josephus, *Vita*, 41-61) A Roman/Jewish committee must have been assembled at Tiberias to no doubt discuss the creation of a new law/religion during the reign of Emperor Tiberius (circa 14-37 C.E.).

'Josephus', in the books *Jewish War*, books 2 through 4, and his *Life* describes the cities of Tiberias and Sepphoris in Galilee. Tiberias, an Israeli city on the western shore of the *Sea of Galilee*, named in honor of *Emperor Tiberius*, may have been the ideal place for a committee, but so too would the city of Sepphoris.

The political structure of Tiberias would have been more Hellenistic than that of Jerusalem, and several indications suggest that Tiberias was not a typical Hellenistic city, but a royal administrative one. 'Flavius Josephus' states that important political assemblies were held (also) in the *proseuche*, an ancient synagogue, as 'Josephus' puts it, in his *Vita*, page 277, "*a huge building capable of accommodating a large crowd*". Sepphoris, we are informed, was a pro-Roman, aristocratic city that '*welcomed the enemy into its midst*', and where Herod's son, Herod Antipas, selected as the provincial capital for his government in Galilee. Those who ran the royal administration of Galilee were of the powerful and wealthy Romanized/Hellenized families, meaning the ruler's position is evidence of Roman imperial rule. The committee members would most certainly have needed to have already been familiar with philosophy and religion, and, again, it is safe to assume that if the new religion was to be based on the current Judaic religion, then the committee would have almost certainly included members of the Herodian leadership. Some of the committee members may also have been those who took part in the assassination conspiracy against Emperor Nero.

Nero was pro-Jewish, so too was his mistress, later his wife, Poppaea, who was described as being '*theosebes*', or god-fearing. So it is unlikely that Nero, possibly under Poppaea's influence, would have allowed a new religion to be constructed, especially if it was going to ridicule the Jewish faith and attempt to manipulate the minds of Jewish people through lies. Nero most certainly rejected the new "Jewish book" plan, which, along with the growing discontent for him among the ruling class, led to an assassination attempt on his life by the Pisos and their supporters, known today as the *Pisonian con-*

spiracy, which the historian **Tacitus** details. This assassination attempt failed when the plot was aborted, instead, Nero had Gaius Calpurnius Piso and Seneca, along with their fellow conspirators, executed by forcing them to commit suicide. Gaius Piso was allowed to die by committing suicide, to enable the Piso family to keep his wealth and property. Nero then exiled **Arrius** to Syria, perhaps because he gave information about the conspirators to Nero, as Tacitus mentions a name of a conspirator which appears to be Arrius, '**Antonius Natalis**', '*Natalis*' meaning birthday (*christ's Birthday*-Christmas Day/Natali Domini?). Antonius Natalis is mentioned as taking part in the Pisonian Conspiracy, and, being threatened with torture, disclosed his fellow conspirator's names and avoided punishment – "*Natalis was the partner of Piso in all his secret counsels...*" (**ref** – Tacitus, *Annals*, XV.54,71 – **ref** – Tacitus, *Annals* 15.50, 54-56, 71). Nero sent Arrius Piso to Syria to act as governor, a post that also gave him command of the legions controlling **Judaea**. Arrius records his service in Judaea in the year 65 CE using the names '**Gessius Florus**' and in 66 CE with the name '**Cestius Gallus**'.

Using the name '**Gessius Florus**', to describe this period of events, Arrius provoked the Jewish revolt in 66 CE, by making the situation of the Jews unbearable. As procurator, he permitted a massacre of Jews in Jerusalem, and the Zealots there began to revolt. When Herod Agrippa II supported Arrius, although urging moderation, the Zealots gained the upper hand, and the case became hopeless. Writing as Josephus, Arrius states that 'Gessius' was the primary cause of the Great Jewish Revolt. (**ref** – Josephus, *Antiquities of the Jews*, Book 20, Chapter 11, Section 1) Arrius must have been trying to start a war with the 'Jewish zealots', so they would cause more problems for Rome and hoped Nero would then back him, his family, and supporters in his attempt to destroy the Temple in Jerusalem. The idea was that with the Temple destroyed, he could then create a more peaceful Messiah, who would eventually be given the name '**Jesus**'. He would predate the New Testament story to **40 years before the Temple's destruction**, so he could write that 'Jesus' makes a prophecy that the Temple would be destroyed, because of the refusal by the Jews to accept a Roman God. This is clear from reading the Gospels (Matthew. 23:37-38), where the Jewish people were unwilling to accept the story his family had created and become, in a way, 'pacified' as they intended. It is worth noting that Arrius when writing as 'Josephus', and speaking of 'Gessius', says –

"...*nor could any one outdo him in disguising the truth; nor could any one contrive more subtle ways of deceit than he did.*"

ref – Josephus, *Wars of the Jews*, Chapter XIV

– Also worth noting, I think, is that Arrius using the name 'Gessius' meant who would have been able to pronounce it as
"**Jes(I)us.**"

The claim Arrius and his family predated or backdated the story to **40 years** before the Temple's destruction is a very valid claim based on a few evidential factors –

First

Apart from the strong personal motives, the fact is there is, even today, an inexplicable lack of non-Roman contemporary evidence for 'Jesus' existing at all.

Second

'Jesus' dies on **Passover 33**, because he is the '***Passover lamb***' of the **New Covenant** or New Testament. The New Covenant *replaced* the **Old Covenant**/Testament. The **Old Covenant** had a **Passover Sacrifice** and 40 years of wandering before the **Israelites** could gain ownership of **Israel**.

We are told '**Jesus**' dies on **Passover 33** and that the Roman war concludes on **Passover 73**, when the Romans gained ownership of Israel. The length of time between **33** and **73** is **40 years**, which is a perfect 40-year cycle for the **New Testament Passover Lamb**. That time cycle leads to the new date of the next **New Covenant** and the new change in ownership of **Israel**. This new date, after the death of 'Jesus', is the date **Rome** owned all of that land. Rome owning Judea led to the new Judaism, which is Christianity, which eventually became more powerful than the old Judaism. Backdating the New Testament story meant the authors could have 'Jesus' appear to predict the fall of Jerusalem, which led to the fall of the old Judaism, and the changes of ownership would also conform to the story structure of the Old Testament.

The 12th legion of '**Cestius Gallus**' (Arrius Piso) was ambushed by the Jewish zealots in the pass below **Bethoron** (Beth Horon) suffering very heavy losses, including being robbed of a large amount of war material. With most of Arrius' troops killed or wounded, he barely managed to escape to Antioch. This incident would create the story of the '**Good Samaritan**'. (**ref** – Josephus, *Jewish War*, Book II, chapter XVIIII, verses 9-11; Tacitus, *Histories* 5.10) Nero's reaction to this was to once again exile Arrius, this time to **Pannonia** in central Europe to command a legion there, which meant he would be far away from Syria and the Jewish people. In 'Josephus' 'Marcus Antonius Primus' becomes '**Antonius Julianus**', but Tacitus describes '**Marcus Antonius Primus**' in his *Histories*, Book II, LXXXVI, pg.299. Interestingly, the third-century "Christian" writer Minucius Felix in *Octavius*, chapter 33 wrote the following: "*Carefully read over their Scriptures, or if you are better pleased with the Roman writings, inquire concerning the Jews in the books (to say nothing of ancient documents) of Flavius Josephus or Antoninus Julianus.*" This implies that 'Antonius Julianus' was a contemporary historian, and well-known, along with 'Josephus'. But there was not any historian known as 'Antonius Julianus', this was another name Arrius used or was used to refer to him. After sending Arrius to Pannonia, Nero then sent *Gaius Licinius Mucianus* to serve in **Syria** instead and sent **Vespasian** to Judaea to put down the Jewish revolt.

Mucianus was a general, statesman, and writer of ancient Rome, and is considered to have played a role behind the scenes in the success of Vespasian becoming emperor. It seems by the year 68 CE, the Pisos and their supporters accomplished their mission to have Nero assassinated. **Epaphroditus**, is said to have conducted the assassination/suicide, most likely because he was made to, perhaps in exchange for a financial reward? When referencing Roman historians, they state that Epaphroditus only assisted the emperor's suicide. (**ref** – Suetonius. *Nero* 49, and Cassius Dio in *Dio Cassius* 63.29) (See also Tacitus, *Annals* XV.55, footnote 2). The chaos of the 'civil war' or the '*Year of the Four Emperors*' followed Nero's eventual suicide, and although Gaius Calpurnius Piso and his conspirators failed to assassinate Nero, Arrius Piso, his family, and royal relatives did manage to kill him at a later date, and once they did, they were then in control of the Roman Empire. However, for the first few years after the death of Nero, some in the family disagreed over just which of them should be emperor. For the first few years the individuals who became emperors were – **Galba**, **Otho**, and **Vitellius**. *Galba*, who was a direct descendant of *Augustus Caesar*, was a very rich, but elderly man, who adopted a member of the Piso family called *Lucius Calpurnius Piso Frugi Licinianus*, Arrius Piso's cousin, essentially to be his successor.

But **Otho**, *Marcus Salvius Otho Caesar Augustus* (who was Galba's son, a fact which was hidden in history), killed his father, Galba, with Piso being murdered four days later, and took control of the Roman Empire. (**ref** – Tacitus, *Histories* I.14). *Galba* was forcibly removed from power by his son *Otho*, who was also removed from power by a royal friend of Nero, Emperor **Vitellius**, who was thrust onto the throne when his supporters managed to kill **Otho**. Vitellius was the father-in-law of *Julius Gnaeus Agricola*, and Agricola was the father-in-law of *Justus Piso* and *Claudia Phoebe* (Arrius' children), and *Domitia Paulina I*, *T. Flavius Clemens*, and *Cornelius Tacitus*. When Vitellius seized power, the Piso family and supporters worked together against Vitellius, resulting in the **Pisos**,

Mucianus, and **Tiberius Alexander**, all joining ranks behind **Vespasian** to overthrow **Vitellius**. (**ref** – Tacitus, *Histories* II. pp. 74-81) An article about Tacitus' *Histories* I, titled '*Four-Day Caesar*', and written by English scholar Dame *Winifred Mary Beard*, for the *London Review of Books*, discusses the adoption of Licinianus Piso by Galba. In the article Dame Mary Beard touches on the subject which Sir Ronald Syme stated in his works, that subject is the fact that, from the start, autocracy (*a system of government by one person with absolute power*) and the city of Rome have gone hand in hand from the beginning, which links to an oligarchy. In the article, Mary Beard says that the adoption scene, presented by Tacitus, highlights the dilemmas of succession, and, as Mary puts it, "..*what arguments could ever count as good when picking a man to rule the world.*"

Whilst the civil war was taking place in Rome, Arrius at this point was still in Pannonia (Austria-Hungary), commanding the 7th legion. (**ref** – Tacitus, *Histories* III.2, footnote 1). But with Nero now dead, **Vespasian** sent **Arrius**, now appearing in **Tacitus** with the name '**Marcus Antonius Primus**', south across the Alps to Rome to defeat **Vitellius**. Vespasian's legions meanwhile marched overland under Gaius Licinius Mucianus from the east towards Rome. When Arrius reached Rome, he defeated Vitellius and his army and secured Rome for Vespasian, Vespasian would now become emperor, because of Arrius' efforts. Vespasian then ordered Mucianus, who at this point had arrived in Rome, to send Arrius, along with his legions, to Judea to help his son *Titus Flavius* with the siege of Jerusalem, which meant Arrius could accomplish his goal of destroying the Temple. But the siege at Jerusalem would not be the end of the battle between the Pisos, Rome, and the Jews.

Arrius must have believed it would be a much smoother path to the Pisos' realization of a new religion, as the Pisos, and the Flavian side of his family now owned the entire known world. The Pisos and the Flavians were now in control of all the books in the empire, including those taken from the Ptolemic Library in Alexandria, Egypt. When the library in Alexandria was burnt, the Serapeum library, named after the Egyptian god Serapis, escaped intact. There is no record of what happened to the religious books contained there, but scholars have stated they may have been removed by the Romans to the Lake of Galilee or Tyberya. But with Jerusalem now destroyed, Arrius would also gain possession of all the books in Judea, as well as gathering up books in Rome so he could re-write history. Once he had all the books he could get his hands on, either by buying them or confiscating them, he burnt all but certain books, and there appears to be a joke alluding to this in **Acts 19:19**, *"Many of those who had practiced magic brought their books together and burnt them in public"* *"In this powerful way the word of the Lord kept spreading and growing stronger."* As we know from history, Arrius and Titus were successful in the siege, and in 70 CE they assaulted the city, then the Temple, burned it, slaughtered many thousands, and sent thousands more to slavery and gladiatorial combat and death.

The Gospels Were Originally A Satirical Play

After the siege at Jerusalem, the Gospels were written in the following sequence:

the present **Gospel of Mark** (73 CE)

the **Gospel of Matthew** (75 CE)

the **Gospel of Luke** (85-90 CE)

The Pisos would create the story and the characters found in the New Testament, and they would place the story into a specific time in history, connecting it with some related people. Those people included the **Herods, Gamaliel the Elder**, a leading authority in the Sanhedrin, the supreme council of the Jews, and the **Roman procurators**, but 'Jesus' and those involved directly with him are fictional characters. As stated earlier, the Gospel of '**Mark**' was the first gospel to be completed, and the new religion would *appear* to have come from or be another '*branch*' of the current *Jewish religion*, the intention being to replace the teachings of the current Jewish sects active at the time. From the evidence presented above, it seems Seneca and Lucius Piso created the first versions of gospels we know today as 'Mark' and 'Matthew'. When looking at Seneca's ideological concepts, it is clear they are *the same* as those that show up later in the Gospels, such as *faith healing, ghosts, angels,* and the ideas of *Heaven* and *Satan* (**ref** – Bruno Bauer, '*Christ and the Caesars*', 1877). Seneca would have had just as much motivation to contribute to this work as the Pisos, because he was an ancestor of Arrius, through Arrius' mother, through her maternal ancestry. Looking at the name 'Arria' *superficially*, you would not be able to work out that Arria The Elder (Arria Sr.) was the sister of Seneca, because the name used for her in public was generally, 'Arria'. However, her real family name was '*Aennea*', as the male form of her brother's name '*Lucius Aenneas Seneca*'. As explained previously, the aristocracy seems to have incorporated components and/or letter uses from other languages when writing in one language, for example, an '**A**' can also be '**Ae**', and, as already shown, the letters 'n' and 'r' were exchanged for one another. Aenneas Seneca and Aennea (Arria Sr.) are descendants of *Mark Anthony* and *Cleopatra* through their daughter **Cleopatra Selene II**. This information seems to have been well hidden, the reason, quite possibly, being that uncovering this relationship, and the ancestry and identity of Arria the Elder (Sr.), uncovers Arrius' identity; it is interesting to note that the word for 'moon' in Greek, which is *Selene* σελήνη is used in Mark 13:24; Matt. 24:29; Luke 21:25; Acts 2:20; I Cor. 15:41; Rev. 6:12; 8:12; 12:1; 21:23. (more information can be read at www.henryhdavis.com/seneca)

The Gospels are written in the form of **Acts** and **Scenes** (such as a play), the reason perhaps being that the Pisos knew Nero would not be easily convinced by the idea of a new religion, which means they would have to appeal to Nero's taste. Their attempt at this was to write the literature for this new religion in the form of a satirical play, complete with acts & scenes, and it is that structure that remained within the finished Gospels, which, to me, acts as a form of proof. Seneca and Lucius Piso must have been composing their own Gospel drafts, and Lucius appears to have been acting as the editor and was in charge of the literary structure, while Seneca was providing most of the various ideological concepts. That earliest version of the Gospel of '**Mark**', the '*New Book by Lucilius*', which no longer exists, but is described in Seneca's letter, must be what scholars refer to as the '**Q**' or '**Quelle**' (source)***document***. The 'Q' document, or 'Q' gospel, is considered a hypothetical document that would explain why 'Matthew' and 'Luke' are substantially based on 'Mark', although some scholars are still skeptical of the Q hypothesis.

"Scholars hypothesized that a collection of such material must have been circulating in the early churches, and they have designated it with the symbol "Q," from the German Quelle ("source")" (**ref** – 'The New Oxford Annotated Bible New Revised Standard Version, page 1380)

'Matthew' contains approximately 90-95% of the verses found in 'Mark', in the same order and, near enough, using the same words, meaning the gospel authors (Lucius Piso, Arrius) copied from the original 'Mark'. But the later gospels of 'Matthew' and 'Luke' also have close agreements with each other, that could not have come from the Gospel of Mark that we have, meaning they were not copied from the present Gospel of Mark, but that their source would have been the version of 'Mark' that no longer exists. The Messiah was a part of the Gospel of 'Mark', but had not been named, as the 'Jesus' character would be created later on, most likely by Arrius. When Nero killed Seneca, Gaius Piso, and other members of the committee, the task of completing the literature would have gone to Lucius and Arrius Piso. Once the Temple and Jerusalem were destroyed, Lucius Piso and Arrius would have been free for a few years at that point to create the Gospels of 'Mark' and 'Matthew' we have now. Nero, in *this* particular situation, was not the bad guy we have been led to believe he was by those in control of writing the historical accounts after his death.

King Herod's descent from Eleazar Maccabeus (Auran) of the Hasmoneans:

Mattathias ben Johanan (d.165/166 BCE)

M. (a royal cousin)

|

Eleazar Auran (Eleazar Auraneas/Aureneas Hasmoneaus, d. 163 BCE)

M. (a royal cousin)

|

Jason Auran (Jason Auraneas/Aureneas Hasmoneaus, circa 130 BCE)

M. (a royal cousin)

|

Antipater I Antipas (Antipater Antipas/Antipos Auraneas Hasmoneaus, circa 80 BCE)

M. (a royal cousin)

|

Antipater II Antipas (Antipater Antipas/Antipos Auraneas Hasmoneaus II)

M. Cypras/Cypras Of Idumia (circa 30 BCE)

|

King Herod 'The Great' (d. 4 BCE)

M. Mariamne I (Mariamne Hasmoneaus, dr. of Alexander & Alexandra Regent)

The references shown below, shown earlier, are connected to and can be found in Whiston's translation of the works of 'Flavius Josephus'

Jason, son of Eleazar (Auran), is found in two places on the same page; pg. 256.

Eleazar, who was called 'Auran' (of the Maccabees); pg. 258.

Eleazar (Auran), brother of Judas of the Maccabees (Hasmoneans); pg. 263.

Antipater (I), son of Jason; pg. 274.

Antipater II (Antipas), which was his father's name also; pg. 289.

Antipater II (Antipas), King Herod's father; pg. 289, 293, 295, 296, 297, 303, 434, 439, 441.

6. 'ROYAL LANGUAGE'

The use of certain literary techniques used by the aristocracy to present information, for example, abbreviations on coinage, is well known. But these same techniques seem to have been used within the New Testament, as mentioned earlier and briefly explained. Taking a more detailed look will hopefully result in a better understanding of how it was used and what it looks like. To begin, it is important to understand that the Roman aristocracy was privileged enough to be given an education that was far beyond the standard of education that the common people of the day would receive. Even today, our standard education system is a fairly recent creation and, right from the start, those from a more privileged background have the opportunity to receive a better education than those from poorer backgrounds.

Today we enjoy modern luxuries such as *TVs*, *computers*, and *smartphones*, but, of course, these devices did not exist in ancient times, instead, Rome's aristocratic population became experts in using many languages, especially Latin and Greek. The aristocracy used Latin for imperial administration and legislation, and Koine (common) Greek was the language used for the majority of the populations of the Roman Empire, which included the Jewish population. The wealthy enjoyed various forms of entertainment, one form of entertainment was the Roman orgies documented in history, but sex played a much more important part in the Roman culture than just orgies, it was also an important form of pleasure and a necessary belief of their society.

Rome had its prostitutes of various classes and homosexual relationships, and they were fond of what we would call 'porn' in the form of explicit art. But there was a dark side to this Roman culture, which was the use of slavery, and the use of slaves significantly contributed to the vast growth of the Roman Empire. Most slaves were prisoners of war and had no rights and were at the total mercy of his or her master, who could use them for sexual gratification if desired. At the height of Rome's power, slaves represented 10-15% of the total population of the empire. Other forms of entertainment were the reading of books and other reading material, and a huge amount of books were being written and had been written in Greek. However, the official language of Rome was Latin, so for royalty and members of the aristocracy, being able to understand more languages, and how they worked, meant that not only would they be able to read many more books, but it would also allow them the opportunity to write using those languages. Now although the overall language used within the New Testament is **Koine Greek**, parts of it incorporate other languages, such as – **Latin**, **Hebrew**, **Aramaic**, **Egyptian** and **Phoenician**, and within the scriptures, these languages are used along with certain literary techniques to present information.

For example, in **the Book of Revelation,** the number '**666**' is not written using *words*, such as **six hundred and sixty-six**, as it easily could have been. In **Revelation 7**, '**144,000**' is written using 'ρ' (100), 'μ' (40), and 'δ' (4), all Greek letters, with the word '**thousand**' being written as a word using all Greek letters. So '**666**' could have been written using all **Greek** words or letters, but it was not, the Greek glyph '**ς**', which is the letter '**F**' and has a numerical value of '**6**', could have been used instead. But '**666**' was written using **3 different letters**, each with their own numerical value – '**Chi**' (600), '**Xi**' (60), and the **Phoenician** letter '**Bau**', which has the numerical value of '**6**', was used to present the number 6. The question to ask is *why* the number '**6**' was not presented using a **Greek** letter. But what has also been observed within these texts is the use of **acrostic initials** and **abbreviations**.

Acrostic initials –

An acrostic is a form of writing in which the **first letter** (or syllable, or word) of **each line** (or paragraph), spells out a **word**, **message**, or **the alphabet**. The word comes from the French '**acrostichis**', which comes from the post-classical **Latin** '**acrostichis**', which is from the **Koine Greek** '**akrostichis**', which is from the **Ancient Greek** '**akros**' meaning "highest, topmost". As a form of constrained writing, an **acrostic** can be used as a *mnemonic device* to aid memory retrieval, which assists in remembering something.

Abbreviations –

An abbreviation is a shortened form of a word or phrase used to represent a larger, more complex message.

Scholars are well aware of these techniques being used within the New Testament, but what has been discovered is that a *combination* of these techniques was used. An example of a famous **acrostic** is one that was made in **Greek**, which spells out one word meaning one thing, but also reveals another message which is – JESUS CHRIST, SON OF GOD, SAVIOUR, and the initials spell '**ΙΧΘΥΣ**', which is pronounced "**ichthus**" and means '**fish**', and is the word used for 'fish' in the Gospels (Matthew 7:10, 14:7, etc.)

The letters in Greek are:

Ι – represents **Iesous** 'Ιησος', which is the Greek word for 'Jesus'

Χ – represents **Xristos** 'Χριστος', which is Greek for 'Christ'

Θ – represents **Theos** 'Θεος', which is Greek for 'God'

Υ – represents **Uios** 'Υιος', which is Greek and means 'Son'

Σ – represents **Soter** 'Σωτηρ', which is Greek and means 'Saviour'

One example of the techniques described above that was used in the New Testament is as follows:

The word '**πειθων**', which is '**peithon**', the Greek word for 'persuading' used in **Acts 19:8**, is being used to present the meaning of **two words** because it is made up using the parts of two words.

One of those words is the name '**Piso**', which in **Greek** is

'**Pei**(son)' and the other is the Greek word for '**God**', which is '**Th**(e)o', so those words combined create '**peithon**'.

If you separate those two words, what we have is '**Peison Theo**', which reads as – '**Piso God**'.

The part that is '**Pei**' is an **abbreviation** for '**Peison**', but why does '**Thon**' become '**Theo**' ('**Theon**')? The reason is because of how the vowels in ancient languages worked, where double letters could be used to produce a certain sound. Here, the '**h**' in the '**Th**' is doubled and the '**h**' becomes '**e**', but in Hebrew, vowels could drop, so now '**Thon**' becomes '**Thhon**', but with the language rules being used it looks like this '**Theo(n)**. To spot the above example requires knowledge of the Greek and Hebrew languages, but, as explained before, the Pisos appear to have used the rules for these languages in their own way.

The reason the Roman royals and aristocrats in this period would have been able to create their own language *within* a language, using the various languages of the time, is because, as stated above, they had a vast knowledge of multiple languages. They could fully create *'another language'*, for themselves only, using different methods from the languages of the time, such as vowel switching and syntax arrangements. Vowels were never written in the beginnings of languages, and words were only recognized by their consonants, meaning the Pisos could switch the vowels and even drop them, depending on what was trying to be presented.

For example, they could use the syntax rules used in *one* language, for example, **Hebrew**, but use those syntax rules when writing in **Greek** or **Latin**. But to add to this, the American/Jewish author and historical researcher Abelard Reuchlin also noticed that the Pisos used a number system to present the names of the authors within the New Testament, and that number system used the numbers associated with the letters of the alphabets of the time. The Pisos presented the names and messages in such a way that allowed the surface story to '*crossover*' in usage within various languages. So this vowel changing, coupled with the techniques described above, meant the New Testament surface story could still be read if the texts were translated, but only the royals would know and understand the hidden words in the original Koine Greek texts. What the above means, is that royalty could use the languages of the time any way they wanted to, they could use a certain word in one language in place of another, so it would have a specific meaning in another language, such as 'God' or 'Phallus' for example. These individuals also used *compound* words, meaning they would use one word to create two or more words, and this technique would be combined with the use of the different syntax rules of one language when writing in another. That meant they could create sentences but experiment with the structure so that words were arranged to present a certain name or meaning. Lastly, they also used inference, meaning they did not have to use certain words at all within a sentence. They did that by setting precedent examples, an example from the past, by creating a memorable line or phrase and then calling attention to it indirectly in what they were writing. When they did this they only needed to reference, or state, a part of a line or phrase to say something without saying the entire line, in effect, these words were "invisible words".

7. THE MAIN AUTHOR - ARRIUS PISO

The time has now come to examine the evidence that points to a Piso family authorship of the scriptures, with that evidence coming directly from the New Testament. To make your judgments, it is recommended that you purchase a good **Interlinear Greek-English New Testament**, such as one by Professor *George Ricker Berry*, who was an internationally known Semitic scholar and archaeologist and used the King James Version of the New Testament that was translated from the original Greek. I am aware that some individuals have issues with the King James Version, but considering the information below is *still* presented within it and connects to the history discussed in this book, it means the King James Version is a valid tool for this investigation. When studying this information, it is important to remember that the **Book of Revelation** means a revealing of something, or in this case, someone. Not only does the Book of Revelation provide us with clues to discovering what is being said, but historical and contemporary literary evidence also confirms these findings. In terms of religion and theology, the Book of Revelation is seen as disclosing a *truth* or *knowledge*, and, based on the overwhelming evidence seen so far, that revelation is revealing who the main creator of Christianity was.

A good place to start would be to examine the connections between the alias names and the real names that Arrius Piso and the authors of the Gospels used, so that is what we shall do. First '*Josephus*' (Arrius) introduces himself as '**Joseph bar Mathias**', which means '**Josephus son of Matthias**', '**bar**' means '**son**' (of) in **Aramaic**, in Hebrew the name appears as '**Josephus Ben Matthias**', '**ben**', meaning '**son**' (of) in **Hebrew**. Josephus in Latin is **Joseph**, but 'Josephus' is Arrius Piso, because, again, of the overwhelming evidence. So 'Josephus' introducing himself as '*a son of Matthias*', is Arrius introducing himself as 'a son of Matthias', which he was, through his mother's ancestors. But the name Piso has the same four letters in Hebrew as the name Joseph (Yosef) – **Piso** = פיסו   **Yoseph** = יוסף, which means the name '*Flavius Josephus*' can also be seen as **Flavius Piso**, and so '*Josephus son of Matthias*' can also be seen as **Piso son of Matthias**. Next, we have the name '**Joseph of Arimathea**', a name that was briefly mentioned in the '*Gospels and Josephus: The Parallels*' chapter. The similarity between the name '*Joseph of Arimathea*' and the '*Josephus son of Mathias*' name was noted as sounding *phonetically* the same, but if this name is examined again, it appears the techniques described in the previous chapter are being used –

> '*Joseph*' can be '*Josephus*', and '**Arimathea**' can be two names brought together, using the abbreviation and acrostic techniques, those names are **Arrius** and **Matthias**. Looking at that name now, we can see it meaning '**Joseph**'/'**Josephus**'/**Piso** (of) **Ari**(us) (of) **Matth**(ias), with the vowels 'e' and 'a' switched.

Next, we have the name '**Mary**', which is the English version of the **Latin** name '**Maria**', which in turn came from the **Greek** name 'Μαριαμ' (Mariam). In Latin Christianity, the *Greek* form

'**Mariam**', *which is the Aramaic form of the biblical name* '**Miriam**', *became* '**Maria**', which is found in the New Testament. But again, when we look closer at the original **Latin** and **Greek** versions of those names, we can see another name within them, that name is **Aria**, the Greek form of the name of Arrius Piso's mother. So the Latin and Greek version of those names can be seen like this– M-**aria** and M-**aria**-m, which for the authors, would create further *'Messiah authenticity'* to the 'Jesus' character, as this would act as another link to 'Moses', whose sister was called 'Miriam', the 'Moses' story being a sequel to the 'Joseph' story. However, in the Greek alphabet, the letter **Pi** '**π**', which is the first letter in the name Piso and has a numerical value of **80**, and when the two '**M**'s are attached either side of the name Aria, they total 80 because M in Greek has the value of 40, making the name **Aria Piso**. But, in the New Testament 'Mariam' is sometimes spelled '**Marias**', which is **Arius** plus the **12**, as the letter 'M' is also the twelfth letter of the Greek alphabet. In **Luke 8**, we read *"...and the* ***twelve*** *were with him, and certain women, which had been healed of evil spirits and infirmities, Mary called Magdalene, out of whom went seven devils, and Joanna the wife of Chuza, Herod's steward, and Susanna, and many others, which ministered unto him of their substance"*. 'Magdalene' or 'Migdalene', is a name created from the word '**Migdal**', which is Greek for '**almond**', which had the shape of the female organ and was a name referring to temple prostitutes, or "almond" woman, and when **Luke 7:47** reads *"...her sins many, for she had loved much..."*, it is referring to her profession in the story. In biblical times they considered this profession a *"holy calling"*, as the Kadeshoth (Hebrew for 'dedicated women'), were female priests dedicated to the temples, as the whole temple revenues came from prostitution. 'Migdal' also means 'tower' or 'keep', and it is where these 'holy' prostitutes were secluded for the use of the priests. But to create the name, '**Mari Magdalene**', two languages are used, Hebrew and Greek, '**Mari**' in Hebrew means "*she who urges the god to action*", which is appropriate for 'Mary' or 'Mari' the mother of 'Jesus'. '*Magdalene*' means "*almond*" woman, which refers to her sex organ being at the service of the priests. The almond is an ancient symbol for the '**membrum feminum/feminine**', meaning 'female member', so, in essence, the name or title Mary/Mari Magdalene/Migdalene, means Mary "*of the almond*".

Letter and word interchanges or exchanges

Certain letters in The New Testament were used in lieu (instead) of other letters that would appear too obvious if used. For example, an '**a**' could be used in place of an '**o**', and vice versa, and, certain words could be *switched* or used instead of other words, so the real meaning of a statement or piece of information could be secretly presented because of that switching of words or letters. That switching has today made us believe that the texts were written by people who were far less educated, as the words would appear to be misspelled and would never appear to have been written by members of the aristocracy. Sometimes, certain words were used close to each other to present and give *names*. For example, the **Greek** word for '**fornicate**', is '**pournios**' πορνοις, and could represent the name '**Calpurnius**'. This is the case when the word '**pournios**' was used next to or close to the **Greek** word '**kai**' και, which is the word for *and*, *even* or *also*, depending on the context, and that word was seen as the '**Cal**' part of the name '**Calpurnius**'. So the authors used little opportunities like this to present the words '**kai-pournios**' within a sentence, and you can find examples of this in **Revelation 21:8, 2:14**, and **2:20**. In one of the examples given, **Revelation 2:14**, the word is seen like this "*...and fornicators...*", which in **Greek** is και πορνοις (kai-pournios) and would have been seen in **Latin** as '**Calpurnius**'. There is also a letter exchange happening, with the '**i**' and '**l**', because the '**i**' and the '**l**' were seen as the same by the authors, as the small **Greek** '**i**' looks like this *ι*, which looks identical to how the **Latin** small **l** is written.

Most people would never see these original words because our Bibles have been translated into our languages, to make the stories easier to understand, and they were translated based on what words the translators thought they should be. But scholars and historians alike have noticed that when reading ancient texts, particularly the New Testament texts, and the rest of the Bible, there are *multiple word* and *sentence meanings*, but in terms of the New Testament, this was deliberate. In my opinion, the authors did this to cause confusion and conflicts between people, who would read them differently, which is what is happening today. The authors also wanted to make sure the texts presented different messages depending on the situation, which left a lot of the New Testament texts open to the discretion of the bishops and other clergies of the time, who must have been either Piso family members, or their supporters. They would decide how they read those texts to early Church members, because that's how Christianity first began to be accepted and known to the people, and the texts were read by those who were appointed to do so by Arrius Piso and his supporters.

For example, the "Bishops" would decide whether to use the sexual messages contained within the New Testament, depending on who they were preaching to, and they could, in effect, claim their statements referred to one thing at one time, then claim it meant something completely different at a later date, because of the difference in meaning between words. There were secret or "*sacred sex*" words used in the Bible because, as mentioned earlier, sex was an important part of Roman society, but *on the surface*, they would have one meaning, but another *sexual meaning* that related to the Roman culture of the time. We can expect to find this sexual theme in the literature produced by Rome in that time, and Pliny the younger even hints at it by saying, "*In literature as in life*", (**ref** – Pliny The Younger *Letters* Loeb Classical Library Edition, Book II, pg. 65 in a letter to Maturus Arrianus). The **Encyclopedia Biblica**, which was created by Oxford University and produced at the beginning of the 20th century, had listed and explained many of the sex words used in the Bible. It was a work compiled by scholars who carefully researched the word meanings and usage within the Bible. These scholars did not know of the connection between the Piso family and how they used the languages of the time, so the *Encyclopedia Biblica* unknowingly supports these discoveries.

Joseph Jay Deiss, author, businessman, historian, and archaeologist says:

"All living things (depicted), even the sprout of a fountain (as a phallus), respond in kind, for this was all a (running) joke".

(**ref** – Joseph Jay Deiss – "*Herculaneum: Italy's Buried Treasure*", 1985, Harper&Row, New York).

Initials and Abbreviations

As explained before, the literary techniques used within the New Testament were already used on the Royal Coinage as identifying information. For example, the ancient Roman coin on the left above says – "**IMPTITVSCAESVESPAUGPM**" which translates as "**Imperator** (Emperor) **Titus Caesar Vespasian Augustus Pontifex Maximus**", the coin on the right says – "**IMPCAESTAELHADRANTONINVSAVGPIVSPP**" which translates as "**Imperator Caesar Aelia Hadrian Antoninus Augustus Pius Pater Patriae**". This is how the Romans used abbreviations and it was a method of identification that royalty had used for a very long time, and was an established practice within the royal community. They used initials and abbreviations to display *words*, *names*, and *symbols* on their coins, and they would transpose what they were doing, meaning two or more things would exchange places. By shortening information on their coins, they did not have to spell out *entire names* to present them. Ancient royalty established various kingdoms and were the creators of the languages that the people they ruled over would use.

The Evidence

Again, please be aware that to view the information below properly for yourself, you must read the statements in the original Koine Greek language, as you *cannot* see any of the below in simple translations, plus, there is *syntax* involved, which is the grammatical structure of sentences, which means words and phrases are arranged to create sentences.

The Name Piso in the Gospel of Mark

Beginning with **Mark 1:7**, it says "...*He comes who [is] mightier than I after me*..."

7 Καὶ ἐκήρυσσεν, λέγων, Ἔρχεται ὁ ἰσχυρότερός μου ὀπίσω
And he proclaimed, saying, He comes who [is] mightier than I after

μου, οὗ οὐκ εἰμὶ ἱκανὸς κύψας λῦσαι τὸν ἱμάντα
me, of whom I am not fit having stooped down to loose the thong

In Greek, this statement says "*he (that) comes who [is] mightier than I, **the Piso**/οπισω [is] me*..." The words '**after**', '**before**', or '**behind**' seem to be used to present the name '**Piso**'. The omicron 'o' when viewed as a *word* in front of the name Piso/πισω, can become the word '**the**', however, because of how vowels worked in ancient languages, the 'o' could become an 'a'. For example, in Hebrew, *Aleph* (a) could be used in the absence of a vowel, and in Greek, the vowels α, ε, o could contract with one another, becoming one long sound or a double sound. But if using these 'rules' for your own motives, you could use them how you pleased, which is what is happening here. The 'o' changes with the letter '**A**' meaning it can also be seen as the initial 'A' for Arrius, which renders, **A**(rrius) **Piso**. This could be argued as being mere wordplay, however, we have previous information and the context, plus prior examples of literary codes being used, e.g., King Ferdinand's 500-year-old code.

Mark 1:17 says:

"And said to them Jesus, Come after me, and I will make you to become fishers of men."

> 17 καὶ εἶπεν αὐτοῖς ὁ Ἰησοῦς, Δεῦτε ὀπίσω μου, καὶ ποιήσω
> And said to them Jesus, Come after me, and I will make
> ὑμᾶς γενέσθαι ἁλιεῖς ἀνθρώπων. 18 Καὶ εὐθέως ἀφέντες
> you to become fishers of men. And immediately having left

Which says, again in Greek, "And [Jesus] said to them, Come **the Piso** /οπισω me, and I will make you to become fishers of men..."

Mark 1:20 says:

"...the hired servants, they went away after him."

τῶν μισθωτῶν, ἀπῆλθον ὀπίσω αὐτοῦ.
the hired servants, they went away after him.

This sentence says: "...they went away **the Piso**./οπισω him" Again, where it says "the Piso", οπισω, it also reads **A**(rrius)**Piso**".

Mark 2:16 says:

"Why [is it] that he [Jesus] eats and drinks with the **tax-gatherers** and **sinners**?"

This statement references the fact that the Calpurnius Piso family was related to the Flavian family, who collected many taxes.

Mark 4:15 says:

"...immediately comes Satan and takes away the word..."

ὁ λόγος, καὶ ὅταν ἀκούσωσιν, ʳεὐθέως‖ ἔρχεται ὁ σατανᾶς
the word, and when they hear, immediately comes Satan
καὶ αἴρει τὸν λόγον τὸν ἐσπαρμένον ʷἐν ταῖς καρδίαις αὐ-
and takes away the word that has been sown in their hearts.

Looking carefully at this statement, we can see that it says "*...immediately comes Satan [and]* **Kai** *α(i)ρει(ous)/airei(os)/Arrius [takes away] the word...*"

When the syntax is adjusted, this sentence then says: "**Satan** [is] **A(i)rei (ous) Kal (pournius), the word**..." So this statement is saying that **Satan** is **Arrius Piso**, and he is "**the word**". But remember, what seems to be the case is that the Pisos, mainly Arrius and Lucius at this stage, were using words that could present names *phonetically*, meaning the words did not have to be spelled like the original spellings of the names. Phonetically A(i)rei is pronounced **ah'-ee-ro**.

Mark 8:33 says:

Jesus rebukes Peter and says: "*Get behind me, Satan, for thy thoughts are not of the things of God, but the things of men.*"

Ὕπαγε ὀπίσω μου, σατανᾶ· ὅτι οὐ.φρονεῖς τὰ
Get behind me, Satan, for thy thoughts are not of the things
τοῦ θεοῦ, ἀλλὰ τὰ τῶν ἀνθρώπων.
of God, but the things of men.

This statement is meant to be Jesus speaking to Peter. In Greek, this sentence says: "Get **the Piso**./οπισω/**A**(**rrius**) **Piso** *me (Jesus), Satan...*" or "Get **the Piso** me (Jesus), Satan". This statement can be seen as meaning two things, 1) Piso is Jesus, and 2) Piso is Satan. To me, this appears to be Arrius stating that he is "*playing the part*" of "Jesus", "Satan", as well as playing the part of "God" of the New Testament. The following statements show the satire of the Gospels that are based on the events of the Roman-Jewish War. The statements "*How can Satan cast out Satan?*", found in **Mark 3:23**, "*If a kingdom is divided against itself, that kingdom cannot last*", found in **Mark 3:24**, and "*Now if Satan has rebelled against himself and is divided, he cannot stand either – it is the end of him*", found in **Mark 3:26**. These are all satirical statements based on the point in the war where the Jewish sects were fighting each other, which ultimately led to their downfall. *The Jewish War* depicts Jerusalem as the "*House of Satan*", so "*Satan casting out Satan*" is a satirical statement regarding Arrius, along with Titus Flavius, destroying Jerusalem and casting out the Jewish people.

Mark 8:34 says:

"*Whoever desires after me to come, let him deny himself, and let him take up his cross, and let him follow me.*"

```
34 Καὶ προσκαλεσάμενος      τὸν ὄχλον σὺν τοῖς μαθηταῖς
   And    having called to  [him] the crowd  with      ²disciples
αὐτοῦ εἶπεν αὐτοῖς, ᵗ"Ὅστις‖ θέλει ὀπίσω μου ᵛἐλθεῖν,‖ ἀπαρ-
¹his  he said to them, Whosoever desires after me  to come,    let
νησάσθω ἑαυτόν,    καὶ      ἀράτω       τὸν σταυρὸν αὐτοῦ, καὶ
him deny  himself,  and  let him take up     his cross,          and
ἀκολουθείτω μοι. 35 ὃς γὰρ ʷἄν‖ θέλῃ    τὴν ψυχὴν αὐτοῦ
let him follow me.    For whoever may desire    his life
```

When taking a look at this particular statement in Greek, it says: "*Whoever desires **the/A(rrius)Piso** me to come, let him* *deny himself, and let him take up his (own) cross, and let him (then) follow me."* The next part, **Mark 8:35**, says *"For whoever may desire his life to save, shall lose it, but whoever may lose his life on account of me and of the glad tidings, he shall save it."* This statement seems to be implying that those who *retain* their Judaic faith will die, but those who *convert* to the new religion will 'live on in Heaven'.

As you can see from the information above, the name/word The Piso/Piso/APiso appears within key statements six times in the Gospel of Mark. Now it is time to examine what has been found within the *Book of Revelation*, a book that was removed from the New Testament canon by Cyril, Bishop of Jerusalem in 340 C.E., and later the Council of Bishops in Laodicea also agreed to omit the Book of Revelation in 364 CE. In the year 370 C.E., the book was re-instated by Bishop Epiphanius, but five years later, Bishop Gregory Nazianzen omitted it yet again, and then so too did Bishop Philastrius in 380 CE. The question is, why would the Bishops want to omit the Book of Revelation, what did it contain that they did not like?

Well, the Book of Revelation contains many hints and allusions to Arrius Piso and the later Piso family, more so than any other part of the New Testament. To begin, I should first note that the author of the Book of Revelation does not appear to have presented the name or word, 'Piso' or 'Pisone', as '**Piso**', as that would have been too obvious, the name was presented as '**Pis**', just as *Christ* was abbreviated to '**Chi**' or **X** using the literary techniques already discussed. For example, in **Romans 3:22**, we find the word '**faith**' in Greek, which was '**pisteos**', being used to say the phrase "...*faith* (*of*) **Jesus Christ**...", which reads like so "**Pisteos Jesus Christ**", but reading this phrase again, whilst remembering what we have already found, it would say "**Pis(o)-teos Jesus Christ**". The word '**teos**' can also be '**Theos**' θεος, in Greek, meaning '**God**', that means the whole phrase would read as – "**Piso God Jesus Christ**". In **Rev. 13:3**, the author used the word '*after*' in **Greek**, which is '**opiso**' (οπισω), to give the name '**Piso**' in the phrase "... *after the Beast*", so to those in the know, the aristocracy, it would read '**Piso the Beast**', or '**APiso the Beast**' another word for after in Koine Greek is **meta**, but the word 'opiso' was used. It is also worth noting that the word '*panthera*' means '**beast**', and the relevance of this word will be explained later in regards to how it was used by the Jews in the **Jewish Talmud**, as there is a lot of debate over what exactly this word refers to regarding the name '*Yeshua ben Panthera*'. But regarding the word '*opiso*', it is fair to say that unless someone discovered the information in the previous chapters, no one would ever associate '**O Piso**' with **Arrius Piso** or the Piso family in general. The vowel letters '**o**' and '**a**', were interchangeable, as already shown, so '**opiso**' could also be read as '**apiso**'. But if we keep the '**O**', we then have the initial of one of Arrius Piso's *other* alias names, which was '**Optimus**', a name which can be found in the works of Pliny The Younger, in his '*Panegyricus*', which, again, will be explained.

The Evidence in The Book Of Revelation

In **Revelation 1:8**, we find the phrase "*I am the Alpha and the Omega, beginning and ending...*".

8 Ἐγώ εἰμι τὸ ᵃA‖ καὶ τὸ ʽΩ,‖ ʳἀρχὴ καὶ τέλος·‖ λέγει
　I　am　the　A　and the　Ω,　beginning and ending,　says

The author is stating what 'Jesus' is supposed to have said, but this statement should logically have read "**Aleph and Tav the beginning and the end**", since 'Jesus' would have spoken Aramaic to the Jewish people of the first century, and **Aleph** is the beginning of the **Hebrew** alphabet and **Tav** is the end. The correct **translation** into **Greek** would be **Alpha** and **Tau**, since the Hebrew **Tav (T)**, corresponds to the Greek letter **Tau (T)**. If translating the words of 'Jesus' for a Greek-speaking audience, however, then '**Alpha and Omega**' could be correct, since **Omega** is the last letter of the **Greek** alphabet. But if in the story 'Jesus' said '**Tav**' to '**John**', then he should have recorded '**Tav**', because in the story 'John' was preserving the '*truth*' that Jesus is the '**Aleph Tav**' of the scriptures in **Hebrew**, and it would have been understood that he is both the '**Alpha and Omega**' and the '**Aleph and Tav**'. The reason this can be argued is that in other places the Gospels record when 'Jesus' spoke in Aramaic, such as in **Mark 15:34** and **Matthew 27:46** and when the words '**Eli**' and '**Eloi**' are presented, and **Mark 14:36** when 'Jesus' is reported as saying '**Abba**'-"*And he said, Abba, Father, all things are possible unto thee; take away this cup from me: nevertheless not what I will, but what thou wilt.*" Other places in the New Testament that contain Aramaic are *Mark 5:41*;

7:34; 11:9; *Matthew* 5:22; *John* 20:16; *I Corinthians* 16:22. If 'Jesus' spoke to 'John' in Aramaic/Hebrew and 'John' recorded the actual words of 'Jesus' in 'Matthew' and 'Mark' and provided their meaning, then there is no reason for it not to have been done in the above example. If 'Jesus' spoke in Greek to the Aramaic-speaking Jews, which is incredibly unlikely to have been the case, then he would have said '**Alpha**' and '**Omega**', since 'Omega' is the last letter of the Greek alphabet. The correct translation then, into **Hebrew**, would be '**Aleph**' and '**Tav**', since the Greek alphabet contains **2** more letters than the Hebrew alphabet. So there is no way to render Omega into Hebrew, and since Jesus is saying he is the *"beginning and end"* to first-century Jews, he would have been the '**Aleph Tav**' and that is what should have been recorded.

But with the words, '**Alpha**' and '**Omega**' presented, it again reveals Arrius' name, this time in full, albeit 'chopped up'. Arrius starts with an '**A**' (alpha) and **Piso** ends with an '**O**' (omega), but with the word '**kai**' presented, which is '**and**', this phrase reads as:

"I am the **A(rrius)lpha kai(purnius)** the **(pis)Omega**", with the 'i' in 'kai' being seen as an 'l' (L).

So Arrius Calpurnius Piso's full name can be seen, which should not be the case, and it is used in a phrase that should have been recorded in Aramaic, and this phrase can be found repeated in **Revelation 1:8**, **21:6**, and **22:13**.

In **Revelation 1:13**, 'Jesus' is described as *"**the son of man**"*, which means **"descendant of Adam"** or **"the second Adam"**. This phrase is said elsewhere in the New Testament, but as before with the "*Alpha and Omega*" phrase being repeated, it is said more than once to bring attention to it. The reason 'Jesus', which appears to be Arrius, was referred to as "the **second Adam**", was because the person who may have 'played' the first "**Adam**" in **Genesis** was the same person who seems likely to have initiated the creation of the religion that would become **Judaism**. That person was the Pharaoh **Adamenemhept I** or **Amenemhat/Amenemhet I**, who founded the Twelfth Dynasty at Thebes, Egypt. Amenemhet I, was *not* of royal lineage, and the composition of some literary works (the *Prophecy of Neferti* and *the Instructions of Amenemhat*), and then the return to the pyramid-style complexes of the 6th Dynasty rulers, are often considered to have been attempts at legitimizing his rule. But this phrase seems to imply that Arrius was now playing the part of **his** creation 'Jesus' in the new Christian religion.

Revelation 1:14 says "*...and his head and hair (is)* **white as if white wool**, *as* **white as snow**". This means the facial hair of 'Jesus' was white and his whole head of hair appeared "white". According to the story though, 'Jesus' dies in his 30's, so it is highly unlikely that his hair would have been "white". Another explanation for this statement could include 'Jesus' appearing as God, but again there is no evidence for that argument. The more logical conclusion is that the author is talking about Arrius when in old age, as Arrius Piso lived to be quite old. He was born in the year 37 CE and died in, approximately, the year 119 CE, so that would make him about 82 years old.

Another clue that it is Arrius being referring to, is that the word for '**wool**' is '**erion**' εριον, which is "Arrion/"Arrian" and so can refer to either "**Apion**" or "**Arrius**". That points to both Arrius as 'Josephus' and Arrius as himself, because 'Josephus' wrote: "**Against Apion**", which was Arrius writing, and because "**Apion**"/ "**Arrian**" is just another form of **Arrius** using letter exchanges.

Revelation 1:16 says "*out of his* *mouth, a sharp double-edged sword going forth*..." From what we have learned, this tells us that 'Jesus' or Arrius 'spoke' two ways, or used two weapons to achieve his goal. One was using the language spoken by the people to manipulate them, the other was using the writing techniques developed by the aristocracy.

Revelation 4:3 describes the breastplate of someone (*Arrius?*) sitting on his throne, which indicates that this someone was both a priest and a king. The breastplate contains twenty-four stones and the author even says that a particular council is made up of twenty-four elders. Those elders all wear white garments and are all kings because they all wear gold diadems or crowns. The author is simply saying what the real situation was, to enable us to understand the actual meaning behind his words and phrases.

In **Revelation 5:8**, 'Jesus' is stated as being the "*the Lamb*": "*And when he had taken the book, the four beasts and four and twenty elders fell down before the Lamb*...", The word for 'Lamb' in **Greek** is '**Arnion**' αρνιον or '**Amnos**' αμνος. What was written in this instance, however, is the *genitive* of this word, which is '**Arnius**' 'αρνιου', but Arnion αρνίον being a neutral noun means the word can appear the same in the accusative (direct object, i.e., 'the Lamb') and become feminine or masculine by personification. Under a normal reading, the word 'Arnius' may not look suspicious, but because of our previous findings, the author must have chosen this version of the word as a convenient way to present Arrius' name, by saying that '**Jesus**' is the **Arrius** (arnius/lamb). Remember, **r**'s and **n**'s were switched, as in the example found regarding Arria and her name being presented as **F.Annia**. It is clear the '**Arnius**' word was seen as **Arrius.** Another telling clue is in the fact we find the word 'Amnos' used in *John* 1:29, 1:36; *Acts* 8:32; and *I Peter* 1:19; it is interesting to note here that in John 21:15 the plural word '**Arnia**' is used (plural being more than two). 'Arnia' is another form of Arnion, but, as above, this word can also be seen as *Arria.*

Revelation 5:10 reads "*And hast made us unto our God kings and priests: and we shall reign on the earth.*" This is stating exactly what was happening at that time, *kings* and *priests* ruled over the entire known world and had the authority.

In **Revelation 6:12**, the author is writing about how the natural occurrences, that we now know in our time to indeed be natural, were used in that time to fool the 'ignorant masses' by priests. The author speaks of *Earthquakes, the eclipse of the Sun,* as well as the *red moon.* In **Revelation 6:13**, the author talks about "*falling stars*", which we now know are meteors, through scientific study, research, and testing.

Revelation 6:16 talks about the '**wrath of the Lamb**' and uses the word '**Arnius**' for Lamb again, so the author is referring to the '*wrath of the* **Arrius**' that was inflicted on the Jews.

ὥπου τοῦ καθημένου ἐπὶ ᴾᵃτοῦ θρόνου,ᴵᴵ καὶ ἀπὸ τῆς ὀργῆς
of him who sits   on   the   throne, and from the wrath
τοῦ ἀρνίου· 17 ὅτι ἦλθεν ἡ ἡμέρα ἡ μεγάλη τῆς ὀργῆς
of the Lamb;   because is come the ²day   ¹great   ᵃwrath

Revelation 7:14 has the phrase **"The blood of the Lamb"**, with the word 'Arnius' being used again. Now the author could be stating "the Blood of the Lamb" means "the blood" (and sweat) of the Arrius, saying that **his** blood was given to save his people, i.e., his family and supporters. Using this phrase, the connection between the two may be made, i.e., **'Josephus'** leads us to **Arrius**, which leads us to **"the Lamb"** which leads to the character **'Jesus'**. And in this example, two different spellings for Lamb were used. The word Lamb in the phrase "*The blood of the Lamb*" is spelled **'Arnius'**, but only a few lines later in **7:17** we have the word '*Lamb*' again, but Lamb is spelled as **'Arnion'** αρνιον, and there is no reason for this unless of course to point to Arrius. We then have another use of the word Arnius in 14:10 *"...and he shall be tormented in fire and brimstone, before the holy angels, and before the Lamb* αρνιου."

ᵃστολὰςᴵᴵ ᵇαὐτῶνᴵᴵ ἐν τῷ αἵματι τοῦ ἀρνίου. 15 διὰ τοῦτό
²robes   ¹their   in the blood of the Lamb. Because of this
εἰσιν ἐνώπιον τοῦ θρόνου τοῦ θεοῦ, καὶ λατρεύουσιν αὐτῷ
are they before the throne   of God, and   serve   him
ἡμέρας καὶ νυκτὸς ἐν τῷ ναῷ αὐτοῦ· καὶ ὁ καθήμενος ἐπὶ
day   and night in his temple; and he who sits   on
ᶜτοῦ θρόνουᴵᴵ σκηνώσει ἐπ' αὐτούς. 16 οὐ πεινάσουσιν
the   throne   shall tabernacle over them.   They shall not hunger
ἔτι, οὐδὲᵈ διψήσουσιν ἔτι, ᵉοὐδὲᴵᴵ μὴ πέσῃ ἐπ' αὐ-
any more, neither shall they thirst any more, nor at all shall fall upon
τοὺς ὁ ἥλιος, οὐδὲ πᾶν καῦμα· 17 ὅτι τὸ ἀρνίον τὸ
them the sun, nor any heat;   because the Lamb which [is]

Revelation 8:2 says Seven *"trumpets"* for seven *"angels"*. "Angels" is a euphemism for *'leaders of the church'* and "trumpets" refers to the *'thunder tubes'* the high priests used at the alters. They used these 'thunder tubes' to fool those into thinking they were talking to God, whilst they were taking part in a sacrifice. So each of the heads (priests) of the seven churches were given a 'thunder tube' to use at their altars to fool the 'ignorant' or uninformed people. The trumpets were used like megaphones to make the priest's voice echo around the church and sound authoritative.

And we can tell "angel" means high priest and not a winged being, because 1) there is no evidence for the "winged angel" and 2) in **Revelation 1:11**, it says *"the seven stars (weapons) are "angels" of the seven churches"* (of Asia, which were the seven major churches of early Christianity – **Rev:1:20**. And in **Revelation 8:2**, we have the phrase *"And I saw the seven "**angels**" (of the seven churches) which stood before God (King/Ruler/Arrius Piso), and to them (the "**angels**"), were given seven trumpets"*. This means the trumpet was a *"sacred"* device given **only** to **priests**, so, the only answer is that the word "angels" refers to the priests.

Revelation 9:9, says *"and the sound of their "wings" (were) as (the) sound of chariots of many horses running to war"*. The author is telling us that *"flying angels"* does not mean flying, but that this is a euphemism for *'traveling fast by chariot'*. So "angels" were the church leaders/priests traveling fast by chariot, and **Revelation 4:10** says the word *"holy angels"*, but why would the angels need to be described as "holy". The reason is that *"holy"* and *"sacred"* are the same and mean "secret", so now we read "holy angels" as "secret angels" and we know that "angels" means priests, so the saying reads *"secret priests"*.

In **Revelation 9:17**, we have *"...the heads of the horses (were) as lions..."* In ancient history, and in current times, the lion is a symbol of royalty, and the **Greek** word used for a horse, in this case, is '**ippos**' ιππους, which can be assumed was used because the words can be arranged to spell **Piso**. So this phrase means the heads of the **Pisos** were as lions (royals) because the family eventually gained full control of the empire.

Revelation 10:7 says *"...when he is about to sound (the) trumpet, (he) should also **finish/end the mystery of God**, as he did **announce/say/promise in the glad tidings (Gospels) to his bondsmen, the prophets**..."*. So it was agreed by all involved in creating Christianity that the mystery would end one day, and, as seems to be the case, for that to happen, they would insert ways in which to explain, or reveal, who created the religion, and why.

Revelation 11:2, says "And the holy city (Jerusalem) shall they trample upon **forty-two months**". Forty-two months is a very specific number and appears to be talking about the **Bar Kochba War,** which lasted from late 131 C.E., until late 135 C.E., which is a total of **42 months**, or three and a half years; some scholars hold the view it lasted from 132-136 CE. Stating this gives us a way of dating the Book of Revelation to a time just *after* the war, around **136-137** C.E., but interestingly, this forty-two-month number is mentioned more than once, so we take notice of it.

In **Revelation 11:3** it says "And I will give (power/authority) to *my two witnesses, and they shall prophesy a **thousand, two hundred and sixty days**....*". A **thousand, two hundred** and **sixty days** is again **42 months**. This will be mentioned again in Revelation, which means it is important. When someone wants to make sure someone understands and remembers important information, it is usually repeated until they understand it, and that is exactly what is happening here.

Revelation 12:3, says "*a dragon*", and as mentioned earlier in the book, "dragon" is a reference to 'Jesus', because the word for dragon also means "baby boy", and the only "baby boy" that we have in the story of the New Testament is the baby 'Jesus'. **Draken** is a *baby boy* name in **Greek** and in **Latin** it is **Draco**.

Revelation 12:4 reads "*And the dragon stood before the woman who is about to bring forth (give birth), (so) that when she should bring forth, her child* (which is also Arrius' "Son", because this is Arrius Piso's *invented* or *created* child, 'Jesus'), *he might devour (the child/'Jesus')*". This statement is a play on the concept and an allusion to the Greek myth of the *Titan* **Cronus**, who devoured his sons at birth, for fear of being overthrown. This is a way for the author of the Book of Revelation, who will be examined later, to hint at the ancestry of Arrius. Arrius, through his great-grandfather, *Aristobulus*, was a descendant of the person to who the character the *Titan Cronus* has links, via the God *'Pan'*, that person being *Antigonus Gonatas*, notice the name 'Gonatas' backward contains the name 'Satan'. The author writing about the woman giving birth to a baby and then offering it to be consumed by a male is reflected in Arrius' work as '**Flavius Josephus**'. In the War of the Jews, the Jews were starving during the war, and the woman 'Mary' was forced to resort to cannibalism to survive, by killing her son, and then cooking and eating the child, by preparing the body in the same way as in the Old Testament.

Revelation 12:6 says "*a thousand two hundred and sixty days.*", which again is **42 months**. This again is giving us a clue regarding the period of authorship of this book, the author wants us to know the Book of Revelation was written (finished) **after** the last revolt of the Jews (Pharisees), which happened in the **Bar Kochba War** after 135 C.E., and there are a few reasons for this. As said before, there are other places in the New Testament where things are mentioned *after the fact* and are presented to the reader as if they wrote the text *before* the events, to give the illusion that this was a "prophesy" that was fulfilled. The author was trying to point out that the event had already happened, by giving a very specific number that links to a specific event.

In **Revelation 13:4** there is a question "*who is* **like** *the* **beast**? *and* **who** *is able to make war with it?*" Firstly a reader needs to know who the beast is, but we *do* know who "the **beast**" is, it is '**Piso**', because "*beast*" in this instance can only mean '**horse**', and there is no evidence for the type of beast described in the Book of Revelation, and we know that a word used for a horse in this book is '**ippos**', which, as mentioned before, is '**Piso**' rearranged. Once this is figured out, then the answer to the question "*who is able to make war with it?*" can be known, the answer is those who are in a position to make "war" with the "beast" (Arrius) can do so, i.e. a member of the Piso family. This was the "*war in Heaven*" that is spoken of, and "Heaven" was used as a euphemism for more than one thing, in *this instance,* it was used as a metaphor for royalty because those who were royal lived in a paradise or "Heaven" (on earth) compared to the common people. From reading the available material, written by the Piso family and their relatives, there appears to have been a dispute happening between the Piso family members, which led Arrius' son, *Julius*, to write the Book of Revelation- that dispute will be examined shortly.

But in **Revelation 13:3**, Julius Piso has already given us the answer to the above question, "*who is like the* **beast**?", because in **13:3** he says the phrase "*after the beast*". Now normally that phrase would not look like an answer to the above question, but when we realize that the Greek word used for '**after**' is '**opiso**' οπισω, the phrase "**after the beast**" does indeed become an answer. The phrase in the *original* words reads as "o**piso** *the beast*", or taking into account the use of inferred words, it would read as "o**piso** (is) the beast". Another word for "**after**" in Koine Greek is '**meta**' μετα, which would read μετα του θηριο (meta/after the beast), but of course, that was not what was written.

αὐτοῦ, καὶ ἐξουσίαν μεγάλην. 3 καὶ ⁿεἶδον⁰ μίαν° τῶν κεφα-
  ¹his, and ²authority ¹great.   And I saw   one   ³heads
λῶν αὐτοῦ ὡς ἐσφαγμένην εἰς θάνατον· καὶ ἡ πληγὴ τοῦ
¹of ²its as   slain   to   death;   and the wound
θανάτου αὐτοῦ ἐθεραπεύθη, καὶ ᴾἐθαυμάσθη⁰ ᵠἐν⁰ ʳὅλῃ τῇ
³death ¹of ²its was healed: and there was wonder in ²whole ¹the
γῇ⁰ ὀπίσω τοῦ θηρίου. 4 καὶ προσεκύνησαν ˢτὸν δράκοντα⁰
earth after the beast.   And they did homage to the   dragon,

In **Revelations 13:11**, Julius talks of a **beast** (*horse, ippos, Piso*) with two horns like a **Lamb** and who spoke like a **dragon**. As we have learned from earlier, he is saying yet again that the beast is **Piso** and that Piso is "the **Lamb**", i.e. "**Jesus**", and that he is also the '**dragon**' (Satan), with the word 'dragon' referring to 'baby boy', as we know. Saying these words all at the same time links them together, and this is indicated repeatedly in the Book of Revelation; the word for Lamb used here is Arnio ἀρνίῳ.

Revelation 13:18 says "*Here is wisdom. He who has (the) understanding (of what is being said in 'The Revelation'), let him count the **number of the beast**: for (the) number (of) it is a **man's** and the number (of it is)* **666**." Many things have been written and discussed concerning the *'number of the beast'*, but no satisfactory answer, *as far as I can tell*, has ever been agreed upon within academia, but the answer points to what Arrius wrote in his works as 'Josephus', which, again, will be explained shortly.

Revelation 14:11 mentions "*the beast*" and the "*mark*" by saying "*...who worship the beast and his image, and whosoever receiveth the mark of his name.*" When the apocryphal Christian texts and ancient Egyptian words and meanings are researched, it is realized that Julius is trying to tell us that the "mark" (of the beast/Piso) is a cross.

In **Revelation 14:13**, the word "**spirit**" is mentioned, as well as being mentioned in many other places. This word again points to the Pisos, because of *Phonetics*, which is the study and classification of speech sounds. The word "**spirit**" can be seen as the word 'pneuma' πνευμα (also spelled **Numa** or **Nooma**) which is an ancient **Greek** word for "**breath**", but in a *religious* context, it is used for "**spirit**" or "**soul**" and is used in Greek translations of the **Hebrew Bible** and the **Greek New Testament**. The word 'spirit'/'numa' is another word that links to the ancestry of the Piso family, as **Numa Pompilius** is one of the main ancestors from which the Piso family claimed descent, through his third son Calpus.

Revelation 14:14, speaks about *"(the) son of man"*, and the word "**son**" means different things in the ancient languages, but in this case, it means "**descendant**", as in the "*descendant of* **Adam**", or the Egyptian Pharaoh 'Amenemhept I'.

To clarify, the word '*man*' is A*tum* in Egyptian, A*dmu* in Assyrian, and A*dam* in Hebrew. Intriguingly, the Egyptian Pharaoh, **Amen/Amun/Atum/Adamenemhept I**, founded the Twelfth Dynasty at Thebes and had "A*dam*" as a part of his name, and the evidence is compelling that he played/created the character "**Adam**" in **Genesis.** This Pharaoh had a son called "Seth"/"Sesostris", a son which is mentioned by 'Flavius Josephus' (Arrius Piso) who calls him "Seth", who was known as "Sesostris" when he was Pharaoh, but "**Seth**" and "**Sesostris**" are the same. The reason why the evidence for this Pharaoh creating the Genesis story is so interesting is that when the ages given for 'Adam and 'Noah' are counted back, *in terms of the average lifespan for people living at that time*, we end up at the time of this Pharaoh, and this period is when the first legend declaring the king to be the '**Son of God**' originated.

In **Revelation 16:2**, Julius mentions the "*mark*" of the "*beast*" again, bringing attention to it.

Revelation 16:10 says "*the throne of the beast*", this simply means that Arrius was royalty and became a "king" or emperor when he co-ruled the empire.

Revelation 16:13 says *"out of the mouth of the **dragon**, and out of the mouth of the **beast**, and out of the **false prophet**..."* Why are '**dragon**', '**beast**', and '**false prophet**' mentioned? This is Julius again referring to the words associated with his father. Arrius played the '**Draco**' (dragon, baby), he was the "**beast**" and he most certainly was a "**false prophet**", as in the Gospels, 'Jesus' was also considered a 'false prophet' by the Jews.

In **Revelation 19:13** it says *"and his **name** is called, **The Word of God**"*, so Jesus' name is called the *word* of God, what does that mean? If we remember what we have learned up to this point, 'Jesus' of the New Testament only exists in **words**, and those are the words of **Arrius Piso**, who must have considered himself the new "God", just like past emperors. Christians would be forgiven for thinking this means that 'Jesus' was the *"mouthpiece"* for God on earth, but, again, there is no proof of that. What this saying means is that 'Jesus' was the *creation* of someone, or "**the logos**", which points to **Philo of Alexandria**, but Philo makes no mention of 'Jesus', but "the logos" idea first appears in his works and then in the New Testament.

Revelation 19:14 says *"and the armies in "heaven"* (royals in their 'paradise' of luxury), *were following him* (Arrius) *upon horses white, clothed in fine linen, white and pure"*. Can you imagine royalty in that time in Rome wearing anything less than pure white fine linen?

Revelation 19:16 says *"And he has upon his garment* (clothing/veil), *and upon his **thigh** a name (that) is written, King of Kings and Lord of Lords"*. This statement seems to point to something that happened to Arrius as a general (recorded using the name '*Cestius Gallus*') in the war against the Jews (Pharisees). When

Arrius wrote about the incident where he and his troops had to march through a narrow pass next to the village of Beth-horon, he wrote that the Jewish rebels had gathered there, he says "*and covered the Roman army with their darts.*" *There was no escape for the beleaguered, exhausted soldiery. Above them on the hillsides their enemies were as thick as olive groves. Below were steep precipices down which the cavalrymen on their* **frightened horses** *"frequently fell."* Because of various things being stated, both in the New Testament and the Talmud, the statement "*...and upon his* **thigh** *a name (that) is written, King of Kings and Lord of Lords*" seems to be suggesting that Arrius may have fallen from his horse and had his leg crushed, causing him to become lame and unable to walk without difficulty. Julius seems to be telling us that his father not only hurt his leg, but ended up losing it completely, which would mean his thigh was certainly not flesh, but wood, and being wood it could be written on quite easily without hurting his father.

A god called '*Balaam*' appears in the Torah, whose story begins in Chapter 22 of the *Book of Numbers*, but the Babylonian Talmud (Sanhedrin 106b and Gittin 57a) also speaks of a Balaam, a second Balaam, which is applied by the writers of the Talmud to 'Jesus', or so it is thought. (**supporting ref** – '*Jesus in the Talmud*', Peter Schafer) But Balaam also appears in the New Testament in *2 Peter 2:15, Jude verse 11*, and *Revelation 2:14*, and each time the believers are chastised for following Balaam's doctrines. But because the New Testament seems to be authored by the Pisos, the Balaam passages seem to be Arrius, and possibly his sons, teasing that those converting to their religion were following Piso in the guise of Balaam, but why?

The reason is that the Talmud attacks Arrius under the name of Balaam by referring to his fake leg, by creating the legend of the '**Lamed Vav/Vov**', which is '*Balaam*' re-arranged in Hebrew. But the Talmud also asks whether Balaam was 33 or 34 years old when he was killed, the same age 'Jesus' is supposed to have been when he died; interestingly, the number 36, is the total of the name **Josephus** Ιωςηπος in Greek but viewed from a *Latin* perspective (zeros omitted-which will be explained in 'The 666 Riddle' chapter). Arrius looks to have spelled the Josephus pseudonym with a **P** instead of an **F**. *Etymologically* this is correct in Greek, but spelling it that way would total 36, not 33. Making the name total 36 makes it the same total as the name of the ancient Greek philosopher, **Pythagoras** (when viewed from a Latin perspective) from whom Arrius/the Pisos looks to have borrowed, but refined, the alpha-numeric numbering systems. In Luke chapter 3, an additional 21 generations counting back to Adam and God are added to the 57 generations between Jesus and Abraham. Therefore, Arrius deliberately made the total, **78**, and comparing the 78 generations in Luke chapter 3, to the 42 generations (3 *times* 14) presumed in Matthew 1.17, gives a difference of **36**—the name, *Josephus*. The Jewish reply was to light 36 candles during the eight nights of *Chanukah*; and with the legend of the Lamed Vav; and by spelling and choosing the hymn title **Adon Olam** ('Eternal Lord' or '*Sovereign of the Universe*') which totaled 36.

Revelations 20:8 says "**the four corners of the earth**", and this indicates simply that the Pisos, and those of a similar position, knew the Earth was round. We know the Earth is not flat and all of the royals of that time knew this, but the common people of that day were kept uneducated by those in charge and did not travel too far off places like royalty.

Revelations 20:12 says "*and books were opened; and another book was opened, which is "the book of life". And the dead were judged out of the things written in the books according to their (own) works*". Julius is telling us that his father and supporters read and learned from the Jewish books, to create their book, the "*book of life*", which led to the dead Jews being judged based on their own beliefs presented in their books. The "**book of life**" being spoken of was primarily the **New Testament**, and secondly the Bible as a whole book, and then generally all books that recorded information about the lives of royals, their relatives, and ancestors.

In **Revelations 21:6**, we again see the phrase "I *am the* **alpha** *and* **omega**, *the beginning and end*", and the reason for this phrase was explained earlier.

Revelation 21:10 uses the word "**spirit**" and says "*great mountain*". "Spirit" refers to Arrius through the word '**Numa**', as mentioned earlier, but remember, the Egyptian word "**Veru**" means "**Great man/men**", and Arrius used this for one of his alias names, "**Verus**". So the word '*spirit*' and '*great*' points to Arrius, but so too does the word '**mountain**', as Arrius also used the alias name '**Montanus**', which means '**Mountain**'.

Revelation 22:13 repeats the phrase "I *am the* **alpha** *and* **omega**, *the beginning and the end, the first and last*".

In **Revelation 22:16**, it says "I, Jesus, sent my angel (priest/church leader) to testify to you these things in the assemblies (churches). *I am the* **root** *and the offspring ("descendant") of King David, and the* **bright morning star**". Here is how this passage should read, it should say that he is "**a**" descendant of King David, and not "**the**" descendant of King David, because the author, Julius, knows full well that there were many descendants of King David. In regards to the reference of the *"bright morning star"*, this is shared with *'John the Baptist'*, a character created to represent the Pharisee leader, **Yochanan ben Zakai**. But "the bright morning **star**" is a "**spear**", which in ancient Rome referred to "**penis**", which is understood when ancient history and the classics are studied. This statement is referencing **Achilles**' "**spear**", which was as *bright* as the *evening star*, and Arrius Pisos' "**spear**"/**weapon** was the character 'Jesus', which is as *bright* as the *morning star*. (**ref** – Achilles, in 'The Illiad', by Homer).

Revelations 22:20 says *"Yes, I am coming quickly,"* "Amen," *yes come Lord Jesus"*. Some people have concluded that this phrase is rude, but knowing that the New Testament is indeed full of completely disgusting phrases, this is no surprise. No evidence has been found to suggest that the word "coming" in ancient texts means what it is said to be referring to today. What this can be assumed to mean, is that the real 'Jesus' is coming, as in will be *discovered*, and the use of "**Amen**" refers to the royal ancestors, the Pharaohs, as they received the title "Amon" (as in "Amon Ra") through their rising to important positions and taking their thrones. And because of all the evidence we have, the words *"yes (even so), come Lord Jesus"*, can be seen as meaning "Yes indeed come and be known for who you really are."

Key phrases

Below are examples of 'key phrases' that also present Arrius' name, using the techniques explained earlier.

John 3:2 says "...*that from God*...", which in Greek is "**oti apo Theou**" "οτι απο θεου", but when reading this from the perspective of the Pisos and the aristocracy, it reads – "**o** (the) **ti** (for 'titan') **a** (rrius) **p** (iso) **o** (ptimus) (is) God/Theou". Remember, that syntax is incorporated in these words and phrases, which means the words can be switched around to better understand what is being said, meaning the above phrase could also be read as "**The Titan Arrius Piso is God**". But this phrase also connects **Arrius** with the name **Trajan** that **Pliny** speaks about in his **Panegyricus**, when he says that *'Trajan'* received the name *'***Optimus***'*; Pliny the Younger's possible role in the creation of Christianity will be examined shortly. Arrius Piso was likely a (silent) co-ruler with Emperor Trajan (as he was with Vespasian and Titus) as Trajan was Arrius Piso's son in law, and further information regarding this can be found at – *The Optimus In Pliny's Panegyricus*, Roman Piso Academia

In the **Epistles of Pliny**, the phrase "**the name of Christ**" is mentioned when talking about Christians, and it is said twice for emphasis. In Greek, the word for "**Christ**" is '**Xpistos**' Χριστος, which can be seen as – 'X' (**Ch**), 'ris' (**pis**), 't', 'o', 's'. So that means we have "**Ch**(rist) **Pis**(o) **T** (for Titus or 'Titan') **O** (for Optimus), and **S** (for Sabinus, Arrius' great-grandfather)" or "**Christ Piso Titus Optimus Sabinus**". But using syntax the phrase can also be read as "*Piso (is) Christ (the) Optimus Titus Sabinus*"; I should note that "**Optimus**" has **Latin** origins and means "**one of the best, aristocrat, noble**"

In **John 4:36**, we see the word '**reaps**' used to say "**The God Piso Nichomachus**", as '**reaps**' in **Greek** is '**o Therizon**' θεριζων, and here's why – "**O** at the start means '*the*', then the '**The**' part of *The-rizon* is an acrostic for '**theo**' (God), **rizo** is saying '*piso*', because remember '**r**' is seen as '**p**', and the '**z**' is used to give the '**s**' sound, the '**n**' at the end represents '*nichomachus*'. In 'Antiquities of the Jews', created in around 100 CE, Arrius is the '*mathematician*' called '**Nichomachus of Garasa**', because, as we know, Arrius was writing as 'Josephus' and because '**Nico**' means 'Victor' or 'Winner', and '**Machus**' means 'of the battle' (of Garasa). When we read Josephus, we find Arrius as a Roman General at the battle of Garasa, which took place in **66** CE, and 'Josephus', or Arrius, was the first person in history to mention Garasa.

8. A FAMILY AUTHORSHIP

The information in this chapter will perhaps be the hardest to verify/explain, as it involves attempting to understand who the authors of the later gospels/epistles were, by trying to understand/decipher their real names using their alias names. The task which involves the process of deduction and educated conjecture, from reading not only the Gospels but also the historical writing we have available, is made somewhat easier due to the logical realization that 1) the Pisos/aristocracy only appear to have written about their immediate family, and 2) the fact that the scriptures could only have been written during a certain time, again, based on what has been examined so far. This chapter will not examine every epistle, as doing so would require a whole book in itself, as the amount of information connecting the family members to each epistle is not only complex but also vast. I would suggest reading the work of the researcher '*Roman Piso*', located on *Academia.edu*, for more information regarding each epistle and information regarding the names of the later Christian writers, for example, the paper titled '*Who was the often quoted "Tertullian"*', provides information about which descendant of the Pisos used this name.

During the time the Piso family would have written the New Testament, it was not unheard of to force a slave to write literature. If Arrius wrote or oversaw the creation of the scriptures himself, he must not have thought it a big deal to have variations floating around. However, because we can not know exactly who physically wrote what, I will assume that Arrius wrote much of the scriptures himself, with help from his family. The main author of the version of the Gospel of Mark that we are familiar with, which would have been completed in about the year 73 CE, must have been Arrius Piso. In that Gospel, he wrote that 'Jesus' was greater than the Jewish commander and rebel, **Eleazar ben Yair**, the leader of the Jewish sect the Sicarii at the siege of Masada, why would Jesus be greater?, because Jesus is Arrius and he was the general in charge of the siege of Masada. This is clear when Arrius was writing as 'Flavius Josephus' because he shows genuine hatred for Eleazar. Arrius must have written '**Luke**' *after* the death of *Eleazar ben Yair*, as there is only a slight difference between the statement concerning God declaring 'Jesus' as his son in '**Mark**', and the statement in '**Luke**', giving more evidence to connect the author of Mark with the author of Luke.

Mark 1:11

And there came a voice from heaven, saying, "Thou art my beloved Son, in whom I am well pleased."

Luke 3:22

And the Holy Ghost descended in a bodily shape like a dove upon him, and a voice came from heaven, which said, Thou art my beloved Son; in thee I am well pleased."

Mark 9:7

And there was a cloud that overshadowed them: and a voice

came out of the cloud, saying, "This is my beloved Son: hear him."

Luke 9:35

And there came a voice out of the cloud, saying, "This is my beloved Son: hear him."

Arrius' son, Julius, strongly appears to be the author of the Book of Revelation, for reasons which will be shown. One of those reasons is that he gives hints relating to incidents involving his father, one of which seems to involve the loss of his leg, as, in Revelation 13:12, it reads *"the first beast whom was healed of its death-wound."* So the 'beast' was healed from a *death* wound, which seems to most likely be from a damaged leg, which was possibly fractured and may have become infected. Our attention then is brought to **Luke 4:23**, which was written in 85-90 CE, where it reads *"And he said unto them, Ye will surely say unto me this proverb, Physician, heal thyself: whatsoever we have heard done in Capernaum, do also here in thy country."* What we essentially have then is *Jesus* in the Gospel of Luke referring to himself as a physician, a doctor, and 'Luke' was also meant to be a physician. Taking into consideration that being a physician was not common at the time, and also taking into consideration what we have already looked at, to me this gospel is stating that 'Luke' and 'Jesus' are the same person, Arrius, and Revelation 19:11-14, etc., gives further hints, "And I saw the heaven opened, and behold a white horse (**ippos – piso**); and (**kai – Kalpurnius**) he who sits upon it, called Faithful and True, and in righteousness he judges and makes war. And eyes his [were] as a flame of fire, and upon head his diadems (crowns) many, having a name written, which no one knows but himself, and clothed with a garment dipped in blood: and is called his name The Word (Logos) of God. And the armies in the heaven (Rome) were following him upon horses white, clothed in fine linen, white and pure."

Arrius Piso wrote both *Mark*, *Matthew*, and *Luke*, but at different times, however, when Arrius began to work on this gospel, it seems logical to think that he was helped by his cousin, Herod Agrippa II, who was officially named, *Marcus Julius Agrippa II*. Arrius inserted himself by playing not only the role of 'Jesus' but also playing the role of the '**Josephs**', because he and his father before him must have felt that the identity of a second or new 'Joseph' fit well with them. The reason is that the name '**Piso**' has the same four letters, *rearranged*, as the four Hebrew letters – **Yud – Vov – Samech – Fey**, and these letters in *Hebrew* spell the name 'Joseph'. This must be the reason so much of the story of Joseph in Egypt is secretly redone to create the story of Jesus, a new Savior, who would preach different principles than those which were being taught in Judaism. '**Mark**' or *Marcus* was one of Arrius Piso's names, a name he must have inherited from his grandfather, *Marcus Calpurnius Piso*, and so the Gospel of Mark may have been titled after Arrius' grandfather, who in the very beginning possibly contributed to the development of ideas for the content. However, yet another reason for the name of the gospel could come from the old Latin "*Mart-kos*", which means "*consecrated to the god Mars*", but can also mean "*God of war*". If we remember back to one of the names used for Arrius, which was 'Montanus', and "**Mar's Hill**" being mentioned in the New Testament, which in Greek is "**Areios Pagos**", '*pagos*' of which can also be "*opus*" (Piso, with vowels, changed), then, yet again, we have a link which fits within the context of what was happening. I feel that all the above are plausible reasons for the name Mark being chosen, I don't think that we will ever know the absolute reason for the name of this gospel, but the above certainly follows the same trend as that of the information we have already examined.

Regarding the Gospel of Luke, again, no certain answer can be made, but Arrius' mother married his uncle Lucius Calpurnius Piso, which means the Gospel of '**Luke**' may well have been named after Lucius, again, because Arrius had inherited the right to use that name. Concerning the name 'Matthew', or '**Ur Matthaeus**', as well as inheriting the use of this family name and the right to use it from one of his royal ancestors; writing as '*Flavius Josephus*', Arrius Piso gave his ancestry from the **Maccabees** or **Hasmonean** rulers, and he gives it through the Gospel of '**Matthaeus**' or '**Matthew**', but he did not present the genealogy in a straight forward way. There is also a link from the name Matthew to *Moses*, that link being the rod that was found by him. The rod is variously named mate, matiola, matia and mashia, and finally "mace," for short, with the usual incorrect pronunciation of the letter A in English. The word 'mate' forms the name 'Matthew', as in Latin it is Matteus, French Matthieu, and English Matthew, but in Hebrew, this name also means '*gift of the Lord*', so this can be seen as another reason this name was chosen.

The original researches have stated that the ***Gospel of John*** was written by Justus Piso in approximately 105 CE, in history, in the letters of *Pliny the Younger*, he is known as *Fabius Justus*, and if we remember, Arrius gave the names of his sons in his *Vita* as Josephus, one of those names was Justus. The naming of this gospel seems to have followed the naming tradition of the previous ones, in that it was named according to ancestor worship, in this case honoring his grandfather Gaius, as '**John**' is another form of '**Gaius**', as *Giovanni is* from the Latin **Ioannes** and is the Italian equivalent of John, and *Giovanni* is frequently contracted to Gaou(n), Gianni, Gian, or Gio. It is also possible that it was named to honor his brother Julius Piso, who Arrius called '*John*' in his Vita by naming one of his sons '*Hyrcanus*', the only other person with that name at that time would have been Arrius' ancestor **Jonathan Hyrcanus** of the **Hasmonean** royal house.

As mentioned earlier in the book, Justus appears as '**James**' in Josephus' Vita as a bodyguard, and that same bodyguard is named *Justus*. In his *Vita* writings, Arrius makes Justus an alleged Jewish historian, *Justus of Tiberias*, who had written a conflicting history of the Jewish War and "*accused*" his father, Arrius ('Josephus'), of causing his native Tiberias to revolt against Rome. Arrius as Josephus says Justus' father was Pistos (faithful), perhaps because this word could be seen as akin to the name Piso. If we remember, the name Piso in Hebrew is Joseph re-arranged, and in the Old Testament, Hebrews 11 has the "*faith chapter.*" Interestingly, 'Josephus' also says that Justus had a '*brother*', or *brother-in-law* named Jesus. In this gospel, Justus emphasizes the importance, repeatedly (especially in chapters 10, 12, 14, and 16), that he was sent by his *father* and is *his representative*, in other words, he is saying he is continuing Arrius' work. It would appear that Justus played the role of Jesus in this gospel, as there is no disciple named James within it, despite the importance of James being one of the three loyal disciples in the Synoptic Gospels, perhaps for some reason he felt he could not "play" two characters at once? Interestingly, the Epistle to the Colossians, again stated by the original researchers to have also been written by Justus, referrers to Justus as Jesus in 4:11 by saying "*Jesus who is called Justus.*" Arrius also hinted in his Vita that the names Justus and Jesus had become identical because after talking about Justus of Tiberias, the revolutionary leader, he later gave Tiberias' chief magistrate the name Jesus:

> "*The principal instigator of the mob was Jesus son of Sapphias, the chief magistrate of Tiberias...*" – Josephus *Life* 27-28
> 134-139

The '**Acts of the Apostles**' was written by Arrius and Justus, with some help from Pliny the Younger, in 96-100 CE, according to the original researchers. There is a portion of Acts that is missing from most English translations/interpretations and that is the 29th chapter, which has 10 verses. It is a short text that apparently contains the account of Paul's journey to Spain and Britain, where he preached to a tribe of Israelites on Ludgate Hill, the site of St. Pauls Cathedral. It is said to be the concluding portion of the "Acts of the Apostles" and reads like a continuation. It is said to have been translated in the late 18th century by French naturalist *Sonnini de Manoncourt* from a Greek manuscript discovered in the archives at Constantinople and presented to him by Sultan Abdoul Achmet, which is why this lost chapter is also known as the Sonnini Manuscript.

The *Acts of the Apostles* and the *Book of James* are the only two New Testament books that do not end in amen, and Acts ends abruptly with Paul being under house arrest in chapter 28, leading some Bible scholars to believe they are incomplete in the form in which we have them. The original researchers say Justus Piso shared the writing of Acts and the Pauline Epistles with Pliny the Younger, stating that Pliny's first chapter in Acts was chapter 18. They say in verse 7 Pliny inserted Justus as 'Titius Justus', as at that point Pliny was writing as 'Paul', so Justus, who had written the Epistle to the Colossians using the name 'Paul', needed a new identity. In Acts 18:24 and 19:1, Pliny seems to give Justus another name, Apollos, which is a variation of his former Paul name as Paulus/Pollus, with an 'a' added. Pliny would write 1 Corinthians a few years later, and, again, would repeatedly insert Justus as Apollos (1 Cor. 1:12, 3:4-6, 22, 4:6, 16:12), because Pliny was the writer and so was 'playing' Paul. Pliny died in 116 in western Parthia while fighting the Jews and Parthians, a war that was connected with the second great Jewish revolt of 115-117 CE against the Roman Empire. His death was recorded under his military name, Maximus, *'the great one'*. Later, the expression 'Maxima Culpa' would be produced, which is the feminine form of Maximus combined with the name of the Piso family founder, Calpus, but with a vowel change. Contained within a letter to "Maximus", Pliny gives the following information:

"For what can be better for society than such government, what can be more precious than freedom? How ignominious then must his conduct be who turns good government into anarchy, and liberty into slavery? To these considerations let me add, that you have an established reputation to maintain: **the fame you**

acquired by the administration of the quaestorship in Bithynia, the good opinion of the emperor, the credit you obtained when you were tribune and praetor, in a word, this very government, which may be looked upon as the reward of your former services, are all so many glorious weights which are incumbent upon you to support with suitable dignity".

Now might be an appropriate place to say that 'Roman' also claims to have discovered that *every other word* in certain places within the Epistles of Pliny The Younger and the Pauline Epistles match, which should not be the case. But he says a reader would need to know both Koine Greek and Latin to see this and understand it because, as is known, the Pauline Epistles were written in Greek and the Epistles of Pliny were written in Latin. If this can be proven, it would mean that Pliny The Younger could read and write in both Greek and Latin, which is stated in his epistles as Pliny. (**ref** – Loeb Classical Library Edition, Pliny, *Letters And Panegyricus* I, Book IV, epistle XVIII, page 297, the epistle to Arrius Antoninus (Arrius Piso) & Penguin Classics, *The Letters of Pliny The Younger*, page 126.) It would show that Pliny The Younger must have been the author of the Pauline Epistles, and this intrigues me, as when comparing the journeys of Pliny the Younger and 'Paul', they appear to be identical.

But the reason why someone would need to understand Koine Greek and Latin to see the above being the case is that there are differences in syntax between the two. Because of the ways those languages work, it means the words do not have to match in sequence for the statement to be the same. Greek has a certain syntax for words in sentences, but in Latin, words can be mixed around and still mean the same as a Greek sentence, as long as the word used at the end of the sentence is of a certain type. At this point, however, Pliny being 'St. Paul' can only be a claim, as 'Roman' has stated that his list of matching words was destroyed and is working on producing it again. It must be noted that 'Paul' is only known to us from the Acts and the Epistles attributed to him: and in a very learned analysis of the research on this subject, the Encyclopedia Biblica produced by Oxford professors says, in Column 3627 — "*The principal Epistles cannot be the work of Paul*", and Abraham Dirk Loman, professor at the Lutheran seminary in Amsterdam, and theology professor at the University of Amsterdam states – "*upholds the entirely symbolical character of the whole Gospel story.*" Column 3624 of the Encyclopedia Biblica states: "We cannot regard 'Acts' as a true and credible first-hand narrative of what had actually occurred. The Book bears in part a legendary historical and, in part, and edifying and apologetic character."

Pliny was carefully educated, he studied rhetoric under *Quintilian*, a Roman educator, and rhetorician, and other famous teachers, becoming the most eloquent pleader of his time. While still young he served as military tribune in Syria, and on his return, he entered politics under Emperor Domitian. In the year 100 CE he was appointed consul by Trajan and later, while he was governor of Bithynia, he produced letters of correspondence between Trajan and himself, which were later published. A letter of Pliny's which stands out to me, among others, is one addressed to an individual called '**Titius Aristo**', in that letter he says, "*I am not in the least offended, though, at their low opinion of my* **morals** *(philosophy, rhetoric), and that those who are ignorant of the fact that* **the most learned, the wisest, and the best of**

men have employed themselves in the same way, *should be surprised at the tone of my writings:* ***but from those who know what noble and numerous examples I follow, I shall, I am confident, easily obtain permission to err with those whom it is an honor to imitate****, not only in their most serious occupations but their lightest triflings. Is it unbecoming me (I will not name any living example, lest I should seem to flatter), but is it unbecoming me to practice what became Tully, Calvus, Pollio, Messala, Hortensius, Brutus, Sulla, Catulus, Scaevola, Sulpitius, Varro, the Torquati, Memmius, Gaetulicus,* **Seneca***,* **Lucceius***, and, within our own memory, Verginius Rufus?" …* **"And so if any one of my audience should have the curiosity to read over the same performance which he heard me read, he may find several things altered or omitted***, and perhaps too upon his particular judgment, though he did not say a single word to me. But I am not defending my conduct in this particular, as if I had actually recited my works in public, and not in my own house before my friends, a numerous appearance of whom has upon many occasions been held an honor, but never, surely, a reproach. Farewell.*

Who was Titius Aristo? This was another name used by, or for, Arrius, because *Titius* is a form of Titus, and *Aristo* means 'dinner', linking to Jesus and the Last Supper. Another name that Pliny uses is Claudius Ariston, in the index of the Loeb Classical Library edition it is presented (Ti), for Titus, Claudius Ariston. As Claudius Ariston, Arrius was the leading citizen of Ephesus, in Bithynia, where the Pisos governed and is the location of one of the early churches, to which 'Paul' wrote a letter. As mentioned, the original researchers have stated that Pliny the Younger wrote as 'Paul' and they also state he wrote has "St. Ignatius", in his book 'The True Authorship of the New

Testament', Abelard Reuchlin says *"...we can see him writing to the various family members and friends, such as "***St. Polycarp***", who was* **Proculus Calpurnius Piso,** *as they are starting the first churches in* **Bithynia** *and* **Pontus** *in Turkey. Also the main evidence for Pliny being "***St. Ignatius***", is the same evidence for others involved in the creation of this religion, and that is the fact we find the two people in the same places at the same time."*

Pliny the Younger as "**St. Ignatius**" is interesting, as, again, the original researchers have said Pliny was adopted by Lucius Calpurnius Piso when his uncle, Pliny the Elder died. If we examine the name '*Ignatius*', we can see the literary techniques described earlier being used. "**Ignatius**" would stand for the following – The '**I**' was also seen as an '**L**', because the L's in *Greek* and *Latin* are written similarly, which means we have '**L**' for "**Lucius**". We then have the '**G**' which can be seen as a '**C**' in the Latin language, for '**Calpurnius**', and the word '*natius*' means "**The Younger**" or '*belonging to the hour or day of one's birth*', with 'boy' inferred. So the Piso's and others who were in the 'know' would have seen "**Ignatius**" as "Lc-**natius**". If Pliny The Younger did indeed play 'Paul', then the characters he played were placed at different times to fit the story being told, as were the Gospel stories themselves. This being the case would mean when researchers try to find information about who the possible authors were, they would have been unsuccessful, as they would be searching in the wrong time frame. It would provide a reason as to why the authors have remained hidden for so long and why the Gospels "*predict*" certain events.

The '**Epistle to the Romans**' was written by **Proculus Piso**, a son of Arrius by his third wife, Queen Berenice. Proculus used the alias name "**St. Polycarp**", *'polycarp'* meaning 'much fruit' in Greek, which would connect this name to the name 'Frugi' as used by a branch of the Pisos, as 'Frugi' means 'fruits of the earth'. But Proculus' name can be seen in the Polycarpus name, whilst also honoring his father's name, like so – **Proc**(k)**u**(y)**lus A**(rrius) **P**(iso). It would seem both *Proculus Piso* and **Claudia Phoebe** wrote this epistle about the year 100 CE. *Claudia* is known in history as the wife of the emperor **Trajan** (as **Pompeia Plotina**), and she appears to have written the last few verses of this epistle, **Romans 16:25-27**, which many copies of the New Testament in English leave out, as that portion was written by a woman. Her name is shown in the picture given as '**Phoebe**' right at the end, and you can see where the previous male author finished and the female author begins, as the male author '*signs off*' with '**Amen**'. By approximately 110 CE the initial parts of the New Testament had been written; all of the four gospels, Acts of the Apostles, and nearly all the epistles that were attributed to 'Paul'.

```
commandment of the    commandment of the   eternal   God,    for obedience    of faith   to     all
everlasting God, made
known to all nations  τὰ ἔθνη      γνωρισθέντος.    27 μόνῳ σοφῷ θεῷ, διὰ Ἰη-
for the obedience of  the nations having been made known—[the] only   wise   God, through Je-
faith ; 27 to God only
wise, be glory through σοῦ χριστοῦ,    ᾧ   ἡ δόξα εἰς τοὺς αἰῶνας·    ἀμήν.
Jesus Christ for ever. sus  Christ,   to whom be glory to   the    ages.       Amen.
Amen.
                       ᵏΠρὸς     Ῥωμαίους ἐγράφη ἀπὸ Κορίνθου, διὰ Φοίβης τῆς
                        To [the]   Romans    written   from Corinth.   by   Phoebe
                      διακόνου τῆς ἐν Κεγχρεαῖς ἐκκλησίας.ˡ
                       servant of the ᵃin  ᵃCenchrea   ˡassembly.
```

Epistle of James (in Hebrew *Ya'aqov* '**Jacob**') was written by **Arrius & Justus Calpurnius Piso** around 110 CE. By writing this letter, Arrius and Justus accomplished the following things: It was entitled after James, the name of his son *Fabius Justus* in the synoptic gospels, which gives the reason for the conclusion that Justus helped him write it. It indicated that James was still among the disciples because when "James" wrote the Gospel of John, about the year 105 CE, he had "played" the lead character, Jesus, and so did not insert his name as 'James' in that gospel. Instead, this disciple seemed to just vanish but returned to write this letter for the later New Testament. Arrius had written the book of **Job**, but he needed to historicize it and he used various means to accomplish that. First, he inserted the name into the Greek translation of *Ezekiel* (chapter 14), so that it referred to Job. Then he had written *Ben Sirach*, and within that writing, (49:8-9), had said the righteousness of Job was mentioned in Ezekiel. Doing that meant he had historicized his recent creation of Job, first in the Prophets portion of the Old Testament, and then in his '*Ben Sirach*' creation for the *Greek Apocrypha*. That left only the New Testament to be historicized. While writing 'James' for the New Testament, he inserted into *James* 5:11 praise of the endurance of Job, which meant his book of Job was now historicized in all three religious works.

The **first** and **second Epistle of Peter** were written by **Arrius** with help from **Proculus Piso** between 110-115 CE. The first of these epistles appear to have been written by Arrius, with perhaps help from Proculus. It consists of five chapters, just like 'James' and totals 105 verses. Five was a number the Pisos started using once Arrius became a fictional priest of Apollo at Delphi, and as Plutarch, he wrote a treatise explaining that five was holy to Apollo at Delphi. The number 105 alludes to Arrius, as 105 is the cumulated total of 14 (1+2+3+4...), and 14 was equal to 60, in Greek small numbers, and spelled 'Kalpournios Piso'. The number 105 was also the total number of verses in 1 Peter and 1 John, and 105 is present as the years of life for Judith.

Second Peter also seems to be Arrius' creation, as in 2:5 he historicizes his prior book of Noah, just like in 1 Peter 3:20, and each time a total of 8 people were spared. 8 cumulates at 36, which spelled 'Josephus' as 'Josepos' (**ref** – 'Josephus', *Jewish War*, Book V, Loeb Edition), in Greek small numbers/'*Piso numbers*' (which will be explained). Arrius must have been very old at the time of writing this because he says as long as he is alive, and knowing that his death is imminent (2 Peter 1:13-14) he reserves the right to stir the brethren up by reminder.

The **first**, **second** and **third Epistle of John** were written by **Arrius** with help from **Julius Calpurnius Piso** between 110-115 CE. The first epistle contains five chapters and 105 verses, which is the same as 1 Peter. This epistle starts in a similar way to 'Luke', as in 'Luke' 1:2 it says that eyewitnesses from the beginning have handed the account down to us. In the first Epistle of John, at the start, it says in 1:1 that *"what was from the beginning, we have seen and heard"*, and also in 2:24, 3:11, it says you had "*heard from the beginning,*" as well as a commandment from the beginning (2:7). The language is very similar and the tone of this writing is authoritative, so it would appear it is being written by someone in authority. Julius wrote the second and third epistles of 'John', and true to the family custom, he left hints connecting his writing and authorship of them. The letters are attributed to John the Evangelist, son of Zebedee (meaning *gift of God*) and disciple of Jesus (Arrius), the writer calls himself "presbyter" (elder), which Julius Piso was, as at the time he wrote this, he was the eldest son of Arrius at that point as Alexander was dead. The second and third letter strongly urges a church, called the "*elect lady and her children,*" to boycott heretics who deny the reality of the incarnation, which is interesting, because *elect* in biblical terms means to be *"chosen by God."*

The elect lady Julius seems to be referring to is Queen Berenice, Arrius' third wife, with whom he had two children, Justus Piso and Proculus Piso (Agrippa). The third letter is addressed to a Gaius and complains that "**Diotrephes, who lies to put himself first**, does not acknowledge my authority", this too is interesting. The Greek word Dios means "of **Zeus**", or "*of God*", like Dionysus, who was the Greek god of wine, and, according to legend, was born of a Virgin on December 25th, came from Zeus. As a whole, the word "Diotrephes" means nurtured/cherished by Zeus, but why is the meaning behind Diotrephes important? The word 'Diotrephes' links to Arrius, yet again. Jesus is associated with the God of wine, among other traits from other gods, and when Emperor Hadrian rebuilt Jerusalem to establish a Roman colony, he named it *Aelia Capitolina*, after his family name, *Aelius*, but he also built a new temple to *'Jupiter'*, called the *Temple of Jupiter Optimus Maximus*, also known as the Temple of Jupiter Capitolinus, which was built on the Temple Mount, the site of the destroyed second Jewish holy temple, which contributed to the Bar Kokhba revolt of 132-136 CE:

"At Jerusalem Hadrian founded a city in place of the one which had been razed to the ground, naming it Aelia Capitolina, and on the site of the temple of the god he raised a new temple to Jupiter. This brought on a war of no slight importance nor of brief duration, for the Jews deemed it intolerable that foreign races should be settled in their city and foreign religious rites planted there."

– Cassius Dio, *Roman History*, 69.12.

The importance of the name *Optimus Maximus* in regards to Arrius will be examined shortly, but the fact the new temple was named '*Jupiter*' is important, as Jupiter is the Latin form of Zeus, who, of course, *created* Dionysis, and is linked to Jesus through parallel concepts. Could it be that either Arrius thought of himself as, or his family likened him to Zeus, the creator of a god who is associated with wine, performed miracles while traveling, and was the God of the Vine (Jesus says "I am the True Vine" – John 15:1), again, I cannot see the connection as mere coincidence.

Continuing, mentioned in 2 John are *two* elected ladies, John (or Julius) says "*The children of thy (your) elect sister greet thee (you)*" – 2 John 1:13, KJV. That means we have an "*elect lady*", a lady who was chosen by "God", who has and "*elect sister*", whose children know John (Julius). Queen Berenice had two sisters, one called Drusilla who had two children, a daughter, and son, however, the son appears to have died with Drusilla during the eruption of Mount Vesuvius. The other sister, called Mariamne, had two children, a daughter called Berenice, whom 'Josephus' mentions in *Antiquities of the Jews*, Book XIX, Chapter 8 and 9, and a son called Agrippinus, who is also mentioned by Arrius in his *Antiquities of the Jews*, Chapter 4, page 377.

The **Epistle of Jude** was written by **Arrius** & **Julius Calpurnius Piso** also between the years 110-115 CE. The reason to think this is because this letter only consists of one chapter and 25 verses, which in Greek totals 26, which makes KP by the sequence system (explained later). As Arrius appears to have created the various Judases, and even a feminine version called

Judith, it is reasonable to speculate that he created another one using a shorter name of Jude. With this letter, the author, 'Jude', claims to be the *'brother'* of *'James'* (Justus). The reason, it seems, for the creation of this letter was to name and quote Enoch (verse 14), to again historicize it, Enoch being another early creation by Arrius. This letter was written after the Pauline epistles, as it tells the reader (believers) to "remember the words spoken beforehand by the apostles" (verse 17), and this letter also has an authoritative tone.

The **Revelation of John The Divine** was written by *Julius Piso*, in or about the year 137 CE, as we have already examined, but will go into detail shortly. Julius was killed by Hadrian under name of *Julius Ursus Servianus*, so Julius' son or grandson may have carried on the work of writing the Revelation, as Julius would have been very old by this time. The Book of Revelation was not the book of the New Testament, it was written as the end of the story.

Hebrews was written by *Flavius Arrianus*, a grandson of Arrius, in approximately 140 CE. Flavius Arrianus was the real name of the historian who wrote as '**Appian**' (**r**'s switched with **p**'s) and was the brother of Emperor **Antoninus Pius**, who again, according to the original researchers, also wrote history under the name of '**Suetonius**'. Arrianus' mother was *Claudia Phoebe*, Arrius' daughter, otherwise known as *Pompeia Plotina/Arria Fadilla*, and these two sons were from her marriage to *Rufus Corelius* (who also had other names) before she married Emperor Trajan. Flavius Arrianus also wrote other works, most notably under the name '**Ptolemy**'. As "*Claudius Ptolemy*", Arrian produced work on astronomy and posited the idea that the sun rotated around the earth, because naturally when promoting Christianity the earth would need to be the center of the universe if God had sent his son to earth. That idea, however, disagreed with what the Greeks had long known, but because the church was in power, Ptolemy's idea was taught by the church for 1500 years; teaching the opposite was regarded as a serious error and heresy.

The Greek Translation Of The Septuagint

Arrius was in charge of the Piso family after the destruction of Jerusalem, meaning he would continue with the Christian writings started by his family. After 'Mark' was completed, Arrius went to continue the story of Jesus by creating additional versions of his life and career. To do so, however, even though Arrius came from Jewish royalty and no doubt knew many words and phrases, he needed to familiarize himself with Hebrew religious beliefs and history, in the existing bible. He would need a fluent translation from which to work from to compose his stories about Jesus. As is known within the academic field, Arrius' cousins, the Herods, fled to Rome, and they were fluent in Hebrew and Greek and available to assist Arrius. Judging from the years in which Arrius was active, it is most likely that Herod Agrippa II would assist him with the translation of the *Hebrew Torah*, *Prophets*, and *Psalms* into Greek. Once the Greek translation was complete, Arrius would continue to work from it.

In his *Jewish Antiquities*, Arrius wrote an account regarding how the Greek translation had been created several centuries previously. Within this account he alluded to his name to take credit, for example, *King Ptolemy II Philadelphus* of Egypt

(285-274) writes to *Eleazar*, a high priest of the Judaeans in Jerusalem, that he had decided to have the law translated into Greek and deposited in his library. In response, Eleazar sends six elders from each of the 12 tribes, along with the law, to translate it.

The clues that Arrius inserted hints into this account to claim authorship are as follows:

1. *Aristaios*, a Jewish friend of the king, convinces him to free Jewish captives taken in the overcoming of Judea. This leads to the king's decision to also commission the translation. Aristaios in Greek totals **19**, which is the same total as the name **Piso**. Aristaios is **1)** a longer form of **Arias** (Arius), and **2) Aristaios** Ἀρισταῖος, is a Greek name derived from ἄριστος **(aristos)**, which means '**best**'.

2. **Aristaios** was the son of **Apollo**, who appears in a virgin birth story similar to Jesus', which was referenced by later Christian writers, for example, the third century CE Christian theologian, known as '*Origen*', retells a legend of Plato's mother Perictione virginally conceiving him after the god **Apollo** had appeared to her husband **Ariston.**

3. **Ariston** ties in with the New Testament, because in **Matt 26:26** 'Jesus' says: '*Take, eat; this is my body.*' Then looking back to **Matt. 22:4**, it says: '*... Behold!* **My dinner**, *I (have) prepared...*' The word for dinner in this instance is '**ariston**' (Aristo). The word is also used in **Luke 11:38**, and **Luke 14:12**. So the name used here links to 'Jesus'.

4. The story of the twelve tribes is fiction as ten of the twelve tribes were deported and lost 500 years previously.

5. An individual named '**Nicanor**' is the official who receives the translators. This name also appears in **I Maccabees** as the Syrian general whom the Judaeans defeat and kill, and in **Acts** he is one of seven deacons of the young church in Antioch. Arrius may have used this name because it derives from the Greek νικη (nike) meaning 'victory' and ανηρ (aner) meaning 'man'.
6. **Dorotheos** is ordered by Nicanor to provide and serve food to the arriving translators. In Greek, **Dorotheos** meant '**gift of God**', the same meaning as the Hebrew name **Mattathias**, a longer form of Josephus' apparent family name, **Matthias**, in the fictional *Vita* (Biography).
7. The translators supposedly work until the **ninth hour**, the same hour 'Jesus' is said to have died on the cross (Matthew 27:45-50, et al).
8. The very first account of the Septuagint's creation appears in the *Antiquities* of 'Josephus'. To take the focus away from this being the first account, Arrius' grandson **Arrian**, three-quarters of a century later, wrote 'The Anabasis of Alexander' account, allegedly being from the "400 hidden years", to make the *Antiquities* version seem not the original account.

The Talmud also hinted at Arrius being responsible for the creation of the Septuagint with the statement "**Arayin key Matai**," which meant "Ari (*Arius*) **of the ayin** wrote '*Matthew*', (*ayin* meaning 70, which equaled Septuagint). Perhaps this meant Arrius *used* the Septuagint?, but by using the word '*of*' the Septuagint, it must mean that Arrius created it. The account in 'Josephus' speaks of the translators as totaling 72, but the account also calls them "*the 70 elders*." That is because the

Greek spelling of Piso is '*Peison*', which totaled 29, which, combined with *Kalpournios*, which totaled 41, makes 70. Arrius also wrote in his Vita that a delegation of twelve and then of 70 were dispatched, and in 'Luke' 10:1, Jesus dispatches a delegation of 70.

It is logical at this point to assume that the translators were the Herodians, Arrius' kinsmen through his mother. The New Testament hints at this, with the clearest hint being "*Greet Herodian my kinsmen*," seen in Romans 16:11, 'kinsmen' meaning 'blood relation'. This is written by "*Tertius*", seen in Romans 16:22, an alias name for Arrius' third living son Justus, as 'Tertius' means '*the third*'. 'Tertius' was with 'Paul' in Corinth, and Claudia Phoebe was allowed to write a portion of the epistle Romans. Justus Piso being the third son, after Claudia, means it is logical to think Justus would have been close to Claudia, as would Pliny the Younger have been. In the index of the Loeb Classical Library edition of *Pliny's Epistles and Panegyricus*, we find Justus addressed as "*Tullius*" Justus. At least two of the fictional disciples in the gospels are given the names from Herod's people (just as they appear in Josephus' public writings). One of these disciples is called *Philip*, who was Herod's son by Cleopatra, and another is *Bartholomew*, which meant '*son of Ptolemy*', and Ptolemy was the name of a general (*Jewish War*, I, 314 – *Jewish Antiquities*, XIV, 431-432), and also the name of a friend of Herod (*Jewish War*, I, 280 – *Jewish Antiquities*, XIV, 378). What is remarkable about these names being used for disciples, is the fact the disciples were meant to be poor working men, *not* aristocrats, and according to the New Testament story, the Herodians (and the Pharisees) were persecuting Jesus.

As has been examined, 'Josephus' even names his youngest son *Simonides, Agrippa*, presumably after *King Herod Agrippa* II, a close friend of 'Josephus' (*Jewish War* VII Appendix (13) p. 651). In the *Book of Revelation* 2:13, in about the year 135 CE, Julius expressed his sorrow over the death of his 'witness' *Antipas* who was killed. It can be assumed that this was the Antipas who, whilst besieged in and defending the royal palace at the start of the revolt of 66-70 CE, met his death (*Jewish War* II, 557). All these names, *Agrippa, Herodian, Antipas*, were names used in the family of the Herodian aristocracy. The members of the Herodian aristocracy who had been fighting and collaborating with the Romans fled to Rome and joined their Pisonian relations and friends, no doubt taking what wealth they could with them. Given their clear knowledge of the Hebrew language, their relationship to the Piso family, and their fluency in Greek, it is logical to conclude that they were the ones who would have been willing and able to translate the Hebrew Bible into Greek.

The Apocrypha

The Piso family were already busy with two other types of writings which would help historicize the religion, one of those writings were additions to the Septuagint Greek Bible. The Pisos, or most likely Arrius, would *"require"* the surviving Judaean rabbis and scribes to translate these additions into their biblical books. The other writings, which Arrius would dictate most of, became the so-called Apocryphal books. The Apocrypha comprised tales said to have been written in the prior centuries concerning the "*400 lost years*" since the completion of the Hebrew Prophetic books. It seems there were various purposes for these additional writings, one concerned the number of places Arrius' *Antiquities* writings had gone in a different direction from Jewish history, as told in the Hebrew Bible. To correct these "*errors*," Arrius would either write the new "ancient" books with which those errors would be consistent; or, his new writings would correct his errors and be consistent with the Hebrew Bible. Either way, it appears Arrius wanted to show that any errors had been deliberate.

Judging by what he wrote, it is clear he wanted to make both prior Judaism and Judaean heroes more consistent with Christianity, and the heroes would appear as resembling savior-like deliverers of the people. He wanted to glorify the Judaean foundation on which he had created the new faith, as the New Testament was intended to be read to, and therefore accepted by, the pagan slaves and poor people of the empire. The book of *Judith* seems to be an exceptionally good example of that, with the speeches phrased to more fully agree with Arrius' view of the law. In both *Judith* and *Susannah*, Arrius inserted partially concealed attacks on those who were preventing the Judaean people from being converted to Christianity, the Pharisees. The goal was for this new faith to act as a kind of *social security* for the slave's masters; for the millions of poor people, the goal was to make them view the new faith as a comfort. But for it to be accepted, the Judaism of the prior unwritten centuries had to be perceived as *brave* and *victorious*, so, in his *Jewish Antiquities*, and later in book form, he had created two stories of great Judaean victories. Both these showed Judaeans to have been very brave and triumphant against overwhelming governmental oppression, but *not* Roman oppression. The events described were the **Persian** oppression at the time of *Esther*, in the *Septuagint*, and the Greek/Syrian oppression at the time of the **Maccabees**, in the *Apocrypha*, both of which would be described as having ended in Judaean holiday celebrations.

Once these additional works for the Septuagint and Apocrypha were completed, the family would historicize them by inserting mentions of them into the New Testament writings which they were finishing. Enoch of the Apocrypha would be mentioned in *Jude* 14, and years later in *Hebrews* 11:5; and the Apocryphal Noah (which no longer exists) would be mentioned in 1 *Peter* 3:20 and 2 *Peter* 2:5, and then later in *Hebrews* 11:7. To historicize *Daniel*, which would be written for the Septuagint, his name would be added to *Matthew* 26:15 and added by implication to *Mark* 13:14. Daniel also appeared with *Baruch* (a book written by Arrius for the Apocrypha) in Septuagint *Nehemiah* 10:6. At that point the Judaeans would be "required" to add this verse to their Hebrew Bible, appearing as *Nehemiah* 10:7. The Book of *Job* would also be historicized, after having only been mentioned in Genesis 46:13 in the Old Testament, Arrius added praise for his endurance in the Letter of James 5:11. Then the Judaeans at **Bnei Brak** would again be *"required"* to add him visibly along with Daniel and Noah to their existing Ezekiel in Chapter 14, where he would be praised for his righteousness. It may sound odd to some that the Judaeans would cooperate with the Pisos in this way, but after 96 CE, the Piso family was in semi-control of the empire and full control of all its writings. However, it is still startling that they could force the Judaean sages and scribes in faraway Bnei Brak to add verses to their existing bible.

There are many books in the Apocrypha which need to be explained, but for this chapter, we will look at one of them, the **Letter of Aristeas,** which gives information that the author was Arrius. He wrote both accounts of his day, describing how the Septuagint was created; one in his *Jewish Antiquities*, in which the central character is *Aristaios*, which totaled 19 in small numbering in Greek, 19 being the total of the name *Piso*, and the other was entitled the Letter of *Aristeas*, which totaled 16 in small numbering, Pi (Piso) being the 16th letter of the Greek alphabet. *Antiquities* had been created in 93 CE, so it must have been seen that a more ancient account would have been helpful to validate the recent account in Josephus' Antiquities. To accomplish this, the *Letter of Aristeas* would be written and would be stated to have been several hundred years old, if that is the case, then could the mention of the letter in the *Life of Moses* by Philo of Alexandria be a later addition to that work by the Pisos? (**ref** – *The Apocrypha and Pseudepigrapha of the Old Testament* in English. by *Charles*, R. H. (Robert Henry), Fellow of Merton College, Oxford, 1855-1931. Publication date 1913, vol II pp. 83-122) This letter became part of the *Pseudepigrapha*, which was a collection the church felt was of even lower importance than the Apocrypha, which shows its authorship was suspect.

This letter is written to Aristeas' brother *Philocrates*, a name which in Greek means *"lover of strength"*. The letter requested details of Aristeas' motives and the objectives in his mission to Eleazar the high priest, requesting that Eleazar send translators of the law to the Egyptian king. Aristeas tells Philocrates that he (Philo) had recently come to them from the island with a disposition toward holiness and sympathy toward men who live according to the law. He also reminds him he had sent him information about the Jewish race from the priests in Egypt. In this letter, Arrius is secretly addressing his kinsmen Pliny, who had created Christian writings as both Paul and then Ignatius Theophorus until the year 105 CE. How can it be known that 'Philocrates' is an alias for Pliny?, because we find the name Theophilus as the first translator from the ninth tribe, as listed among the names by Aristeas. That is the same name that Arrius had his son Justus address at the start of Luke and Acts. In Luke 1:3 Arrius sends Theophilus an account of what they had accomplished among the *disciples* and *apostles*, and in Acts 1.1, he sends him the first account of all that Jesus began to do and teach. Now, similarly, Arrius writes to Theophilus under Pliny's other alias name Philocrates, Arrius had written *Daniel* by the time he writes this letter, as that is the final translator's name listed from the ninth tribe, as Theophilus was the first listed from that tribe. Theophilus being mentioned early in Luke and Acts can be seen as Pliny the Younger because using the pseudonym of *Ignatius*, he carried the title Theophorus, "bearer of God." That means Pliny's pseudonyms can be traced from **Theophorus** (bearer of god) to **Theophilus** (love of god) to **Philocrates** (lover of strength). Philocrates (Pliny) had returned from the island where he was separated from his family because he was in exile for molesting a small boy when acting as military governor in Egypt. They relieved him of his office and exiled him to an island; The name recorded for him was (G)C. Vibius Maximus. (**ref** – Syme, Sir Ronald, Roman Papers Vol. 1, Clarendon Press, Oxford Univ. England 1979)

So now Arrius reminds Philocrates that he has returned to them from the island renewed *"with a disposition of holiness"*, and with "*sympathy toward those who live under the law.*" It appears that Pliny was the only family member to be openly scandalized for this type of activity, but of course, they used an alias name. Aristeas (Arrius) ends the account by saying he has sent him the complete story, and by praising him as finding greater pleasure in such things than in the writings of mythmakers, and as being devoted to things which benefit the soul and spending much time on them. Now although this letter states to have been written several hundred years earlier, it must have been written by Arrius when he was back in Rome and just before Pliny was killed leading his legions in western Parthia. Regarding Pliny, he was in Pontus and Bithynia many times between 85 and 112 CE, and understanding his pseudonym as *Maximus*, repeatedly followed by various second names in his public letters, is key to working out his activities. In his letters he appears as *Terentius Maximus*, procurator for Emperor Domitian in Bithynia; he was also there in 85-86 CE as proconsul under the name, *Lappius Maximus*, all the careers of various people named Maximus—each of which was Pliny—appear in his public letters.

9. THE JEWS REJECTED THE STORY

"If I had not come and spoken to them, they would not be guilty of sin; but now they have no excuse for their sin, whoever hates me ('Jesus') hates my Father (creator Arrius) as well".

"They would not have been guilty of sin if I had not done among them the things that no one else ever did." – John 15:22 -4

The above statement is stating that the Jews were only guilty of sin because they rejected 'Jesus', and is stating that if the Jews hate 'Jesus', then they also hate Arrius. When looking at the history regarding this, the only sin that the Jewish population committed, in the eyes of *the aristocracy*, was a sin against the culture of slavery, the extortionate taxes imposed on them, and their diminished quality of life as a result of Roman rule. The Pharisees, on the other hand, were attempting to fight for human rights, an end to slavery, and an honest governmental system. The Jewish leaders, which consisted of the Pharisees and Scribes at this point, knew that while finishing the Gospel of 'Matthew' and writing his account of the war, Arrius was the Roman general who in 73 CE had destroyed the last three Jewish outposts, which were –

1) **Machaerus**

(Which, according to 'Josephus', is the location of the imprisonment and execution of '**John the Baptist**'),

2) **Herodium**

and

3) **Masada**

(Which, according to 'Josephus', was the place of capture of **Eleazar Ben Jair**, but 'Josephus' is the *only* source for the Battle of Masada).

In his semi-fictional story of the war, Arrius gave himself the fictional name '**Flavius Silva**', when writing about the siege of *Masada*. 'Silva' in Latin means 'forest', 'woodland', 'thicket' or 'bramble' which links to the '*root*' story in the works of 'Josephus', that focus on the Eleazar individual. But the apparent full name of 'Flavius Silva' is '**Lucius Flavius Silva Nonius Bassus**', a created name that uses parts of Arrius' family names, and words that relate to 'God' or 'Christ'. **Lucius** is, of course, Arrius' uncle, **Flavius** is an inherited name, '**Silva**' becomes '**Salva**' if the vowel '**i**' is switched with an '**a**', using the Hebrew language rules, with Salva meaning '**Saviour**'. We then have the word '**Nonius**' which means '**horse**' (beast), which in Greek can be spelled as '**ippos**' (Piso), and finally, we have '**Bassus**', which is just another form of '**Bacchus**', a copy of Dionysus, the god of wine. With Arrius being the conqueror of Masada, he would know the details of that battle very well, and would later write that the defenders who committed suicide totaled **960**. I find it difficult to believe that the dead bodies of this siege would have been counted, even if they were, I doubt the number was 960, as, yet again, this number links to Christianity.

The number '**960**' was used because –

'**Christ**' in **Greek** is **Xpistos**, the Greek glyph 'χ' represents '**Chi**', which had the number **600**, so 600 stood for **Christ**.

300, which is represented by the Greek glyph 'τ', stood for the **Cross**, because **Revelations 14:11** mentions the '**beast**', and the '**mark**', and that is because in Egyptian writing '*a mark*' is represented by a '**T**'. When searching the apocryphal Christian texts, we find that the 'mark' of the beast is a **cross**, and the Egyptian form for the 'mark' is how the early Christian cross was represented.

60 stood for the name **Calpurnius Piso**, as '**6**' in the eyes of the aristocracy/Pisos was a small **60** and stood for '**Kalpournios Piso**' (Greek spelling, small '*Piso*' numbers, which will be explained).

After the year 75 CE, he placed into the Gospel of Mark the fallen Jewish commander of Masada, **Eleazer ben Yair**, who he names as '*Jairus*' in **Mark 5:22**. That is because '*Yair*' is Biblical Hebrew and '*Iairos*' is the Biblical Greek, '*Iairus*' is Biblical Latin and '*Jairus*' is the Biblical version we are familiar with. In **Luke 8:4**, he appears as '**Lazarus**', because that is the **Greek** form of the **Hebrew** name **Eleazer**.

The destruction which resulted from the war meant Judaea was desolate and underpopulated after the year 70 CE, and with little left to tax, the Herodian aristocracy had gone to live in Rome. The Saducean priesthood, who were the appointees and in-laws of the Herods, were all dead because of the rebels, and even the Essenic visionaries in the desert were dead, all because of the Pisos, Flavians, and Herodians working together. The remaining population, around 2-3 million, had scattered to in and around Rome because there was nothing left in Judea, and there was nowhere else to make a living, but of course, the Jews brought their religion with them to Rome, so the tension did not cease to exist. In that time there were a lot of people living in and around Rome that we would think of as 'ignorant' or uneducated, which may be a harsh description, but unfortunately, a realistic one. Those uneducated individuals would be all the slaves and the people who worked in the homes doing the cooking and the cleaning, and other tasks they were being used for.

The non-political Pharisees were the only surviving Judean leadership, who, after the year 70 CE, changed their names to **Rabbis**, and the remaining Judeans looked to them for guidance. The word 'Rabbi', comes from the Aramaic/Hebrew word '*rav*', which means greater/larger, and in this case, it is used as '*master*' and 'Rabbi' is a combination of '*rav*' and the word 'sheli', which means 'my'. The Rabbi/Pharisees leader, and the first sage, was a man named **Yohanan ben Zakkai**, who had been granted Vespasian's permission to establish a school at Yavne, which in the Bible is known as *Jabneh*, on the condition that Yochanan would not resist Roman rule and not participate in the rebellion. Respecting the imperial wishes of Vespasian meant the Rabbis were now teaching pacifism and accommodation, but even though the Rabbis accommodated Vespasian's wishes, they still refused to accommodate the Piso's, or Arrius' wishes for a new religion. They refused to teach and instruct their people to accept his story, so, even at that stage, the Pharisees (Rabbi) were not fully cooperative, and we can only imagine how this must have angered and frustrated Arrius Piso. Considering the events of the war, and after the Jews had been defeated, the fact they still refused to teach this new religion only made matters worse.

The act of Rabbi Yohanan ben Zakkai accommodating Vespasian's wishes would explain why the **Babylonian Talmud** speaks of a supposed Prophecy that Yohanan ben Zakkai makes, before the destruction of the Temple in 70 CE. The *Babylonian Talmud* records a story about the Roman siege of Jerusalem, right before the destruction of the Second Temple is recorded (**ref** – Gittin 56a-56b; *Avot D'Rabbi Nathan* A, Chapter 4; *Avot or:* B, Chapter 6; *Lam. Rabbah* 1:29). This story says that apparently Rabbi Yohanan ben Zakkai encouraged the Jewish people to surrender to the Roman general Vespasian, a group of rebels however refused and instead wished to battle. When Rabbi Yohanan ben Zakkai realized that the rebels' actions would lead to the destruction of the Temple, he told his students to carry him out of the city in a coffin to deceive the rebel gatekeepers into allowing them to leave for the sake of burying the dead. After he escaped, Rabbi Yohanan ben Zakkai apparently went to the Roman camp, approached Vespasian, and predicted or made a prophesy that Vespasian would become the new emperor.

Soon after this Prophesy, the word was delivered that Nero had died and that Vespasian had indeed been crowned the new emperor. When offered a reward for his correct prediction/prophecy, Rabbi Yohanan ben Zakkai requested that he be given the city of Yavne, to re-establish Jewish life, this request was granted but Jerusalem was destroyed, as Rabbi Yohanan ben Zakai had expected. It should be noted that there are many discrepancies amongst the rabbinic versions, but even so, there are some major problems with this story. If we remember back to the 'Gospels' chapter, we learned that 'Josephus' apparently makes the *same* prophecy or prediction. In the works of 'Josephus', the story goes that after being "captured" by Vespasian and Titus at the battle of Jotapata, during the Great Revolt, he escaped into a cave with 40 other people (**ref** – *Jewish War*, Book 3, Chapter 7-8), they all committed suicide instead of surrendering, but, by luck of the draw, 'Josephus' and one more person are still alive. 'Josephus' apparently convinced the other man to surrender with him, and afterward, 'Josephus' approaches Vespasian and says *"You believe, Vespasian, that I am merely a prisoner, but I come to you as a herald of greater destinies…You will be Caesar, Vespasian. You will be emperor…"* (**ref** – *Jewish War*, Book 3, Chapters 8-9). As we know, according to the story, Vespasian became emperor and 'Josephus' was granted Roman citizenship.

So both the Talmud and 'Josephus' talk about a leader who surrenders to the Romans, in opposition to other Jews, makes a prophecy about Vespasian becoming emperor and is rewarded. The account of 'Josephus' fits into historical context, but we know why that is, it's because Arrius wrote it that way, and because Arrius and his supporters had Nero killed. But also, when Jotapata was captured by the Romans, along with the rest of the Galilee in 67 CE, Vespasian was still a general who was commanding the legions there. (**Supporting ref** – Amram Tropper, *Rewriting Ancient Jewish History: The History of the Jews in Roman times and the New Historical Method* (New York: Routledge 2016), pages 149-157) (**ref** – E.D. Huntsman, "The Reliability of Josephus: Can He Be Trusted?" Brigham Young University Studies 36, no. 3 (1996), pages 392-402). The version written by Rabbi Chazel/Hazal in the Talmud does not fit the historical context, because we know that the Roman siege of Jerusalem took place in 70 CE, and at the point, Vespasian was already back in Rome as the emperor. So Rabbi Yohanan ben Zakkai could *not* have met Vespasian outside Jerusalem or made the prophecy. It can be logically assumed that this version of the story was created from what Arrius wrote as 'Josephus', to accommodate the new teaching of pacifism and accommodation to the new generation of Jewish people. The Jews felt uncomfortable under the rule of the Romans and felt there was no hope without a Temple, but Rabbi Chazel/Hazal would have wanted to teach the Jewish people that Jewish life could continue and adapt without the Temple. Rabbi Yohanan ben Zakkai would have been considered a hero since, after the destruction of the Temple, he was the one responsible for making various religious enactments that agreed with Vespasian's wishes. These enactments allowed for Temple-bound Jewish practices to be done outside the Temple, which would allow Judaism to thrive in a new diaspora.

The problems between Rome and the Jews did not go away, the Roman aristocrats noticed that the Judeans were bringing the slaves and the other uneducated masses into their Temples or the Synagogues, and indoctrinating them into Judaism. They were teaching them that Christianity was a fraud, even after everything that had happened, and this, of course, would have been seen as another major problem. Because the aristocracy both hated and were afraid of the Pharisees, who were the leaders, or '*warriors*', fighting for the Jewish people and were refusing to give up and accept the lie about 'Jesus', even after a great many deaths had occurred, they never excepted it, because they knew the story was made up. The fear was that if the Pharisees had converted enough slaves and enough of the population of Rome to Judaism, from whatever else they had believed in, what would happen if another war came along between Rome and the Pharisees (Rabbis). Rome's leaders were worried that the Pharisees might tell those uneducated people to fight for Judaism, to fight for the Pharisees, and some of those people were even in the Roman military. If enough people had been converted and were told to fight against Rome, the aristocracy would have lost, because there would have been too many people fighting against them, including their soldiers.

So the Roman aristocracy had to try and put a stop to this new problem, and the way they decided to do that was to stop the spread of Judaism by the Pharisees, by destroying all the scriptures the Pharisees were using, which would have been considered the 'root' of their Judaism. Because of the Pharisee's resilience, which must have annoyed, frustrated, and angered Arrius Piso, given his status and motives for writing what he did, he created a picture of the Jews in the successive Gospels as being increasingly evil. In **Acts 23:12**, written between 96-100 CE, it is the Jews and not just the Pharisees or Sadducees who form a conspiracy to kill Paul, and by the time of the **Gospel of John,** in the year 105 CE, the author, who was Justus Piso, writes that Jesus tells the Jews who challenge him, "*You are of (your) father the devil ...*" (**John 8:44**). In **Luke 23.34** 'Jesus' doesn't excuse the Jews, he excuses the **Roman soldiers** – "*Father, forgive them, for they know not what they do.*" The New Testament pictures the Jews as the enemies of '*Jesus*', '*Paul*', and of the message of the Gospels. Arrius Piso's son

Proculus, writing the **Epistle to the Romans 11:28**, explained the reason the Jews were being pictured as the enemies of the new believers –

"Because they rejected the Good News, the Jews (mainly the Pharisees) are God's (Arrius') enemies for the sake of you Gentiles (people).

But because of God's (Arrius') choice, they (the people) are his friends because of their ancestors (the Jewish leaders/royals)."

The above statement is saying that the Jews refused to accept the Good News, with regards to the Gospel, so they became God's enemies. But the Jews are still God's chosen people, and he loves them very much because of the promises he made to their ancestors (royalty, the aristocracy, Herodians). This is literary manipulation and is playing on the emotions of the people. The author of **1** and **2 John** (Julius Piso) admits the Jews were then opposing the Gospel, they were refusing to confess that 'Jesus Christ' had come *"in (the) flesh"* (**1 John 4:3** and **2 John, verse 7**) and the response was to label these opponents as deceivers and *"anti-Christ"*. In **Matthew chapter 23**, Jesus repeatedly calls the scribes and Pharisees hypocrites and even vipers but does not include the people. **Matthew 3:7** says that the Pharisees and Sadducees are called offspring of vipers, but this time it is '**John the Baptist**' that insults them, but by the time of **Luke 3:7**, it is not just the leaders but the crowds as well who '*John the Baptist*' calls the offspring of vipers. The reason Arrius had the character 'John the Baptist' insult both the Pharisees and Sadducees, is because 'John the Baptist' was a character created to ridicule the Pharisee leader, or Rabbi, **Yochanan ben Zakai**. This famous Jewish leader was ridiculed because he was a leader in the war against the Romans and because he further refused to accept Christianity. And we can tell Yochanan ben Zakai was '**John the Baptist**' because of the name translations.

'**Zakkai**' is translated as '**Zacchaeus**' in **Greek**, but its root is found in the Hebrew word **tzedakah**, and means '*righteousness*', which means the name **Zakkai** means '**righteous**', and the Greek spelling '**Zacchaeus**' Ζακχαιος is found in **Luke Chapter 19:5-8**. But Yochanan ben Zakai is ridiculed even more, by saying '*John the Baptist*' was the "son" of '**Zacharias**'. The name '**Zacharias**' was created by combining two names, the **Greek** version of '**Zacch**(aeus)', with the name **Arrius**. That brings us to the name **Yohanan**, which is '**John**', so '**Yohanan ben Zakai**' is translated as '**John the Righteous**'. The English name '**John**' comes from the **Latin** names '**Ioannes**' and '**Iohannes**', which in turn comes from the **Greek** name '**Ioannes**' ιωαννης, which comes from the **Hebrew** name '**Yohanan**'. But by the Pisos, or mainly Arrius, going even further and by combining the word '**Zacch**' (Zakai) with '**Arias**' (Arrius), this would create the name '**Zacharias**', and with the knowledge that the word '**ben**' means '*son of*', that produces '**John** the **Baptist/Righteous** '*son of*' **Zakkai/Arrius**'. In reality, 'John the Baptist' was another creation ("son") of Arrius Piso, but another cruel element about this is that in the New Testament story, 'John the Baptist' paved the way for Christianity. So by creating the name 'John the Baptist', the Pharisee (Rabbi) leader had a version of his name help Christianity, as he refused to accept the religion.

Yeshua ben Panthera

The name *Yeshua ben Panthera*, as mentioned in the Jewish Talmud, has been debated as having a religious context and being a reference to 'Jesus Christ'. This is because the name '**Jesus**' used in the English language comes from the Latin form of the Greek name '**Iesous**' ιησους, which comes from the Hebrew '**Yeshua**', which also has the variants Joshua or Jeshua. The first thing to note about the name *Yeshua ben Panthera/Pendera*, are the different meanings for the Panthera word. Firstly, it is a general word for *'mother'*, which could include *'mother-in-law'*, and secondly, the word was also used to describe a '**beast**'. The word '**panther**' comes from the classical Latin word '**panthera**', which comes from the Greek words '**pan**' παν, which means "**all**", and '**ther**' θηρ, which means "**prey**", so those words combined give the meaning of "**predator of all animals**". But the use of word '*Panthera*' as a word for '*Beast*' originated in antiquity (meaning the ancient past before the Middle Ages) in the Orient, from India to Persia to Greece, and the word 'Panthera' is used to describe all beasts, including the **lion, tiger, jaguar,** and **leopard**.

The reason the word 'Panthera' being used to describe a 'beast' is important is because of the context in which the word beast is used in the '**Book of Revelation**', as previously shown. The word 'beast' is mentioned multiple times and is used to point to Arrius Piso. For instance, in **Revelation 13:2**, we read "*And the beast which I saw was like to a leopard, and feet its as of a bear, and its mouth as the mouth of a lion...*" Now in history, the lion has always been associated with royalty, going back to Egyptian times, and was a secondary attribute of the gods and kings, because the lion represented power and vitality. But in regards to the situation in which the name '**Yeshua ben Pan-**

thera is used in the Babylonian Talmud, logic tells us this name can only be a reference to one person who has a long history with the Jews, and has the word 'beast' used to refer to him, that person is Arrius Piso. If we examine the name closely we can see why –

'**Yeshua ben Panthera**' means **Yeshua/Jesus** 'son of '**Beast**', because '**ben**' means '**son of**', and the words for 'son' also meant '*creation*'/'*invention*', as '*offspring*' means the product or result of something. So now this name reads as **Yeshua/Jesus** 'son' ('creation'/'invention') of **Panthera** (beast), which points to **Arrius Piso**. As examined in the 'Main Author' chapter, in **Revelation 13:3**, we have the phrase "*after the beast*" and the Greek word used for '**after**' is '**opiso**' οπισω. So the phrase in the original words read "o**piso** the **beast**", or taking into account the use of inferred words, it would read as "o**piso** (is) the **beast**".

There is also further evidence and many more examples of proof that the writers of the Talmud were referring to Arrius Piso, as we find his name and references to his actions within the Babylonian Talmud's scripture. After everything that had happened, it is safe to assume they could not write about this openly and did not want to risk any more lives, so they inserted the name Arrius Calpurnius Piso very subtly. But the church had so much power that it controlled everything and could seize and censor the Jewish books, and enforce its intent on the Jews. The illiterate populations were taught by the church in the Roman Empire that the Jews would accept Christ, but the "incorrect" opinions regarding Christ misled and blinded them in their Talmud. But the Jews refused to convert to Christianity, despite the forced censorship and the enforced conversion sermons in synagogues. This frustration led to the church seizing and burning the Talmud, and framing the Jews on false charges and forcing those who they had not burned at the stake to leave Rome. The ancient Jewish Rabbi's, who started the school at Yavne, before 100 CE, and their successors who put together the Talmud through the generations, understood Greek very well and knew how the Pisos used the different languages to insert names and messages. So the Rabbis inserted their messages within their text, which were based on the techniques the Pisos had created in Greek. They would not write the nasty comments in Palestine, because that was under Rome's control, instead, they wrote the messages in the *Babylonian Talmud*, which was written in Persia, an area that Rome did not control. The writers of the Talmud made sure that their scholars of future generations would remember it was the Piso family who had destroyed their nation.

While the Jewish leaders were humiliated and ridiculed in the New Testament, they in return did the same to Arrius Piso in the Talmud, which has created a link of proof between the two. The fact that the Rabbis managed to insert Arrius' names in the Talmud, despite the dangers, shows just how resilient these people were. But these scriptures link this long historical story together, because had they not managed to reference Arrius' names, then we would only have the language techniques used by the Pisos in the New Testament to refer to as evidence.

The name **Arrius** appears in the Talmud in a story regarding a visitor to Rav (Rabbi) Yochanan and contains a statement that appears as follows – "**ARI OLAH ME BOBEL**", which means "*a* **lion** *has come up from Babylon*" (Rome) (**ref** – Ib *Bava Kamma*,

117a). '**Ari**' was a shortened form of '**Aryea**', which is Hebrew and means "*a lion*", but as we can tell from previous examples, this is just a secret allusion to **Arrius**, because as before, the word 'panthera' can refer to the lion. Also inserted in the texts is the phrase "**ARAYIN KEY MATAL**", this secretly meant "**Ari**" of the **Ayin**, because **Ayin** is the 16th letter of the Hebrew Aleph-Bet (alphabet) and has a numeric value of **70**, which refers to the Septuagint, which Arrius altered and which was quoted by the author of 'Matthew', that is, Arrius Piso.

The name **Calpurnius** is found as '*Kalpurnius*' within the phrase "*seven types of punishment come to the world for seven capital transgressions*", 7+7 = 14, and the significance of this will be explained shortly (**ref** – 2b *Abot*, 5.10). The phrase "**MEENAY PURONOOYOT**" means "*types of punishment*", but when this statement is included in a discussion regarding various plagues of insects, the phrase "**KOL MEENAY POORONEEYUS**" is also found. This appears to have the meaning '*all types of calamities*', (**ref** – 3b *Taanit*, 14a10). But when the words '**Kol**' and '**Meenay**' are switched around, we have "**MEENAY KOLPOORNEEYUS**", which means '**Min of Kalpurnius**'. '**The Min**' is what the Jews called the Pisos, because Arrius as 'Jesus' is secretly a 'Phallus', or *Rome's power*, this is because the male organ was considered to possess the power to 'wave off evil' and increase fertility. To quote Ian Mcneil Cooke, who wrote a book called '*Sun Disc to Crucifix: The Cross*', – "The erect penis was commonly used in religions of the early Mediterranean and West Asian civilizations, to show the procreative and protective properties of various deities...there is concrete evidence showing the link between the cross and the phallus in classical pagan civilizations, a link which was to continue into Christian art and *mythology in the image of various types of crosses. Even the adoration of phallic pagan deities disguised as 'saints' is associated with phallic rituals. Many of these ceremonies were carried out in the churches as early as the 19th century".*

But 'the Min' or 'Ah-min' was also the Itho-phallic gods of the Egyptians, so they were the female-male gods who were able to '*create life*'. The Jews writing "*Meenay Kolpoorneeyus*" means "*creation of Kalpurnius* (Calpurnius)". But Minos was the ancient lawgiver of Crete and another Minos was king of ancient Crete, but Minos in Greek in small numbering/'*Piso numbers*' (which will be explained shortly), totaled **19**, which is what the name Piso totaled. The Jews making use of this name to point to Arrius Piso is quite appropriate, as Pliny (writing as 'Paul') quotes Epimenides, another Cretan, and says in Titus 2:12 "*All Cretans are liars*". But the 'Min', in Egyptian '*mnw*', was also an ancient Egyptian god whose cult began in the fourth millennium BCE, and he was mostly represented in a human male form, with an erect penis, which he holds in his left hand and an upright arm holding a flail. Referred to by the names *Khem* or *Min*, he was the god of reproduction, and in the Middle Kingdom, his importance grew when he became closely linked with Horus, who, as mentioned earlier in the book, was a name used by Arrius to create the alias name 'Gessius Fl-(H)orus', and was also linked with Amun in the New Kingdom, forming Min-Amun.

In **Matthew 26:34** etc., Peter denies Christ three times before the cock crows, the cock/rooster being a symbol of '**St. Peter**', and "**Peter**" or "**Pator**" does not only mean "**Father**", "**Parent**" or "**Rock**", but also means "**the cock**" or "**penis**", as the word is still used as slang to this day. As Barbara G. Walker's 'The Woman's Dictionary of Symbols and Sacred Objects' says, "The cock was also a symbol of Saint Peter, whose name also meant a phallus or male principle (**pater**). So, the cock's image was often placed atop church towers". The "Savior of the World" image hidden in the Vatican, appears in Walker's book on p. 397, where she says "It is no coincidence that "cock" is slang for "penis." The cock was a phallic totem in Roman and medieval sculptures showing cocks somehow transformed into, or supporting, human penises. Roman carvings of disembodied phalli often gave them the legs or wings of cocks. Hidden in the treasury of the Vatican is a bronze image of a cock with the head of a penis on the torso of a man, the pedestal inscribed "**The Savior of the World**."

The last part of Arrius' name, **Piso**, is found in a story regarding "**PISHON HA' GOMOL**", which means 'Pishon the camel driver' (**ref** – 4b Yeb., 107b), who was using the property of his unnamed minor wife. His conduct was challenged by his wife during his absence and he was given two penalties by the court, and this story was placed in the time of the school of Shammi (and Hillel) circa. 1 CE. By backdating the story to that period, the church censor would not think Pishon/Pison related to Piso, who lived 37-119 CE. But the term 'camel' driver would show who "Pishon" referred to, as the term 'camel' is from the Hebrew 'gamal' and means 'to repay'. So, by the Rabbis inserting nasty comments towards Arrius in the Talmud, they are returning the favor for the nasty comments made towards them in the New Testament. As well as being able to make the name 'Piso' from 'Pishon/Pison', those words also refer to a river of 'Eden', said to compass the whole land of Havilah where there is **gold**, and the word 'gold' is linked to Arrius Piso and will be explained in the next chapter.

10. THE '666' RIDDLE

The New Testament describes a powerful leader and his government or empire as the '**Beast**', and the number associated with that 'Beast' is '**666**'. The writer of the Book of Revelation makes it clear that he is creating a riddle – 666 stands for the name of a man who is the Beast, the world's worst tyrant, and Satan's right-hand man. This number was changed to '**616**' when the Church was deciding whether to continue to include 'Revelations' in the Christian canon. They tried to change '666' to '616' in the manuscripts, because of what '666' meant, and this was done to confuse the numbering system or '*proof/identity system*' the authors used, but still honor the original meaning of the '666' number. The Pisos appear to have used a numbering system that would act as a 'proof/identity system', as a way of '*copyrighting*' the scripture. The author associates the number '666' of the 'Beast' with the mark of the 'Beast', and tells us to:

"***count the number***" and that it is "***the number of a man***".

When reading **Revelation 13:17-18**, it says:

"...and that no one should be able to buy or to sell, except he who has the '**mark**' or the name of the '**beast**', or the '**number** of **his name**'. Here is wisdom, he who has **understanding** let him count the **number** of **the beast**, for it is the number of a **man** and his number is 666."

The Bible story associates the number **six** with **man** because as the story goes, God made man on the sixth day, but '666' is a triple repetition of the number, and so it emphasizes the fact that the 'beast' represents a government of human authority, not God's.

Using all the information that has been discovered and researched, it is clear the answer lies within the alphabets/languages of the time, and the three main alpha/numeric systems being used were – **Hebrew**, **Latin** (Roman Numerals) and **Greek**. Until the year 80 CE, the Greek alpha-numeric system comprised only an old initial system that the Greek philosopher Pythagoras developed. It seems Arrius and the Piso family took this letter and numbering system, developed it, and then used it as a '*signature*' in the New Testament. By combining and incorporating the three different main languages and the numbers associated with the letters of those languages, a '*Piso number system*' was created. Arrius gives hints of what he refers to as '*triangular numbers*' in his works as 'Flavius Josephus', which is what the number '666' is. When we read 'Josephus', we find that Arrius was a Roman General at the battle of Garasa in 66 CE and was the first person to mention Garasa. This information makes sense because writing as 'Josephus', Arrius was must also have been the '*mathematician*' called **'Nichomachus'** ('Nichomachus of Garasa') with the dates given for him being approximately 60 CE and died 100 C.E., and this is because 'Nico' means '*Victor*' or '*Winner*' and 'Machus' means '*of the battle*' (of Garasa).

The Numbering Systems

The Pisos used 3 numbering systems to '*copyright*' their work, those numbering systems are as follows:

1) Small Numbering System – Each letter in Greek had a numerical equivalent, but a '*small numbering system*' was used inside the New Testament, where the zeros were not used because Roman numerals did not have a zero, instead, the word 'nulla' was used, which meant zero. So from a Latin perspective, an '**80**' (Pi/Π) would be viewed as an '**8**'

2) Initial Number System – This system used the full numerical values of the Greek letters, so the zeros were included, but only the *initials* of names were used, for example –

K = 20, **P** =80, so those two combined together make 100 (KP)

C (in Latin) = 100, **P** (in Greek) = 80, so combined they make 180 (CP)

K = 20, and the glyph (symbol) for **P** in Latin looks the same as the letter **R** in Greek, which is ρ and has the numerical value of 100, so the Greek numbering is 100, therefore, combined they make 120 (KP)

C (in Latin) = 100, **P** (as R) in Greek was 100, so that makes 200 (CP)

3) The Sequence System – This was a system that was used as both an extension and *with* systems 1 or 2. Each of the letters in the Greek alphabet was in order, but by *combining* the number systems, i.e. the numbers assigned to the Greek letters, and each letter's position in the alphabet, meant the letters could be used to spell or reference the same name.

For example, if the **Initial Greek Alphabet Letter Sequence** was used with the **Small Numbering System**, then the letter Ξ which is Xi, which is used on the Papal cross, was the **14**[th] letter of the Greek alphabet and had the numerical value of **60**. That means that **Kalpournios Piso**, which totaled **60** in **small numbering**, could also be presented as **14**.

If the **Sequence System** was used with the **Initial Number System**, then **K** would be the **10**[th] letter in the Greek alphabet sequence, and **P** would be the **16**[th], which means **KP** would be presented as **26**.

Examples of these number systems being used as a 'signature' can be found in the two chapters which contain the genealogies of Jesus, which are **Matthew 1** and **Luke 3**. In those chapters, Arrius used the numbers 41, 60, and 26, to present who he was. In **Matthew 1**, 41 is written as the number of generations from Abraham to Jesus, and in **Matthew 1:17**, **14** is presented *three times*, which makes **42**, so when **1** and **17** are added, it makes **60**, 14×3 + 1+17 = 60, which is **KP** in Small Numbering. The first chapter of this Gospel has **25** verses and those verses *plus* the first chapter = **26** (10th & 16th Greek letters = **KP**).

In **Luke 3**, the third chapter has **38** verses, making a total of **41** (38+3=41). The generations from Jesus back to Abraham totals **57**, which means 57 plus 3 (chapter 3) = **60** (KP). **Luke 3:23** gives us **26** (3+23=26), in this verse we also read that Jesus' age was 30. This means that many of the important verses, along with the chapters that contain those verses, are arranged so that the numbers present Arrius' name or initials. Also, it should be noted that **John 3:16** = **19** (3+16) which spells '**Piso**' in Small Numbering, and **John 8:32** = **40** (8+32), ie, the 40 years.

Why would the authors have used a number system like this? There are two obvious answers, 1) because there was no such thing as 'copyright' when the New Testament was written, and the use of these number systems would have allowed the Pisos to identify themselves as the authors, and 2) is the fact that although they wanted to claim authorship, they could not openly admit they wrote the scripture, so their number system was the ideal solution for them, and it worked. The main number system has **50** numbers overall, but those numbers do not include the numbers that were used to point to the meaning behind the number '**666**'. Out of the **50** main numbers, **27** were used as '*main numbers*' for the '*Piso number system*' and **17** numbers were used as '*combined numbers*' (small numbering system and sequence system) and **6** numbers that can be both '*main*' and '*combined*' numbers. It is also worth noting that because of how these numbers work, it means these number systems were deliberately created for a particular purpose, meaning the numbers, and what they spell when totaled up, should <u>not</u> in any way relate to Arrius Piso or the Piso family.

The Piso Number System

Number **8**

The number **8** in the Bible represented a 'new beginning', which meant a new order or creation. But in the 'Piso *number system*', **8** represented the letter '**P**' for **Piso** as it was considered a small Greek **80**, which represented '**Pi**' π. In the passage referenced below, '**8**' is given as the number for '**H**', but why? The only logical reason would be that it is was seen as the Latin H, instead of the letter 'Eta', which looks like an 'H'. But if the New Testament came out of Rome, then it can refer to Horus because of the striking comparison between 'Horus' and 'Jesus', and because it was a name used by Arrius. (**ref** – *The apocryphal book of 'Barnabas'*. Chap. VIIII, Verse 10- 12). (**ref** – See '*Lost Books of the Bible*', pg. 154, published by Bell Publishing Co. NY, NV).

Number **10**

The number **10** represented the letter '**I**' ('**J**'), which stood for '**Jesus**' **Ιησους** in the initial Greek alphanumeric system. But in the '*Piso sequence number system*', it represented '**K**' for '**Kalpournios**', because 'K' was the 10th letter of the Greek alphabet. (**ref** – *The apocryphal book of 'Barnabas'* Chap. VIIII, Verse 12 (See '*Lost Books of the Bible*', pg. 154, published by Bell Publishing Co, NY, NV).

Number **18**

In the *Apocryphal book 'Barnabas'* 18:12, '**18**' is '**10**' and '**8**', which stands for **10** = **Jesus** and **8** = **Piso**, '*Barnabas*' verse 12 says – "*Mark, first the eighteen, and next the three hundred. For the numeral letters of* **ten** *and* **eight** *are* '**I H**', *and these denote Jesus*".

As examined above, '**H**' can be an acrostic initial for '**Horus**', and '**8**' was used for '**P**' in the '*Piso number system*' because the Roman number system did not have a '**0**'. Our number system is the only one known to have a numeral for zero, except for the Mayan system. The Babylonians mark for 'nothing' was used mainly as punctuation and so because of this knowledge, we can be certain that Arrius used the number '**8**' for his system, because the number '**0**' was not recognized by the Romans. 18 is also the Pythagorean 666 (6+6+6 = 18). (**ref** – *The apocryphal book of 'Barnabas'*, Chap. VIIII, Verse 12). (See '*Lost Books of the Bible*', pg. 154, published by Bell Publishing Co., NY, NV).

Number 20

'K' for 'Kalpournios' in the initial Greek system and 'Nicon' in small '*Piso numbers*'.

Number 26

'Suetonius' writes '*Chrestus*', which in Greek small numbers/'*Piso numbers*' totals 26 (KP) by the '*sequence system*', but if spelled normally as '*Christus*', it would total 22.

Number 27

This number honored 'Pliny the Younger' by using his first name '**Pliny**', which is '**Plinios**' in Latin, and the number 27 was created using '*small numbers*' in the '*Piso number system*' –

'**Pi**', which is '**80**' in Greek but '**8**' in the '*Piso number system*', '**Lambda**' ('**L**') is '**30**' in Greek but '**3**' in '*Piso's number system*', '**Iota**' ('**I**') is '**10**' in Greek but '**1**' in '*Piso's number system*', '**Nu**'

('**N**') is '**50**' in Greek but '**5**' 'Piso's *number system*', '**Iota**' again is '**10**' in Greek but also '**1**', and '**Omikron**' is '**70**' in Greek but '**7**' in 'Piso's *number system*'. So 8+3+1+5+1+7+2 = **27**

Number 30

The number **30** represented 'Jesus/Flavius' by the Piso 'sequence system', and also the total of the name '**Flavius**' Φλαουιος in Greek (Piso) 'small numbers'.

So we have –

'**Phi**' ('**F**' sound) which is '**500**' in Greek and '**5**' in the 'Piso number system', '**Lambda**' ('**L**') which is '**30**' in Greek but '**3**' in 'Piso's number system', '**Alpha**' ('**A**') which is '**1**' in Greek and the 'Piso number system', '**Omicron**' (**o**) is '**70**' but '**7**' in the 'Piso number system', '**Upsilion**' (υ) is '**400**' in Greek, but '**4**' in the 'Piso number system', '**Iota**' ('**I**') is '**10**' in Greek but '**1**' in the 'Piso number system', '**Omicron**' ('**O**') again is '**70**' in Greek but also '**7**', and '**Sigma**' ('**s**') is '**200**' in Greek and '**2**' in the 'Piso number system'.

So 5+3+1+7+4+1+7+2 = **30**, and which points to the '30 *pieces of* 'Gold' *for Solomon*. And by the 'sequence system' the '**I**' of 'Jesus' was the 9th letter in the Greek alphabet and the '**F**' from 'Flavius' was the 21st letter, which also totals 30.

Number 36

This square (quadratus – '*Flavius Josephus Never*' Existed chapter) number represented the total of the **original** spelling of

'Josephus' as **'Josepos'** Ιωςηπος in Greek (Piso) *small numbers*, and is shown various times throughout the works of 'Flavius Josephus'. For example, we have 'Josepos' (*Jewish War*, Loeb, Ch. VIII, Paragraph 3); "*Josepos said thus...*" (*pg. 569, Wars of the Jews, Book. VI, Ch. II, Verse I*) and "*..Josepos was taken up,...*" (*Wars of the Jews*, Whiston translation, page 574, Book V, Chap. XIII, Verse III.)

Number 46

Ιηςους Χριςτος 'Jesus Christ' in small (Piso) numbers. John 2:20 states that the Jews tell Jesus it took 46 years to build the Temple.

Number 47

The most famous theorem of Pythagoras. In The Jewish War, Arrius wrote that his defense of Jotapata had lasted 47 days. (**ref** – *The Jewish War*, 3:141–288, 316ff)

Number 60

Is the numerical equivalent of 'Calpurnius Piso' in the Greek spelling, ('*Kalpournios Piso*'), but using Greek (Piso) *small numbers*.

ΚΑΛΠΟΥΡΝΙΟΣΠΙΣΩ

K=2 A=1 Λ=3 Π=8 O=7 Y=4 P=1 N=5 I=1 O=7 Σ=2 Π=8 I=1 Σ=2 Ω=8

Number 66

This was the '6' of '**Xi**' and '6' of '**Bau**' of the '**Chi**', '**Xi**', '**Bau**' from '**666**', in the original language and the total of the name '**Flavius Josephus**' (**Flaouios Iosepos**), which is **30** + **36** in Greek small (Piso) numbering. It is also important to note that the Church later arranged the Old Testament into **39** books, and so combined with the **27** books of the New Testament, it totals **66**.

Number **96**

Is the name '**Alex**' in regular numbering, the name of Arrius' first son. One of Pliny's letters to Emperor Trajan concerning his recent alleged persecution of Christians is made to number 96 in the 10th volume of his letters.

Number **99**

This number represented **Pliny the Younger** as the total of his full name – '**Gaios Kaikilios Sekoundos Plinious**', in Greek (Piso) small numbers.

Number **100**

This number represented '**K**' and '**P**' ('Kalpurnius Piso') using the original Greek alpha-numeric system. But in the Latin numerical system, '**C**' for '**Calpumius**' was also **100**. (**ref** – Suetonius, *The Twelve Caesars*, pg. 99, under '*Augustus*', "*At about this time lightning melted the initial letter of his name on the inscription below one of his statues. This was interpreted to* *mean that he would live only another hundred days, which the letter 'C' signifies..."* (Penguin Classics edition, Penguin Books) '**KP**', with the '**P**' seen as '**R**', was 120 by the initial Greek system and the gathering of the brethren in **Acts 1:15** consists of 120.

Number **300**

This number stood for '**T**', which represented the cross. (**ref** – *The General Epistle of 'Barnabas'*, (the Apocryphal New Testament) Chap. VIIII, Verses 10-14 – *"And because the cross was that by which we were to find grace; therefore he adds, three hundred; the note of which is T (the figure of his cross). Wherefore by two letters he signified Jesus, and by the third his cross"*).

Number **600**

This number represented the '**Chi**' ('**X**') in the Greek alphanumeric system and is pronounced '**Kai**' and stands for '**Christ**', because it is an acrostic initial for 'Christ'. It is used to write '666' ('**Chi**', '**Xi**', '**Bau**' – 600, 60, 6).

Number **616**

As mentioned above, the Church was deciding whether or not to continue to include the *Book of Revelations* within the Christian canon, in the **Council of Nicaea in Bithynia** convened by Constantine I, because of what '666' represented. The Church chose to try and change '666' to '616', as '**616**' still honored

'Christ/Piso', as **600** = '**Christ**' and **16** = '**Piso**', because '**Pi**' is the **16**[th] letter of the Greek alphabet, but the number 616 would not directly link back to the intended individual being spoken of in the Book of Revelation.

'**Ch**' ('**Chi**'/'**X**') is **600** and represents 'Christ' when used acrostically, and 'Piso' is represented acrostically as '**Pis**' using the *sequence system* and *small number system*. So '**Pi**' = '**8**', '**Iota**' = '**1**' and '**Zeta**', which was used for '**S**' = '**7**', which is 8+1+7 = **16**.

Number **666**

This number was used in the Book of Revelation by Julius Piso to point to his father Arrius, and the reason is that Arrius used the number '666' once when he wrote as 'Flavius Josephus'. Julius inserted a number which can be considered a *'proof/identity number'*, which is **2,368**, which is both the total of the names '**Jesus**' and '**Christ**' *combined*, and also the total number of the *entire last phrase* of **Revelation 13:18**, (*"and the number of it"*) when the number '**666**' *was added* to it.

'**Jesus**' – **I** =10, **H** =8, **S** =200, **O** =70, **U** =400, **S** =200 which gives a total of **888**

'**Christ**' –**X** =600, **P** =100, **I** =10, **S** =200, **T** =300, **O** =70 **S** =200 which is **1,480**.

Combined, these two names total of **2,368**.

Next, we have **KAI O ARITHMOS**, which says *"and the number"*, which totals **531**, and **AUTOU**, which says *"of it"* and totals

1,171, together they total **1,702**, but when '**666**' is added, we have **2,368**.

When **2368** is added up using the original Pythagorean math principles, Pythagoreanism of which was prominent in Roman literature during the first-century BCE and first-century CE, it equals '**19**' – (2 + 3 + 6 + 8 = 19), which produces the name '**Piso**' in the Greek (Piso) small numbers. So the total number of this *'proof/identity number'* was created from the Greek initial alphanumeric system, *except* for '**666**', because '666' was not only a part of that total number (2,368) but was also used as a *separate* number in itself. As mentioned before, '666' was not written as it could have been written, for example, the way '**144 thousand**' was written in **Revelation 7:4** ρμδ χιλιαδες. It was written in the form of three letters with numerical values and those letters are, '**Chi**', '**Xi**', '**Bau**'. '**Chi**' stands for '**Christ**' and has a numerical value of **600** and the other letters which made up '**666**' were '**Xi**' ('**60**', which could be seen as a '**6**' in Roman eyes ('Piso *small numbers*') and the Phoenician letter '**Bau**', which also had the value of '**6**'. These two letters created '**66**', which was, and is, the total number of the name '**Flavius Josephus**'/**Josepos** in small Greek (Piso) numbers. The letter '**Bau**' being used is very interesting, and I am sure was not an accident, as it represents the word '**malkûth**' (malkooth) in **Hebrew**, '**malkutha**' (Aramaic), which was used in 'Daniel' 4:3 and means 'kingship', '**royalty**', '**royal power**', '**reign**', '**kingdom**', '**sovereign power**'. This Hebrew word is synonymous with the Greek word '**Basileia**' Βασιλεια, and in the **Septuagint**, the Hebrew word '**malkûth**' is constantly translated as '**Basileia**'. So we know the number of the 'Beast' is contained within the name of a kingdom, which the Greek word 'Basileia' signifies, as the great empires of Babylonia, Persia, Macedonia, and Rome were called 'Basileia', meaning 'kingdoms' and the monarchs of these powers were named '**Basileis**' Βασιλεις, meaning '**Kings**'.

So the number '**666**' is the numerical equivalent of "**Christ/Flavius Josephus**", or in other words, using the knowledge that the Bible used inferred sentences, we know the number of the Beast is – "**Christ (Jesus)** 'was' **Flavius Josephus**, and 'Josephus' was none other than Arrius Piso. That means the 'proof/identity number' of **2,368** reveals the man behind this literary creation. Arrius writing as 'Josephus', uses the number '**666**' to secretly represent himself when saying how '**gold**' was given to King Solomon. He says "*The talents of gold…*", because by saying 'gold' he can also mean '**Flavius**' because that name also means '**Golden**' or '**yellow-haired**' and comes from the **Latin** '*Flavus*', meaning 'yellow, golden'. (**ref** – Josephus, 'Antiquities of the Jews', Chap. 7. verse 3). **1 Kings 10:14** says, "*the weight of gold (Flavius) which Solomon received every year was* **six hundred threescore and six** (666) *talents of gold, besides what came from the tradesmen, from the traffic of merchants, and from all the kings of Arabia and the governors of the regions*". (Jewish Study Bible). This is Arrius hinting at his descent from **King Solomon**, through **King David**, as he does in **Matthew 1:6** when he plays 'Jesus'. And he was saying that 666 was "**gold**" or in other words, "**Flavius**", so in essence his number. Finally, the number '**36**' (in the '**66**' part of '**666**') also adds up to 'Josepos' (Josephus), and cumulates (by the Cumulative Number System) into '**666**', which means that '**666**' is also '**36**' or 'Josepos' (Josephus).

Why did Julius Piso give us this information?

Julius Piso, (who was *John* as a little boy in the Synoptic Gospels), was Arrius Piso's oldest living son, and history portrays him as loyal to his family and a loyal general. Appearing as '*Julius Severus*', in the historical records; **Severus** could be argued as coming from both the '**Verus**' part of one of Arrius' alias names, and '**Servianus**', which came from the family name inherited from his mother Boionia **Servilia** Priscilla, it can also be seen as the Pisos ancestral name of **Sabinus**, with the vowel change of the **E** to **A** and **I**, with **V** being seen as **B**, and the **R** changing to **N**. As Julius Severus, he had just destroyed *Bar Cochbah/Kokhba*, resulting in the final dispersion of the Jews in the year 135 CE, but instead of being rewarded, a rift between he, his brother Justus, sister Claudia, and Emperor Hadrian developed. Justus, who appears as **Marcus Annius Verus II** in history, his father using the name Annius Verus before him, was a favored and close friend of Hadrian, even becoming a consul three times, first as a suffect consul in 97 CE, then as ordinary consul in both 121 and 126 CE, an ordinary consul holding more prestige than a suffect consul.

Justus and his sister Claudia Phoebe Piso announced that they preferred Hadrian to succeed Claudia's husband, Emperor Trajan, and so, when Trajan died, on August 8, 117 CE, his cousin and adopted son Hadrian then became emperor. Hadrian was childless at the age of 50 and so needed a successor, Hadrian treated Julius (Servianus/Severus) with distinguished honor, considering him to be his first successor, however, as Hadrian's reign came to its end, he changed his mind. Julius Piso by this time was in his sixties, so that factor could have contributed to the decision to not make him the next emperor, possibly; although Nerva became emperor at the age of Sixty Six, so I doubt his age was an issue. Hadrian turned his attention to Julius' grandson as his successor, which made Julius very happy, after all, his grandson was Hadrian's great-nephew, as Julius had married Hadrian's sister. Hadrian groomed Julius' grandson to be his heir, giving him special status in his court and all seemed well. However, Hadrian suddenly changed his mind in 136 CE, for reasons not fully understood within current academia, and decided to adopt *Lucius Ceionius Commodus* as his son and heir, sometimes referred to as *Lucius Aelius Verus*. But Lucius Verus died before Hadrian, and instead of Hadrian reconsidering Julius' grandson, he named Claudia Phoebe Piso's son *Antoninus Pius* as his heir. Julius and his grandson became angry at Hadrian, Justus, and Claudia, as Julius was the elder of the Piso family at this point and had done his duty to both Trajan and Hadrian, so he must have felt, quite rightly, that his grandson should become the next emperor, if not himself. Hadrian eventually ordered the deaths of Julius and his grandson, as Cassius Dio says: *"Those who perished at the end of his reign were Servianus and his grandson Fuscus."* – Dio, Cassius, Vol. VIII, Epitome LXIX, verse 5 pg. 429.

"He now began to be sick; for he had been subject even before this

to a flow of blood from the nostrils, and at this time it became distinctly more copious. He therefore despaired of his life, and on this account appointed Lucius Commodus to be Caesar for the Romans, although this man frequently vomited blood. Servianus and his grandson Fuscus, the former a nonagenarian and the latter eighteen years of age, were put to death on the ground that they were displeased at this action. Servianus before being executed asked for fire, and as he offered incense he exclaimed: "That I am guilty of no wrong, ye, O Gods, are well aware; as for Hadrian, this is my only prayer, that he may long for death but be unable to die." And, indeed, Hadrian did linger on a long time in his illness, and often prayed that he might expire, and often desired to kill himself. Here is, indeed, a letter of his in existence which gives proof of precisely this — how dreadful it is to long for death and yet be unable to die. This Servianus had been regarded by Hadrian as capable of filling even the imperial office. For instance, Hadrian had once at a banquet told his friends to name him ten men who were competent to be sole ruler, and then, after a moment's pause, had added: "nine only I want to know; for one I have already — Servianus." (**ref** – Dio, Cassius., Vol. VIII, Epitome LXIX, verse 17 pg. 457, Loeb Classical Library edition, and Anthony Birley, *Hadrian the Restless Emperor*, pp. 291-292.)

As mentioned, current academia has no answer for Emperor Hadrian's sudden change of mind, but judging by Julius' writings in terms of the New Testament, I believe the answer is clear. Julius wrote **John I, II**, and **III** as well as the **Book of Revelation**, which was completed in 137 CE, and within John III he condemns '*Diotrephes*' (meaning "nourished by Jupiter") for his arrogant self-seeking ways and wicked slander; Jupiter, of course, is the Latin Zeus, creator of Dionysis, who is linked to Jesus. Julius describes '*Diotrephes*' as having a self-appointed position and that he wished to be first, he wished to have superiority and acted in the church like an *aristocrat*. He is also described as being *ambitious, proud, disrespectful of apostolic authority, rebellious,* and *inhospitable*. Julius writes in John 3:10 that, "*Diotrephes, receives not us. On account of this, if I come, I will bring to the remembrance of him the works which he does, with words evil prating (talk foolishly or at tedious length about something) against us; and not satisfied with these, neither himself receives the brethren and those who would he forbids, and from the assembly casts them out.*" 2 and 3 John are the shortest books in the New Testament, possibly indicating that Julius did not want to write them, he even says "*Many things I had to write to you but not I desire with ink and pen to you to write I hope however soon you to see and mouth to mouth we will speak.*" This comment coupled with the fact John III contains the frustration, pointing to his father as '*Diotrephes*', indicates that he did not agree with what his father was doing and perhaps did not want to be part of the creation of the new religion.

Julius' family must have been aware of his feelings. Justus seems to have been more like his father, both politically and in terms of writing the scriptures, as a message about '*political juggling*' by Julius (L. Iulius Ursus Servianus) to his brother Justus, as *Marcus Annius Verus II*, suggests. The message is seen as an elegant, self-deprecating and bitter joke, and not complimentary to Justus, and is viewed as a strange poem inscription:

"Ursus, who was the first Roman to play with a glass ball properly with my fellow-players, while the people approved with greatest applause, in the baths of Trajan, in the baths Agrippa and Titus, and frequently in Nero's (if only you believe me) – am I. Gather together rejoicing, o pilicrepi, and lovingly cover the statue of your friend with rose and violet blossoms and many a leaf and ancient perfume; and pour forth the unmixed black Falernian or the Setian or the Caecuban, to one who is alive and willing, from the master's cellar; and sing with one voice of Ursus the old man, merry, full of jest, a pilicrepus [ballplayer], a scholar, who surpassed all of his predecessors with his taste, his dignity, and his most delicate art. Now let us old men speak true words in verse: I have been defeated, I confess it, by the thrice consul Verus, my patron, not once but many times, whose exodiarius I am pleased to be called." (**ref** – Champlin, Edward, The Glass Ball Game, pp. 159-163)

The above inscription was found on a large marble tablet in the sixteenth century at St. Peter's in Rome. In the reference above, speculation over a game played with a glass ball is discussed, as there is no clear evidence of this game in antiquity, as German Classical scholar *Franz Buecheler* is stated to have remarked in the paper above. The statement *'whose exodiarius I am pleased to be called'* is also considered a strange end to the poem, as it is used as a term of self-abasement (a voluntary self-punishment or humiliation in order to atone for some real or imagined wrongdoing) and of contempt. In the closing paragraphs of the paper, M. *Annius Verus*, consul suffect in 97 CE under Emperor Nerva, is identified as the Verus mentioned in the inscription. This man was an ordinary consul in 121 CE and 126 CE under Hadrian and was in his late sixties or seventies, he is also stated as being an *'older contemporary of Dio Chrysostom,'* whose identity will be examined in the next chapter.

Hadrian's sudden change of mind, which must have been influenced by Justus and Claudia, was a strategic move to stop Julius and his grandson from becoming emperor. Justus and Claudia, who appeared to have been fully supportive of the new religion, may have feared that Julius would stop the progress of the development of the Christian literature when he became emperor, just as Nero seems to have done. But before Julius was killed, he ridiculed his father and family, most likely out of anger, in the Book of Revelation, and would use a *'play on words'*, just like other members of his family had done in previous scripture. In the Revelation, Julius used the 'Piso number' **42**, (which was used earlier in **Matthew 1:17**), to hint at the war that he had helped Hadrian to fight, that war being the *Bar Kokhba* revolt in 132 CE, which lasted 42months, or three and a half years, and was led by *Simon bar Kockhba*, and this information helps to date his book because Julius says "**forty-two months**", which is **three and a half years** – "They shall trample upon the holy city (Jerusalem) forty-two months (three and a half years." **Rev. 11:2**. Julius ridicules Pliny the Younger too, who was number **27**, which totals **Plinios**, by making the *'beast'* in **Revelation 13:1**, have **10** horns, **7** heads, and **10** diadems (crowns), which totals **27**, and he makes his dead father into the *'dragon'*, who acts (has authority) for **42** months. In **Revelation 13:5** and **Revelation 15:6**, it says "*the seven angels (priests) have seven plagues*", which is a total of **14**, but **Revelation 13:1** is also **14** – (13+1 and so points to Arrius, his father because **14** was equal to **60** ('*Kalpournios Piso*', in Greek numbers, as explained at the beginning of this chapter). Also in **Matthew 1:17,** *fourteen generations* is mentioned three times, so 3×14 = **42**, that is '*Jesus genealogy*', in multiples of 7)

In **Revelation 13:5**, as examined earlier, authority was given to the '*beast*' (ippos, Piso) to act forty-two months, and just before that sentence, Julius says "*Who is able to make war with the beast?*" This statement means that another "beast" or another Piso (Julius himself), has the ability or means to make war with the 'beast', or in other words, his father Arrius and the other supporting Pisos. He is saying that he can make 'war' with the other Pisos by writing the Book of Revelation, in retaliation for him or his grandson not being named emperor. But Julius retaliates even further in **Revelation 13:18**, by exposing the identity of his father, by saying the number of the 'beast' was '**666**', which was '**Xpistos**' by the initial Greek system, plus **66** (Flavius Josephus) by the '*small number system*', so, as mentioned, that gives us Arrius' alias name 'Flavius Josephus'/Josepos and his creation, 'Christ'. Some ancient manuscripts do present this number as '**616**', but as shown, the result is the same, **16** is '**P**' by the '*Piso sequence system*' (**Pi** *is the 16th letter of the Greek alphabet*), and '**P**' stood for **Piso**, so '616' is **Christ + Piso**. In **Rev. 22:18-19**, Julius warns against adding or taking away from this book, but when he writes this he doesn't mean the Bible or the New Testament, he means his book, the Revelation. He did not want anyone to make any changes to what he had written within it, and this statement was most likely borrowed from his father's book '*Antiquities of the Jews*' Book X, Chapter X, verse VI. In that chapter, Arrius ('Josephus') says-"*In the beginning of this 'history', I intended to do no more than "translate" the Hebrew books into the Greek language, and* *promised them to explain those "**facts**", without adding (anything) to them of my own, or taking (anything) away from them."*

Reading on in Josephus we find the letter of Aristeas, where Josephus goes on to hint about his editing the Greek Septuagint (Book XII, Chap. 2, verse 2), the Greek Septuagint also being called the 'LXX' or 'the Seventy', and this is hinted at in **Luke 10:17** (a detailed examination regarding when the Septuagint was actually written can be found at www.henryhdavis.com.) Julius, who seems to have been the Church Father '*Clement of Rome*', the name Clement possibly being used to honor his ancestor, *T. Flavius Clemens*, who was executed for 'atheism' and became regarded as the first 'Christian Martyr'; S and T can replace each other, as in the case of the Hebrew word 'Sur' (rock), which is also presented as 'Tsur', 'Tsar', and 'Tar', Tsur being the name of the stone pillar god. Cassius Dio says that Clemens was put to death on a charge of atheism, for which, he adds, "*many others who went over to the Jewish opinions were executed.*" '*Clement of Rome*' held office from 88 to his "death" in 99, and is considered to be the first *Apostolic Father of the Church*, one of the three chief ones together with *Polycarp* (Proculus/Agrippa) and *Ignatius* (Pliny) of Antioch.

Arrius writing as 'Josephus' was the only ancient author to have used the number '666' in his works (*Jewish Antiquities*, Book 8, Chapter 7, Verse 2), circa 90 CE, right up until it was used by Julius. The number had not appeared anywhere outside of any biblical scripture, but by using that number, Julius could only point to one person, his father. However, after Julius was executed, *Suetonius*, who appears to have been the Emperor *Antoninus Pius*, grandson of Arrius, for reasons that will be explained, would finish writing 'The Twelve Caesars' circa 145 CE, and within the writings of that book, he would associate the number with Emperor Nero. He would do so by writing the statement:

"During his reign many abuses were severely punished and put down, and no fewer new laws were made...Punishment was inflicted on the Christians, a class of men given to a new and mischievous superstition." (Suetonius, 'Nero', 16.2)

Nero at the beginning was the main initial enemy of the Piso family, and 'Suetonius' associated '666' with Nero in his writings because he knew full well that Julius had used it to point to Arrius as 'Flavius Josephus'. Suetonius would use the number and associate it with Nero, as 'Nero Caesar' in Hebrew is NRON QSR and adds up to 666. He would also state that Emperor Claudius had expelled the Jews from Rome for constantly making disturbances at the instigation of *Chrestus*, thereby historicizing the story appearing in Acts of the Apostles 18:2. Later, during the time of Constantine, the aristocracy tried to change the number to 616 but instead decided to translate the New Testament into Latin, so that the majority of what was there in the original Greek could no longer be seen. But the translating of the New Testament into Latin makes no sense if using the *current* understanding of the history of Christianity, and the languages understood by the majority of people. By 1522, Martin Luther, a German professor of theology, had translated the New Testament into German, as the people could not understand the Latin version, even today, Catholic masses are in Latin.

Martin Luther wanted the people to be able to read the Bible themselves, and so he translated it from the original Greek and Hebrew, which worried the church officials, as they no longer had strict control over the word of 'God'; in Latin, when 'Nero Caesar' is put into Hebrew letters, the second 'N' of Nero drops and has the value of 616. Suetonius and other writers of history would continue to paint the picture of Nero as the bad guy, and as is known today, Nero was described, most famously by Tacitus, who published his writings at the end of the first century and the start of the second century, as persecuting Christians and blaming them for burning Rome. But that doesn't make any sense, for one, the term, *Christian*, was not known until the end of the first century, long after Nero had died, and if we resort to the idea for a moment that there *were* "Christians" when Nero was alive, they would have only been known as Jews. If using the current understanding regarding early Christianity, it means the religion had not fully emerged from Judaism at that point, so for Nero to specifically name "Christians" as the cause of the fire does not fit with the period. Professor of Classics, *Brent D. Shaw*, concluded in his paper 'The Myth of Neronian Persecution' that:

"The conclusions are simple. There are no sound probative reasons to accept the mirage, however appealing it might be, that Christians were attacked by the Roman state as a special group and were martyred under Nero, and no good evidence, contemporary or even later, that links them with the Great Fire in 64 C.E." (**ref** – 'The Myth of Neronian Persecution', JRS 105 (2015), pages 73-100.)

Logically, 666 and 616 cannot refer to Nero, as there is no basis for that reasoning, and if there is no basis for that reasoning, then there is no basis for 616 to refer to Emperor Caligula either. Another point to make if thinking about this in terms of the *current understanding* of Christianity, is that the changing of the number indicates that the name behind the number 666 was known, otherwise, how could it be changed? and if the name was known, why write a number, why not just write the name?

In regards to propaganda regarding previous emperors, the Pisos and their supporters would do the same to Emperor Domitian as they did with Nero. Domitian, the son of Emperor Vespasian and brother of Emperor Titus, wanted to take control of the Roman Empire, and in doing so, take Arrius' secret co-rule alongside Titus away from him, a secret co-rule that can be determined by his use of the 'Titus' name, for example where he says his second wife was with *Titus* at the siege of Jerusalem. Because we have determined the birth dates of his sons Alexander and Julius, we can tell Arrius is referring to himself in the third person, just as he does in his *Wars of the Jews*, for example where he describes being trapped in a cave with others and drawing lots on who will commit suicide. Because he does refer to himself in the third person, he is showing us that he has set a precedent (earlier) example of that, almost like a disclaimer. But the fact that this '666' number was changed in the first place and the Book of Revelation was repeatedly removed from the Bible, shows that it contained something that later leaders of the Church did not like.

In terms of co-rule, this was a practice that had already been established in the Roman Republic, which can be seen by the use of the two main consuls or government representatives having coins produced with their images displayed. For example, Diocletian made Maximian a co-emperor, Augustus had shared his office, Marcus Aurelius did the same and Emperor Carus ruled with his sons. That means this practice continued from the Roman Republic through to the Roman Empire, as there was no reason for it not to, but that co-rule would be kept secret and for a good reason. If an emperor was assassinated or as history shows, overthrown, then a replacement was immediately available and there would be no reason for panic, as the affairs of state would remain stable, and this aspect of how Rome was governed brings us back to when Arrius Piso killed Emperor Vitellius and the alias name used for him when recording that event, which was '*Marcus Antonius Primus*'.

Logically, 'Marcus Antonius Primus' should have then become emperor, based on previous examples in history, but he is not recorded as emperor, Vespasian is, so we can logically determine, again based on evidence, that Arrius must have co-ruled with Vespasian and then with Titus, because Tacitus in his *Histories*, Book 4, Chapter 2, mentions 'Marcus Antonius Primus' as exercising the '*supreme authority*', which would have only been possible if he was a co-ruler. But we know that Arrius had already inherited the names 'Titus' and 'Flavius' from Vespasian's brother, Arrius' grandfather T. *Flavius Sabinus* II, and so, again, this would explain the use of the name 'Titus' being used by Arrius to hide in history when writing as 'Josephus'. Although Arrius was friendly with both Vespasian and Titus, unfortunately for him, he does not seem to have had the same relationship with Domitian, and when Domitian became emperor, it seems he refused to co-rule with Arrius and so exiled him, along with his family, to Pannonia, and Julius writing as 'Clement of Rome' even talks about this exile. The Roman aristocracy who had supported Vespasian and Arrius was not happy with Domitian being emperor, and it appears Domitian knew this. Eventually, Domitian was murdered by his wife Domitia, his chamberlain, and the Praetorian Prefect, on September 18th 96 CE, and afterward, the elderly statesman Nerva replaced Domitian as emperor and officially recalled Arrius Piso and his family back from exile.

11. ORIGIN OF THE POPES

In the time of the Pharaohs, the succession of the throne would be given to the firstborn son and the position of High Priest to the second son. If that was not always possible, both positions could be filled by the first Son, and this act of the Pharaohs relates to the beginning of the Popes and who received that title. The Old English word '**bisceop**' is where we get our English word '**bishop**', and that word comes from the Latin word '**episcopus**'. But as with many other Latin words which are connected with religion and the church, this word was borrowed from the Greek word '**episkopos**' επισκοπος, meaning "**overseer**", and was first used for officials in government and was only later used for Church leaders. In the Bible, they used '*bishop*' and '*priest*' to identify the same thing, and then much later a bishop became the overseer of a large district. Because Arrius Piso seems to be the primary creator of the Christian religion, he would be the first 'bishop' of Rome, 'St. Peter', the '*father*' or '*rock*' of Christianity, a title which would later become known as 'pope', which means 'father', the word 'pope' coming from the Greek word 'pappas' παππας, which became the Latin word 'papa'.

Pliny The Younger appears to have been 'Paul', the travels of both are remarkably similar, although it is unfortunate that Roman Piso's list of words that match between the letters of Pliny the Younger and 'Paul' were lost or destroyed, as to see evidence like that would be extremely interesting. If the words of the epistles between Pliny and 'Paul' do indeed match, when viewed as 'every other word', because of syntax, then tests will need to be done to see if this is presented in other works of the time, to verify or rule out this being common. Arrius' Sons would also contribute to the creation of scriptures, later, once they had learned the languages and the literary techniques being used, and would also be given the title of Bishop, although it was most likely just that, a title, as the religion had likely not 'taken off' at that point. The evidence points towards these individuals as the *'root'* of today's Christianity, with the grandchildren of Arrius Piso and Pliny The Younger also later becoming the early Church Fathers and popes of the early Christian Church, just like the position of High Priest was passed down to other royals in the times of the Pharaohs. This must have been done for the control to be kept within the family, because for something as misleading as this to succeed, on a scale that Christianity would reach, it means they would have to of had tight control of it. Had there not been tight control, within the high offices of Rome, these findings would surely have been discovered earlier, would they not? What that means, is that the first 10 bishops of Rome must have come from the same tight-knit family, or oligarchy, who again used alias names, through nomenclature, to hide their identity.

As mentioned before, Arrius Piso must have chosen the name 'Peter', Petrus in Latin, and Petros in Greek, meaning *'stone'*, *'rock'*, as his alias name of the founder of the Christian religion, because he was the "father" ('pater') of the Christian religion. The vowel letters 'e' and 'a' were interchangeable, so the two names 'Peter' and 'Pater' could be seen as the same, this name then became the title of the bishop of Rome, as Papa ('Pater') of the Christian Church; 'pater' is also part of the name 'Jupiter'/*Iūpiter* (Greek Zeus), from the Proto-Italic *djous/dyeus* "day, sky" + *patēr* "father" = "sky father". The Romans used **O**, **U**, and **V**, indifferently, for the symbol of the female organ ('the door of life') and placed the **I** (pillar/phallus), i.e. the rod of *The Ark of the Covenant* represents the male phallus, with the O, creating 'IO', 'IU', or 'IV'. The Romans used sex symbols as the idea of "god-ship" or the power of God to create life, and the supreme God of the Romans was IU-pater (Jupiter/double-sexed (creator) father); O, or Om, or Ooma (Uma, connected with Siva/Shiva) was the universal sign of the female, the Yogis of India made this sign with their forefinger and thumb.

'Papa' was a "granted" or "awarded" title that was bestowed only upon those individuals who had a right to inherit its use, as was the case with other royal titles that were inherited. Not all royals could use or inherit all titles though, certain titles had to be "granted" or "bestowed" upon them by a consensus of other royals, or royal authority, such as an emperor, much like modern times.

Jesus is the *only* character we generally associate as performing 'miracles' within the New Testament, but it seems the Pisos liked the idea of giving Jesus-like qualities to others, even though Jesus is supposed to have been the unique and *only* son of God, how is it possible that so many others have the same ability to work "miracles"? 'Peter' works miracles, this can be seen in **Luke 5:18-26**, **8:41-42**, **49-56**, but if 'Peter' was also Arrius, and Arrius was also 'Jesus', then it cannot be too surprising that 'Peter' is described as also performing "miracles".

The character Peter must have been created as a way to allow Arrius to continue playing his part in the gospels after having killed off the main character, 'Jesus', and so allowing the story to continue through Peter beyond 30/33 CE. As we know, or as those who either study/research this religion, or are religious, should know, 'Peter' is given the *'keys to heaven'*, which means that Arrius was *keeping* the 'keys'. Peter is an alter-ego of Jesus in the story because he is another character being played by the *same person*, Arrius. Later, there was a succession of ordained figureheads of the religion, which were to be headed from Rome, as bishops of Rome – later, to be designated as 'Popes'.

This must have been another reason for the creation of the character 'Peter', it provided the platform to be the first of these bishops, with the successors of 'Peter' (Arrius), filling that position. But this could have only happened on paper, as there was no actual Church to be a figurehead of; and that was surely the case for most of the period between the death of Arrius Piso and the time of Emperor Constantine. Even respected New Testament authority, *Bart Ehrman*, in his book *'The Triumph of Christianity'*, questioned how this religion gained thirty million followers in three hundred years. Erhman says that Christianity probably represented seven to ten percent of the population of the Roman Empire, then, a hundred years later, 60 million inhabitants claimed allegiance to the religion, a number Erhman says is extraordinary. I feel this is not extraordinary if the power behind the Roman Empire was also the power behind this religion. Because of the later Christian texts that we have, it must be the case that the family was either instructed to or wanted to continue writing as if there were an actual Christian Church in existence, even if there was not, in essence, creating an illusion.

'Paul' is also given the ability to perform a miracle or two, and is also acknowledged as a "god", in **Acts 28:3-6** it says "*And when Paul had gathered a **bundle of sticks and laid them on the fire, there came a viper (snake) out of the heat, and fastened (itself) on his hand**. And when the barbarians (that were there) saw **the venomous beast** hang on his hand, they said among themselves, "no doubt this man is a murderer, whom though he had escaped the sea (inference is "by a miracle"), yet vengeance suffereth (him) not to live." And he (Paul) shook off the beast into the fire and felt no harm. But (when) they were expecting him (Paul) to become inflamed (poisoned) and to fall down suddenly dead (he did not), but (rather) for a long time (when) they still expected to see this (yet they) saw nothing amiss (or adverse) happen to him, they changed their opinion (of him) and said that he was a god.*" The stick turning into a snake, links to Moses' staff, "miraculously" turning into a snake and then back into a staff, and is referred to as the "rod of God", a phallic reference.

The snake is called a "venomous beast", which must be a reference to the cobra, which is indigenous to India, perhaps this statement then is reminding us of the fact that the Pharaohs used the cobra on their crowns, even though it is not indigenous to Egypt. Emperor Constantine was made into a new 'Jesus' too by his half brother Julius Constantius' son, Julius Constantius II, who the original researchers say wrote as Church Father Eusebius, which is interesting, as Julius' second wife was called **Eusebia**. According to Eusebius in 'Life of Constantine', in which Eusebius writes a favorable biography of the emperor, Constantine sees something in the sky at the Battle of the Milvian Bridge, as mentioned at the beginning of the book. Constantine looked up to the sun before the battle and saw a '*cross of light*' above it, and with it the words '*in this sign, conquer*', Constantine then commanded his troops to adorn their shields with a Christian symbol, '**chi-rho**' (XP), the first two letters of **ΧΡΙΣΤΟΣ** which is Greek for Christos. We read that Constantine was so moved by his vision of the cross he vowed to worship no other God than the one represented to him. From what we read, we are given to understand that the Bishops who apparently traveled with Constantine made him feel that he could confidently believe that Jesus was the only begotten son of God and that the cross he had seen in his vision was a symbol of Jesus' triumph over death, but of course, we have already highlighted the contradictory statements regarding this.

The Christian religion was not an overnight success, it was initially a failure. It took approximately three hundred years to begin to become what we know it as today when Constantine embarked on reviving it and making it the official religion of Rome. This religion must have only existed on paper through the family's writings, which is why these individuals were only 'bishops' of Rome on paper. Christianity would not be an actual religion with many believers until after the time of Constantine I, around the year 330 CE, and it was then that an infrastructure of churches and bishops was created, which was needed for it to grow and build believers and followers. At the start, Arrius and his family thought they would only need to convert the old altars in the Roman Empire and set up a bishop at each of the first seven 'Churches', for the first stages of their religion to be successful. But there was a big problem, at that point, the New Testament was yet to be completed and so those early potential believers would have been rightly skeptical of the history of the religion, as no early Church history had been written for Arrius, and it appears, Pliny, to base their claims upon. With no early history fully completed, it would have appeared to have come out of nowhere, which was a major issue, and the Jewish population, who consisted at that time of only the Pharisees and the Scribes, the Scribes who were mentioned in the New Testament, were a Jewish sect who was on the same side as the Pharisees. The Pharisees were still around and they knew the truth about Christianity's origins and they informed some of the potential early believers about the actual history of this religion, which meant that for this belief system to be absorbed, Arrius and Pliny The Younger would need to address these critical issues.

It appears the religion may have been tested upon uneducated commoners near where they lived, in Herculaneum and Pompeii, at a much earlier date by Arrius Piso because he and his family had property and land there. The *Sator Square* or *Rotas Square*, which is a 'word square' that contains a five-word Latin palindrome, which is a word, phrase, or sentence which reads the same backward as well as forwards, for example, '*nurses run*' or '*Madam I'm Adam*', was discovered in the ruins of Pompeii, which is only 15 kilometers away from Herculaneum. Herculaneum was an ancient city with a population of around 4,000–5,000 people. It was an elegant and fashionable town on the Bay of Naples and played host to top families of Rome during the hot Italian summers. *Lucius Calpurnius Piso Caesoninus*, consul in 58 BCE, and father-in-law of Julius Ceasar had built a seaside villa of immense scale, today it is known as the '*Villa of the Papyri*'. New archaeological studies suggest the villa should be dated to the 40s or even 30s BCE, a period of great instability, and repeated civil wars that saw Julius Caesar murdered, and his heir Octavian (Emperor Augustus) eventually achieve dominance. That means Piso's son, often known as Piso the Pontifex, comes into play, who was a major supporter of the new regime.

The greatest find from this villa is its library of more than 1,000 volumes of papyrus scrolls, which were carbonized by the heat of the volcanic eruption of Mount Vesuvius in 79 CE. The vast majority of texts found are works of Epicurean Greek philosophy, with Piso being a patron and friend of Philodemus, the poet and scholar. (**ref** – Cicero, *In Pisonem*, pages 68-72, whilst attacking Piso, speaks of Piso's Greek friend and personal philosopher; Jane I. M. Tait, in '*Philodemus' influence on the Latin poets*', 1941, follows *Asconius*' (Roman historian) identification of the unnamed poet as Philodemus the Epicurean – **ref** – Asconius, '*Commentaries on Speeches by Cicero*', R.G. Lewis, page 16.)

By 73-75 CE the only gospels that were finished were 'Mark' and 'Matthew', but with the eruption of Mount Vesuvius in 79 CE, those cities of Herculaneum and Pompeii were buried. Because of this, Arrius and Pliny would have undoubtedly had to re-start the task of promoting their religion, but they would also have to wait until sometime after the reign of Domitian, as in around 93 CE, he had banished the Piso family from Rome, except for Pliny The Younger, who was Arrius Piso's much younger foster brother, and this was possibly done to separate the two. Domitian was hated by the aristocracy, and his major opponents included excessively doctrine-devoted senators, who were friends of Tacitus and Pliny the Younger. Arrius, who was still serving in the military, was exiled by Domitian to Pannonia, which meant he was again far away from Rome, and the historical documents that reveal this information include the writings of 'Flavius Josephus', Tacitus, Pliny The Younger, and Suetonius.

The word square is arranged like this –

SATOR

AREPO

TENET

OPERA

ROTAS

By repositioning the letters around the '**N**' in the center, which is a 'noun' meaning *fish* in Aramaic, and became an acrostic of the declaration of faith "*Jesus Christ the Savior and the son of God*", a Greek cross can be made which then reads as 'Pater Noster', which means "*Our Father*" in Latin. The remaining letters '**A**' and '**O**' can represent '**Alpha** and **Omega**' or as examined earlier, '**A**(rrius) and (**Kal**(purinius) (Pis)**O**'.

It was going to take more than just converting alters in order for Christianity to progress. Because when Arrius and Pliny, and most likely, their royal slave scribes were going around amongst the people, they had to convince them that they were true 'prophets' and that this religion and its scripture had existed long before their time. Their royal power, in this case, would not help, as they were trying to convince people that these accounts were from illiterate people, and certainly not royalty. So before Constantine I, and even during his time, the Christian Church really did only exist as a story, that is why during the time between Arrius and Constantine, the members of the Piso family were busy writing as the other 'Church Fathers' in order to make it appear that Christianity really had existed for many years, that way they would have a basis for it when an opportunity to revive it came along. One way that they made the scriptures and story believable, was to age the paper by placing the books into the granary for days or perhaps weeks, which is mentioned by *Dio Chrysostom* –

"The reason for this is that I do not much care for the writers of Tragedy nor try to emulate them, for I know that it is a disgrace to mention people of the present day in a tragedy, but that it is some ancient event which I should have touched upon and one not very credible either. Yet men of former times certainly were not ashamed to name people of their own day whether in speaking or in writing, but those of the present day strive to name the ancients on any pretext. I shall tell you what wisdom they show in doing this, and don't you declare everything I say is nonsense, perhaps, however, it is anything but nonsense, for surely you have noticed what some of our booksellers do? **Because they, knowing that old books are in demand since better written and on better paper, bury the worst specimens of our day in grain in order that they may take on the same color as the old ones, and after ruining the books into the bargain they sell them as old".**

(**ref** – *Discourses by Dio Chrysostom*, Loeb Classical Library, 21st Discourse, Vol II, p.283)

Dio Chrysostom, who we are told was a Greek orator and philosopher, seems to be yet another alias name of Arrius Piso, which can be logically suggested by hints left about 'Dio Chrysostom'. No exact dates of birth or death are given for 'Dio', but he is said to have been born in Prusa, Bithynia, an ancient town situated at the northern foot of Mt. Olympus. Arria the Younger and 'Fannia' were banished from Rome by Domitian, but because we see no information regarding another exile for Arrius under his alias names during this time, a little investigation needs to take place. It could be thought that he must still be in Rome, but when we consider that Arrius may be '*Dio Chrysostom*', another 'puzzle piece' falls into place. 'Dio Chrysostom' was banished from Rome by Domitian in 82 CE to Prusa, Bithynia, and returned to Rome *after* Domitian was killed, and 'Dio' is recorded as being a close '*friend*' with Emperor Trajan, this is because Arrius was Trajan's father in law. What should be noted as well, is the fact that 'Dio' means 'God' and '*Chrys*-(t)ostom' is a variation of the word 'Christ', but 'Chrysostom' means 'golden-mouthed', coming from 'Chrysos' meaning 'gold', which relates to 'Flavius Josephus', some scholars have even argued that Josephus was particularly influenced by Dio Chrysostom. The writings of 'Dio' also parallelled the 'teachings' and verses of the New Testament, just as Seneca's writings did earlier, and Arrius as 'Dio' making mention of certain books being made to look older would act as another very subtle clue as to what they were doing. Even Pliny the Younger talks about visiting him in Prusa, where he had apartments, in a letter to Trajan, Pliny, *Letter* 10.81.

In regards to the beginning phases of Christianity, the very early churches were not successful, as no one was attending them because of no basis for the religion, so sex was used to try and lure people in. In the Gospels, after the first ones were written, they started to write what can be only be described as indecent sexual material, which in that time, from a Latin reader's perspective, was just barely disguised, because of the meanings behind the words. The 'bishops' would get the 'Church' attendees sexually excited and would then direct them to small '*sex rooms*' that were built into those early 'Churches', where they would choose a "helper". As payment, they were asked for a tithe or donation, a tithe being formerly taken as a tax for the support of the Church and clergy. This was simply a continuation of a practice that was already happening in Rome with '*vestal virgins*', but these were not "virgins" at all, they were Temple prostitutes who were pretending to be inexperienced because that is what a majority of their 'clientele' preferred. This was normal practice for temples since the Sumerians, but once the people of the towns, where these 'Christian' churches were located, realized what was going on, they forcibly closed them down. The *Encyclopedia Biblica*, page 837, states:

"*The offer of the Body, which was in honor of the deity and prevailed in the Northern Semitic religions, where a special class of temple harlots was maintained and a commerce with them was a religious act*".

The Christian or "New" Churches were simply brothels, like the "*high places*" of the Old Testament, where all prostitutes had their fees, as is shown in the story of Tamar and Judah, where she, acting as the professional prostitute says, "*What wilt though give me that thou mayest come in unto me.*" Emperor Titus is reported to have left valuable gifts for the benefit of the maidens, whose "converse" he had enjoyed, and for the temple treasury when he visited Paphos on his way to subjugate Jerusalem.

Paul's (Pliny's) travels to these places, which were known for having great Roman brothels and for vice or sex trade, for example, the mentioning of **Antioch**, **Lystra**, **Salamis**, **Paphos**, **Perga**, **Pisidia**, **Pamphylia**, **Iconium**, **Athens**, and **Corinth**, served as a sort of advertisement for these Churches/brothels, because that's how money for the Church was first made, by taking a cut of the brothels profits. These little rooms of around eight feet by five feet surrounded the temple and were called '*selaoth*' or '*lesakoth*'. 'Selaoth' means "chambers for men and women" or "double-sex chambers", and 'Lesakoth' means "for the purpose of being joined". One place though called **Caesarea Philippi**, would have been considered the equivalent of Las Vegas (Sin City) in first-century Israel, but worse, and was named in 2 CE by *Herod Philip*, son of Herod the Great and his fifth wife, Cleopatra of Jerusalem, to honor Caesar Augustus. It was located in the Golan Heights region of Israel and was established by Ptolemaic Greeks as a Hellenistic city, and was a specific place where the worshipping of the God **Pan** took place. Next to the cave mouth, in the open-air Pan Shrine, there was a large niche in which a statue of Pan (a half-goat, half-human creature) stood, with a large erect phallus.

This God was worshipped for its fertility properties and surrounding him in the wall were many smaller niches in which were statues of his attending nymphs. Regarding 'Paul', his travels, and the God Pan being depicted with an erect Phallus, this might be a good time to mention that the name '**Paul**' comes from the word 'phallism', a word created from Greek and Latin from the Hindu word 'Pala' or *'Phala'*, which becomes in other countries *Pal, Pel, Pil, Phil, Poll,* **Paul**, *Pul, Phallus,* and *Phulus.* These words represent the male organ of reproduction and in Greece 'pala' became 'phallos' and in Latin, it became 'phallus', which created the adjective 'phallic', used to describe all religious worship, faiths, and emblems that referred to the reproductive organs that represented creative power, the creating of life – (see www.henryhdavis.com for a detailed examination regarding this.) So in ancient times, the use of that power, even by public prostitutes, was considered a sacred act. The Encyclopedia Biblica, a concise but detailed work of church criticism, produced by the Professors of Oxford, around 1910, exposed religion as a fraud, and soon after it was published, Christians and other religious individuals attempted to destroy every copy they could find. As mentioned before, 'Paul' is only known to us from the Acts and the Epistles, and the Encyclopedia Biblica says:

Column 3627 –

"The principal Epistles cannot be the work of Paul," and A. D. Loman, of Amsterdam, says, *"upholds the entirely symbolical character of the whole Gospel history."*

Column 3624 –

"We cannot regard the 'Acts' as a true and credible first-hand

narrative of what had actually occurred. The Book bears in part a legendary historical and, in part, an edifying and apologetic character."

Column 3625 —

With respect to the Pauline Epistles in the New Testament, *"there are none of them by Paul."*

"Neither fourteen, nor thirteen, nor nine or ten, nor seven or eight, nor yet even the four so long universally regarded as unassailable. They are all, without distinction, pseudepigrapha."

Column 3630 —

"The conclusions of criticism on our knowledge of the life and activity of Paul are of a purely negative character."

Column 3630 —

"Thus all the representations formerly current regarding the life and work of Paul must be set aside. These representations are very many and various and discrepant in character; far from showing any resemblance to one another, they exhibit the most inconsistent proportions and features. But, however different they were, they all of them have disappeared; they rested upon a foundation, not of solid rock, but of shifting sand. So, too, the 'ideas,' the 'theology,' the 'system' of Paul have irrevocably passed away, the right foundation being wanting. We possess no Epistle of Paul."

Column 4145 —

"The Roman Church was not founded by Peter or Paul."

In essence, the *Encyclopedia Biblica* concludes that: "*it is always better, safer, and more profitable to know that one does not know than to go on building on a basis that is imaginary.*" – *Encyclopedia Biblica* contributor T.H. Huxley's position, who was an English biologist and anthropologist specializing in comparative anatomy and is known for his public support of Charles Darwin's theory of evolution. The Oxford professors concluded that Paul, as a writer, disappears and that not one point of his history or actions has been proven.

Continuing with the niches in Caesarea Philippi, worshippers of Pan would congregate in front of them and join in bizarre sexual rituals, including sexual intercourse with goats, which were worshipped for their relationship to Pan. This reputation meant that Orthodox rabbis in the first century criticized this place, and the Jewish people were taught never to visit there. Caesarea Philippi sits at the foot of Mount Hermon and butts up against a large cliff, referred to as the '*Rock of the Gods*', because of the many shrines built against it. These are shrines to Caesar, Pan, and another god, possibly the fertility goddess Nemesis, and they were all built up against this cliff. In the center of the cliff is a huge cave from which a stream flowed, which after 19th-century earthquakes, began flowing out from the rock beneath the mouth of the cave. This cave was called the "*Gates of Hades*" because it was believed that Baal, who is associated with **Balaam**, would enter and leave the underworld through places where the water came out of it. In **Mark 8:27-30**, it says that Jesus and his disciples went on to the villages around Caesarea Philippi, which would mean that 'Jesus' took his disciples more than 32 miles to this location from Bethsaida, which is the only recorded trip for him to this region or anywhere similar.

We also read that Jesus said, "*Who do people say the Son of Man is?*" *And they answered,* "*Some say 'John the Baptist'* (translated Yohanan ben Zakkai), *others say Elijah, and others say you are one of the prophets*". *And Jesus answers* "*What about you? Who do you say I am?*" *Peter answered* "*You are the Christ*", (in **Matthew 16:13-17** it reads "*Christ, the Son of God the living*"), then Jesus ordered them "*Do not tell anyone about me.*" Now in this location in the Gospels, we read in **Matthew 16:18** 'Jesus' making a statement, he says "*Blessed are you, Simon Bar (son) of Jonah, for this was not revealed to you by man, but by my Father in heaven.* **And I tell you that you are Peter** (pater/father), **and on this rock** (which can also be 'peter') **I will build my church, and the gates of Hades will not overcome it.**" This is simply Arrius "talking" to himself in the story.

In **Mark 8:34-38** 'Jesus' gives a speech in this location, in the Gospel, it says: And having called to (him) the crowd and his disciples, he said to them, "*Whoever wants to come with me, let him deny himself, and let him take up the cross, and let him follow me. For whoever loses his life on account of me and of the glad tidings (Gospels), he shall save it. For what shall it profit a man if he gains the world whole and loses his soul? For whoever may have been ashamed of me and my words in this generation, the adulterous and sinful, (then) also the Son of Man will be ashamed of him when he shall come in the glory of his Father, with the angels (of) the holy*". And he said to them "*Verily I say to you, that there are some of those here standing, who shall not* *taste of death, till they have seen the kingdom of God come with power."* This is saying whoever doesn't follow the new religion will lose their life and soul, and if they don't accept Arrius then they will die from Rome's power.

In **Acts 19:1**, we read about 'Paul' traveling to Ephesus, this is an individual who was claimed to be a notorious Jew, but appears to be someone that no one had ever heard of. He is an individual who managed to convince many people to give up their whole faith in the Jewish texts to follow the writings and stories of a man whose existence cannot be verified. 'Paul' was said to have traveled through Rome, Greece, etc., preaching and debating, even being arrested, and converting people, it would, therefore, be logical to assume that his activities would have made an impression.

But in **Acts 19:1** 'Paul' travels to Ephesus (present-day Turkey), which is where the Temple of Artemis was located, also known as the Temple of Diana, which was a Greek temple dedicated to Artemis. The original structure was completed around 550 BCE and was considered one of the Seven Wonders of the Ancient World, and it features prominently in 'Paul's' missionary journeys. The religious ceremonies at this Temple included athletic, dramatic, and musical contests, and based on a statement that has been found on inscriptions excavated there, Ephesus was proud of the position as "temple-keeper" of Artemis (**Acts 19:35**). The temple treasury acted as a bank in which deposits were made by cities, kings, and private persons and the Greek Ionians brought expensive gifts to the priests. Sensual orgies would also take place in the worship of Artemis, in which great crowds attended and large numbers of female temple slaves or "priestesses", who came as virgins (or possibly acted as 'virgins'), were dedicated to service in the temple, and this dedication may have included ritual or cultic prostitution. When 'Paul' arrived in Ephesus, he asked some disciples if they had received the 'Holy Spirit' (Numa) when they became believers, these disciples said they hadn't heard that there even was a 'Holy Spirit'. 'Paul' asks what kind of Baptism they had received and they replied "*The baptism of John*". Now **Acts 19:7-8** indicates there were 12 men that 'Paul' was trying to persuade to believe in the 'kingdom of God', and so these were not "disciples" of 'Christ' but were self-identified disciples of '*John the Baptist*', who we know was a created name to ridicule **Yochanan Ben Zakkai**, as examined earlier.

So here 'Paul', or rather Pliny The Younger, and most likely, his slave scribes, for two or perhaps more years, are trying to convince the people in Ephesus to convert to the new religion of Christianity. And this is presented in other examples of the places with which 'Paul' visited, where Pliny The Younger as 'Paul' is traveling around the Roman Empire, beginning in approximately 98 CE, and converting certain alters or small Temples and places of worship used for the old Roman gods and goddesses, and turning them into the first Christian churches, but as mentioned above, this alone did not work. Since the Christian stories within the gospels were back-dated to an earlier time, backdating the bishops of Rome to an earlier time would also have been necessary, for the perception of authenticity, that is until enough time had passed that the 'bishops' could be represented within their own time, such as Emperor Antoninus Pius. But when Constantine began the process of making Roman Catholicism/Universalism the state religion, in around 304 CE, it was brutal, temples were destroyed and those people that would not convert were killed. It was indeed a long process that took around 70 years, which unsurprisingly, quite a few Caesars were engaged in. Constantine now appears to have this great legacy for bringing this universal religion into European culture, as the Roman state religion, because it essentially took away the culture of pagan god worshipping.

The fact is that Constantine gave official orders which began the feudal system, which in reality was a slave system. The word *'serf'* is just a synonym for slave, and when researching the hierarchy structure of this system, we find the Pope/Emperor at the top, then below that, you have the Cardinals and the religious and military individuals. But as you get to the very bottom you see the serf (slave) who is an animal, sometimes even a sheep. However, these official orders, which began the transition of Christianity being made into the state religion, are separated from the orders that created the feudal system, which is odd, because they are part of the same process. In reality, Constantine effectively created a feudal system that replaced an existing system that was more democratic. We can see this is true when researching the *Coloni*, which were a whole class of citizens who developed ownership rights by essentially cultivating the wildland.

They would colonize the land, which is where the expression 'colonization' comes from, and they would then turn the wildland into farming land and they could own the product produced from that land. Constantine changed this and began to issue official orders which stated that you couldn't own the land or the product of that land, and if the magistrate decided they needed more population in some other area, then your children could be sold. As far as occupations were concerned, it had to be the same occupation as your father, and you couldn't change your occupation, or ever leave the land. So this was the beginning of the feudal system and the Roman Catholic Church is an element of that feudal system, but when we stop to think, it is obvious how the two worked together. The serf (slave) was given a religious context for slavery, whereby they were told that the representative of 'Jesus Christ' was telling him to accept his hardship. They were told that there was going to be a *"worker's paradise"* for the individual once he dies, but in the meantime do what the magistrates tell you to do and everything will be fine. To Constantine, Christianity was simply a way to control how the slaves thought, so they would think they were doing the work of their God as opposed to following the commands of the emperor. That is why we read of the apparent *"conversion to Christianity"* of Constantine, as he would have needed to give a non-political reason for his conversion, and what is better than a *"divine sighting"* story, that can be neither debunked or proven. It is clear this was just a development of the process of getting rid of rebellion, and as emperor, Constantine would have been well aware of the origins of the Christian religion, because he was related to Arrius Piso, through Emperor Vespasian.

Emperor Constantine's Descent From Emperor Vespasian –

Emperor Vespasian

(born 9 CE, died 79 CE, ruled from 69-79 CE)

Married –**Flavia Domitilla I** (previously married to Emp. Vitellius)

|

Emperor Titus (born 41 CE, died 81 CE, ruled from 79-81 CE)

Married – **Arrecina Tertilla** & **Marcia Furnilla**

|

Julia Flavia Titia (died 91 CE) (Mother was Marcia Furnilla)

Married – **T.Flavius Sabinus IV** (son of T.Flavius Sabinus III)

|

L.Vibius Sabinus

Married – **Matidia I**

|

Matidia II

Married – **Q. Laelius**

|

Laelia The Elder

Married – **Fulvius Pius** (aka Flavius Ulpius Pius, Antoninus Pius, died 161 CE)

|

ORIGIN OF THE POPES | 297

Fulvia Pia (aka Flavia Ulpius Pi(s)a)

Married – **Publius Septimius Geta**

|

Emperor Septimius Severus (born 146 CE, died 211 CE, ruled 193-211 CE)

Married – Paccia Marciana & Julia Domna (died 211 CE)

|

Bassina (aka Septimia Severa Bassina)

Married – **Claudius Apellinus** (Apolli(a)nus)

|

Claudia Apellina

Married – **Flavius Numerius** (Greek Prince)

|

Flavius Crispus (brother of Emperor Claudius Albinus, ruled 195-197, died 197 CE)

Married – **Aurelia** (descendant of Emperor Marcus Aurelius, ruled 161-180 CE)

|

Flavia Claudia Aurelia Crispa

Married – **Eutropius** (son of Gordiana, sister of Emperor Gordian III, ruled 238-244 CE)

|

Emperor (Julius) **Constantius Chlorus** (ruled 305-306 CE)

Married – **Helena Britannia** & **Theodora**

|

Emperor Constantine I

(half brother of Julius Constantius I, aka Eusebius, died 337 CE)

Married – Minervina (303-307 CE) & Fausta (307-326 CE)

Emperor (Julius) **Constantius Chlorus** (father of *Emperor Constantine* & of *Julius Constantius* I), ruled from 305-307 CE, and he was co-emperor with **Galerius**. Emperor **Constantine** was the son of Emperor *Constantius Chlorus* & *Helena* and ruled from 307-337 CE. Other important relatives include **Tacitus**, **Emperor Trajan**, **Pliny The Younger** (as has been examined), and **Suetonius** (Antoninus Pius). But with the knowledge that these individuals are related to Arrius Piso, this information can shed new light on another argument for Christianity existing before and during Nero's reign. These are the mentions of 'Chrestiani', whose leader is 'Christus'/'Chrestus' by Tacitus, who was related to Arrius, and, as we have learned, even uses his alias names when describing events in history. If Tacitus was related to Arrius and used his various alias names within his literature, then the mention of 'Chrestiani' and 'Christus' and the persecution of Christians by Nero, can logically be seen as a pretense, making something that is not the case appear true, and an example of what can be called propaganda against an emperor that angered the aristocracy of Rome, which contributed to his assassination.

These mentions of persecution come from members of the aristocracy during the Flavian dynasty and they appear *after* Nero's death, by supporters of the Pisos, and the mentions of the 'Chrestiani' act as a way to "historicize" the Christian movement. If we go with the currently understood timespan of growth for this religion, Christians would not have been separated from Judaism during the reign of Emperor Nero. The term '*Christian*' at the beginning of the first century would not have been recognized, as one of the world's most prominent biblical scholars, Candida Moss, who advises exercising caution when dealing with Tacitus, argues in her book *The Myth of Persecution* (2013), the term, Christian, was not known until long after Nero's death. For Nero to specifically name Christians as the cause of the fire does not fit with the period; although previously some have said that argument is hard to sustain given clear references to that term in both pagan and Christian sources (*Suetonius, Tertullian*), and the strong early Christian tradition that depicted Nero as the pagan persecutor.

Arrius' son Julius Piso (Severus/Servianus) had a daughter called *Julia* who married Tacitus' son *Pedanius Fuscus*, which means Arrius was related to Tacitus through that marriage. Cornelius Tacitus, the Roman historian, was inserted into the New Testament as the Roman centurion who was devout and feared God, in Acts, chapter 10 and it was most likely Justus who inserted his name, as Tacitus responded by dedicating his *'Dialogues on Oratory'* (oratory being a skill in public speaking) to *"dear Fabius Justus"*, shortly after the year 100 CE. Cornelius Tacitus also mentioned *'Christ'* and said that he had *'founded the Christians and had been crucified by Pontius Pilate'*; he also detailed how Nero had caused Christians to be torn by dogs and burned on crosses (for more information, reference *'Discovering Tacitus as Neratius Priscus'*, *'Roman Piso'*, Academia.edu, with supporting information from the work of *Sir Ronald Syme*.) *Suetonius*, as touched upon earlier, appears to have been a 'pen name' of Emperor Antoninus Pius, a grandson of Arrius Piso, through his daughter Claudia Phoebe, as shown below:

Arrius Calpurnius Piso

(Arrius Antoninus, among other names, consul in 69 and again in 97 CE)

Arrius had several wives, one of which was **Boionia Procilla**)

|

Claudia Phoebe (Pompiea Plotina, Arria Fadilla), was born approx. 70 CE, and died 129 CE.

Married her first husband 'Rufus', aka **T.Aurelius Fulvus**, cos. ord. 89 CE.

Married her second husband **Emperor Trajan** (Claudia Phoebe/Pompiea Plotina was Trajan's second wife)

I

Emperor Antoninus Pius

(Suetonius), born 86 CE, ruled from 138 until he died in 161 CE.

Married **Annia Galeria Faustina I**

'Suetonius', the author, whose full name is given as *Gaius Suetonius Tranquillus*, hints at Julius talking about Arrius in the Book of Revelation when using the word *'beast'*, in his work Suetonius describes this "beast" by saying the following – *"This charger (horse) of his, an extraordinary animal with feet that looked almost* **human – each of its hoofs was cloven in five parts, resembling human toes** *– had been foaled on his private estate.* **When the soothsayers pronounced that its master would one day rule the world***, Caesar carefully reared, and was the first to ride the* **beast***..."* (**ref** – 'The Twelve Caesars', Julius Caesar) Now this 'beast' is a horse and as we have learned, 'ippos' means horse, and 'ippos' can be seen as 'Piso'. Suetonius also describes the horse as having almost human-like feet, as its hooves were cloven in five parts.

Research has shown that horses did once have five 'toes', however, evolution has meant that although horses are capable of developing five 'toes', those extra toes now disappear before a horse is born. That means that Julius Caesar's horse would not have had hooves that resemble human toes, and it means that Suetonius is subtly talking about a *'human beast'*, and I should also note that **four** hooves cloven in **five** parts equals **twenty**, and the 20th number of the Greek alphabet was the letter K, for Kalpournios. Suetonius' father's name is given as Suetonius

Laetus, who was a tribune of the people, who served with the Thirteenth legion in a military campaign under Otho. (**ref** – Suetonius, 'The Twelve Caesars', Otho)

When researching further, however, certain information supports what we already know, and we can then decipher that Suetonius must have been Antoninus Pius. For one, the name 'Suetonius' is a clue, because if we break the name up we can see it linking to his grandfather, but also incorporating what Suetonius wanted to be famous for, his sayings, one of which was:

"Nothing is more unpredictable than the mob, nothing more obscure than public opinion, nothing more deceptive than the whole political system." But the saying which links the name Suetonius with Arrius' name was *'birds of a feather, flock together...'*

He gave info about bird tongues being a favorite food of at least one certain emperor, Vitellius. (**ref** – Suetonius, *Life of Vitellius*, chapter 13) Many hundreds or thousands of birds had to be caught to supply that many tongues, meaning they would use suet as bait, for which they could then be trapped. '**Suet**', pronounced 'sue-it', was a bird food made of rendered fat and seed, and in Greek, the word '**Lipos**' has the same meaning as 'suet', this word rearranged produces '**Piso**'. The other half of the 'Suetonius' name is '**Onius**', which again with vowel switching and N changed to R gives us '**Anius**/**Arius**. Antoninus Pius' father must have been Rufus Corelius and mother, Claudia Phoebe (Pompeia Plotina), her second husband being Emperor Trajan, and Pius' half-brother was Arrian, who wrote histories as Arrian and Appian, as well as other works; I would like to mention here that Antoninus Pius credited his twenty-year reign to the influence of the philosopher, '*Epictetus*', who is described as being '*lame*' and '*very poor*' and when Domitian became emperor and banished all the philosophers from Rome, 'Epictetus' left, and went to live in Nicopolis, a city on the coast of Greece (near Pannonia) (Aulus Gellius, Attic Nights, XV. 11.) He was apparently famed *far and wide*. Emperor Hadrian went to visit him (Historia Augusta, *Hadrian*), and 'Epictetus' words were recorded for future generations by a pupil named **Arrian**, in eight books of the discourses of Epictetus, only four of which remain, as well as some fragments; The name 'Epictetus' is interesting, as '**epic**' comes from the ancient Greek term 'epos,' meaning 'story, **word**, poem', and 'Tetus' can be 'Titus', so it can be read as '*the word Titus*'.

We learn from 'Suetonius' that he was very close to Emperor Hadrian, even at one point describing how he presented a statuette he owned of Augustus to Hadrian, presumably passed down from his family. With this gesture 'Suetonius' either genuinely admires Hadrian, or he was attempting to get on Hadrian's good side; maybe to increase the chances of being chosen as Hadrian's successor? Because we have already learned that Hadrian changed his mind regarding Julius becoming emperor and choosing Antoninus Pius to succeed him instead, and given the time frame when 'Suetonius' wrote his work and Antoninus became emperor, the correlation becomes apparent. Throughout his work, 'Suetonius' makes sure to describe the Caesars as being larger than life and greatly superior to the average man, even giving us the phrase; "Hail Caesar! We (common men) *who are about to die, salute you!*" This phrase presents the death of the common man, in that situation, as simply to entertain the emperor. (**ref** – Suetonius, *The Twelve Caesars, The Life of Claudius*, pg. 195, verse 21)

He also talks about Cleopatra as *"the most famous"* of Julius Caesar's mistresses and being so wonderful as the Queen of Egypt, but when tracing Antoninus' ancestry back through his mother, that particular Cleopatra is revealed as his ancestor, through Mark Anthony. Suetonius' (Antoninus Pius') half-brother, Arrian, was the son of Emperor Trajan, through Trajan's wife, *Ulpia*, before his marriage to Claudia Phoebe; 'Roman Piso' has stated that Trajan and Pliny the Younger shared a mutual ancestry, through a noblewoman called *Sextilia Vistilia* (Sr.), born around 32 BCE, who was a common, or mutual ancestor of many illustrious Roman families. One of her husbands was *Pomponius Secundus*, great-grandfather of Pliny the Younger, through Pliny the Elder's sister, Plina Secunda. Trajan's mutual ancestry to Pliny is through another husband of Vistilia called *Domitius Corbulo* (Sr.); the work by Sir Ronald Syme, a paper titled '*Domitius Corbulo*' (*Journal of Roman Studies*, 1970-71) regarding this important individual is very informative.

Domitius Corbulo is a very important figure in the first century CE for a number of reasons, including his family and relatives. He was put to death under Nero, and the above paper by Sir Ronald gives key details connecting the relationship between the emperor Trajan and Pliny The Younger, Sir Ronald even says "*Corbulo's early career excited curiosity. And, later, the effort is not vain to look for links between Corbulo and certain persons, families, or groups destroyed by Nero in 65 and 66, in the aftermath of the Pisonian conspiracy.*" Undoubtedly Pliny the Younger and Emperor Trajan knew they were related, that connection was just not presented in any forthright way, they even pretended otherwise, which is another reason to be suspicious. Trajan was a son of *Domitia Longina*, daughter of Domitius Corbulo (Jr.), by her husband before marrying Emperor Domitian, so Trajan was Domitian's step-son. A final point to make is that 'Suetonius' seems to know the Caesar family tree intimately, which seems odd in the sense that they would have trusted that information to an apparent outsider, judging by the family connections the aristocracy appears to have hidden. He also states that the 'Aesar' portion of the name 'Caesar' in Etruscan means "God", and that the 'C' was the Roman 100. (**ref** – Suetonius, *The Twelve Caesars*, *The Life of Augustus*, pg. 104, verse 97)

What we have then are five of the early Roman authors who mention *'Jesus'*, *'Christ'* and/or *'Christians'*, who are all related to each other. 'Flavius Josephus' (Arrius) mentions *'Jesus the 'Christ'* and was related to Pliny The Younger, mainly as his stepbrother, through Pliny's step-father Lucius Piso marrying Arria The Younger after Gaius Piso is killed. We then have Arrius' granddaughter who married Tacitus' son Pedanius Fuscus, as mentioned above, and Antoninus Pius (Suetonius) who was the grandson of Arrius, who mentions *'Chrestus'* in relation to Nero; Arrius also uses the name *'Cresus'* in *Against Apion*, a name not seen anywhere else. Another telling clue that 'Suetonius' was Antoninus Pius and a member of royalty, is not only the fact that many of his works were published, but also from the fact he mentions Nero's notebooks and loose pages coming into his possession, but he doesn't say exactly how he got them.

We have been told that he had access to the state archives and private letters of previous emperors, but by Suetonius being a royal and becoming Caesar under the name Antoninus Pius, that would naturally grant him the privileges that came with that position. (**ref** – Suetonius, *The Twelve Caesars*, *The Life of Nero*, pg. 239, verse 52). It is also worth mentioning that the name 'Antoninus Pius' can be created from '*Anton*', short for 'Antony' (Mark Antony, ancestor of the Pisos), and '*Ninus*', which means 'baby boy' (relating to Arrius/Jesus) and the '*Pius*' part can be 'Piso', because '*Pius*' is the masculine form of '*Pia*', which can be the feminine form of '*Piso*'. So here we have relatives of Arrius going down through to Emperor Constantine, who all have connections with the Christian religion and using it to their advantage. Plus, of course, we have Julius Constantius I, who along with his half-brother, Emperor Constantine, was responsible for reviving and promoting Christianity.

12. CONCLUSION

"In all ages, whatever the form and name of government, be it monarchy, republic, or democracy,

an oligarchy lurks behind the facade; and Roman history, Republican or Imperial, is the history of the governing class."

- Sir Ronald Syme, *The Roman Revolution*, 1939

The difficulty of the process of unraveling all the information presented in this book cannot be overstated. The process is not simply one of reading a few books and finding the answers, but, in this case, one of reading, not just the many classical works available, but also the earliest primary manuscripts available, and only finding answers when a little piece of information is given in one book that connects to another little piece of information given in a much earlier book. The genealogies are an example of that, the family links are given, just in a scattered and misleading way, meaning the authors must have been working in concert with one another, to know who was giving away which bits of information. Another thing I found strange was the way in which the ancient authors wrote, in an unclear way, meaning their books would address many important people, but would not include essential information, now, it seems, they wrote that way on purpose. It is clear that to get to the truth behind the initial creation and eventual spread of the Christian religion, the connection regarding the power struggle taking place between the royal families in Rome, the family connections between the Pisos, Flavians, and the Herodians, and the religious and political unrest happening in Judea needs to be made.

The relationship between the Julian Caesars and the Calpurnius Piso family was tense, and it had been that way before 30 BCE and remained as such until 68 CE. The Julians and the Pisos had the same royal ancestry, one piece of evidence of that is through the wife of L. *Calpurnius Piso Frugi*, consul in 133 BCE, and the mother of Julius Caesar, *Aurelia Cotta*, born in 120 BCE, as both women were members of the gens *Rutilia*. The Pisos had intermarried, making them another 'branch' of the Caesars, which is seen by the Pisos use of the name '*Caesoninus*', which means '*The little Caesars*'. They had married into various royal houses, such as the *Balbi family*, the *Julii family*, and the *Marcii (Marcia) family*, and proof of that is reflected in some of the names they used; including some of their alias names, as we have seen, Arrius Piso had the 'Marcus' name, which was passed on to him through his direct descent from Mark Anthony, as demonstrated earlier on his mother's side.

Julius Caesar married a lady called Calpurnia, in an attempt to bring the two families together, but it did not work, and between that time and the time of Emperor Nero, many Pisos were killed by the Julians and the Piso Frugi side of the Piso family attempted to kill several Julians. Meanwhile, in Judea, there was a continuing war happening between the Jewish sects, which led to the Roman aristocracy being asked by the Herodian leadership to help put a stop to the rebellions. Many members of Roman royalty and the aristocracy were in favor of a new religion, however, Emperor Nero was not, and so he became the enemy. Seneca's philosophic (Stoic) literature would become the ideological ideas used in Christianity, but at that point, Lucius Piso had written no public literature, so there was no connection for Nero to use to execute him. The Pisos must have felt that they had as much of a right to the throne of Rome as the Julians, and they wanted it, and evidence for that is in Emperor Galba's (*Lucius Vitellius Salvus II*) choosing his son-in-law, *Lucius Calpurnius Piso Frugi Licinianus*, who had no political office in Rome, to be his successor. Galba's reasoning, according to Tacitus (Tacitus, *Histories*, Book 1, Chapter 13), was that *Otho*, Galba's son, was too similar to Nero, whom Otho had been close with, and Galba's choice was based on Piso's aristocratic background and blameless record, hardly a sufficient qualification for ruling the Empire. Lucius Calpurnius Piso Frugi Licinianus was only blameless as he had been exiled by Nero, so the opportunity to even make a mistake had not been available. Galba's alliance was with the Pisos, so Otho, as a result of Galba choosing Piso to be the next ruler, killed both his father and Piso and took over the empire.

Then *Vitellius*, who was Galba's brother, killed Otho and took the throne, it seems Vitellius did not want Otho on the throne, perhaps because he was only out for himself. Vitellius, on the other hand, was a good guy, he was against slavery and had even helped in a slave rebellion, even rallying together the common people and slaves to fight for their freedom:

"*Antonius marched by the Via Flamina, and arrived at Saxa Rubra, when the night was far spent, too late to give any help. There he received nothing but gloomy intelligence, that Sabinus was dead, that the Capitol had been burnt to the ground, that*

Rome was in consternation, and also that the populace and the slaves were arming themselves for Vitellius." ..."*By this success, the zeal of the people was increased. The mob of the city armed itself. Some few had military shields, the greater part seized such arms as came to hand, and loudly demanded the signal of battle. Vitellius expressed his thanks to them, and bade them sally forth to defend the capital.*" (Tacitus, Histories, Book III Chapter 2)

When Arrius eventually managed to kill Emperor Vitellius, a kill recorded under the name 'Marcus Antonius Primus', Arrius should have taken the throne, but he did not, however, he must have been a secret co-ruler with both Vespasian and Titus, judging by previous examples of co-rulership, as he records some of his activities using the name Titus. Tacitus also hints at this being the case, as he says the '*Supreme Authority*' rested with (Marcus) Antonius Primus, but why? as far as history tells us, only the Emperor should be referred to as the supreme authority. Then later Pliny the Younger, in a formal public speech, now referred to as his *Panegyricus*, hints at Arrius' co-rulership with Emperor Trajan. In his Panegyricus, where he is seemingly highly praising Trajan, he uses the word '*Optimus*' and draws a comparison to *Jupiter*, who is worshipped as *Optimus Maximus*. Pliny attributes Trajan's election as emperor to '*divine agency*', but earlier in his speech when describing Nerva's search for a suitable heir, he states, as fact, that the essential requirement is for the person to be '*the best and most like the gods*'. The end of the speech contains Pliny's justification that Trajan's title is now '*The Best*', *Optimus*, a title that is used relentlessly in his speech, even though when he uses it, Optimus was only an unofficial part of Trajan's monarchical title. It would appear that Pliny is linking Trajan to Jupiter, but is it Emperor Trajan who Pliny is referring to?

The repeated use of Optimus in Pliny's speech and the linking of Jupiter links to Arrius, because as discussed before, Hadrian built a Temple on the exact site where the Second Temple in Jerusalem stood, and the Temple was named *Jupiter Optimus Maximus*, and Jupiter is the Roman version of Zeus, whose son was Dionysus, who parallels Jesus. What we have then, again, are two references from two people related to Arrius who hint at his co-rulership, one uses the term '*Supreme Authority*', the other uses '*Optimus*', for seemingly unclear reasons, when apparently speaking of Emperor Trajan.

As stated earlier, the name of the Messiah was a later component of the Gospels, and the name 'Jesus' or 'Joshua' is not unique to the individual described in the Gospels, but concerning Arrius, a "*Jesus Christ*" existed, but he was not the man written about in the Bible. This 'Jesus Christ' was *Jesus the son of Gamaliel I*, or *Jesus ben Gamaliel*, who was killed in the same year as his father, *Gamaliel I*, leader of the Pharisees, in the year 63 CE. In the New Testament, this individual was a Jewish high priest of the Pharisees and teacher of the Law (Jewish Torah) and was in a position of authority in the Sanhedrin (assemblies of elders appointed to sit as a tribunal in every city in Israel), *after* the revolt of Theudas the Pharisee (Acts 5:36). This Joshua would have been considered an '*anointed one*' or '*messiah*', so *technically* we could refer to him as a '*Jesus Christ*', because 'Christ' is Greek for the Hebrew word 'Messiah' or 'anointed one', but it is unlikely that this person would have been referred to by this name in his own time.

The evidence points to Arrius choosing the name 'Jesus' because this Jewish high priest would have been an enemy of Arrius, which would have been during the time in which he was in charge of the legions in Judea. Jesus, or Joshua son of Gamaliel I, proactively spread the Jewish teaching and is stated as being responsible for creating a large-scale education system in ancient Judea, which, judging by the historical evidence, would have been the exact opposite of what Arrius and the Roman aristocracy wanted. Regarded as the founder of the institution of formal Jewish education, the *Babylonian Talmud*, Baba Bathra 21a states:

"Joshua b. Gamala came and ordained that teachers of young children should be appointed in each district and each town, and that children should enter school at the age of six or seven."

After the death of this Jewish Priest and Pharisee leader, Arrius appears to have used Jesus' or Joshua's name in the same way he used Yochanan ben Zakai's name, by making the 'Jesus Christ' character the leader of the Christian religion, and Arrius mentions this Joshua, or Jesus, in 'Josephus' *Life/Vita* 204-205. The New Testament also has Gamaliel say, in Acts 5:38-39:

"And now I say unto you (fellow Jews), *withdraw from these men, and let them be; for, if this* (new) *counsel or this* (new) *work* (law) *be from* (common) *men it will be overthrown. But if from God* (royalty) *it be, you* (common) *men are not able to overthrow it* (Christianity), (and) *also* (if you do this) *lest* (as) *fighters against God you are found* (to be)."

The question to ask here is how we can tell the 'it' being

referred to is Christianity? The answer is because the statement makes no sense if Christianity is not the 'it' being spoken of, because why would the Jewish people be trying to overthrow the current Judaic law, the one for which they were fighting? This passage emphasizes the Jews as 'freedom' fighters against the 'God-way', to say that Gamaliel is telling the Jewish people to stop rebelling, but, because this is written in the New Testament, it seems to also be a warning to the Jewish Pharisees of royal status, by saying if they go against the Roman aristocracy, they will lose their royal status and become common people. But, if they stopped fighting, they would be allowed, at some point, to write about how Christianity was really created, i.e., in the *Babylonian Talmud*, so the Jewish leaders had a difficult choice to make. The deaths of both Pharisee leaders Gamaliel I and his son, Jesus/Joshua, meant the only main remaining enemy was Eleazar ben Yair, which again, Arrius' details in his writings as 'Josephus' and the New Testament.

The Book of Revelation gives us crucial information in terms of Arrius' name and includes insults aimed at him and Pliny, the reason is that Julius felt betrayed, despite showing disagreement towards the creation of the new religion, he remained loyal to his family, and later, Hadrian. Julius, the eldest son, appearing in history as Julius Severus & Julius Ursus Servianus (**ref** – *Historia Augusta, Life of Hadrian*, XV.8) felt his grandson or son should have become the next emperor, and Hadrian had shown that he agreed. However, after being a loyal general to Hadrian, the Emperor changed his mind and made Antoninus Pius heir to the throne, a decision in which Justus and Claudia undoubtedly had influence.

This angered Julius, who insisted on his grandson or son becoming emperor, but when he persisted in his protests, even possibly helping to organize a coup, an illegal seizure of power against Hadrian, the Emperor responded by having Julius and *Lucius Pedanius Fuscus Salinator* (Julius' grandson) executed. However, Julius' son survived, perhaps because Hadrian liked him, but Julius managed to start writing the Book of Revelation and his son must have finished it, and through it, presented their frustration and anger. Remember, Arrius gave information about his family in his works as 'Josephus', but in a non-forthright or simple manner, and those works give information about Julius under the name 'John', by using the name 'Hyrcanus', a relative of the Pisos and a Hasmonean leader and Jewish high priest. Once you associate the name 'John' with Julius Piso (by building profiles), you will know that whenever the name 'John' is used, unless made clear otherwise, it is likely Julius who is being referred to.

I must note too, that as 'John', Julius was the only disciple not to be martyred, but his brother Justus was, as "*Justin Martyr*", as '*Justinus*' is a derivative of the name Justus; also, in his book '*The True Authorship of the New Testament*', Abelard Reuchlin says, "*Julius played the Judases as well as the Johns.*" Writing the Book of Revelation, Julius gives a lot of information about his other family members, but particularly his father. Hadrian had sent him out to put down the uprising of the Jews (Pharisees), and he tells us in different ways that he had taken part in the last revolt of the Jews (Pharisees), mainly by telling us how long that revolt had been; forty-two months. Being able to tell us that, he is also saying he wrote the Book of Revelation *after* that war had ended, meaning Revelation had to have been completed after the year 135 CE. Julius was married to Emperor Hadrian's sister, *Aelia Domitia Paulina* II, and he had done his duty to Hadrian whenever asked to, even being sent to govern in Britain, which he did.

Without the information that Julius provides, we may never have known the true context behind the creation of this religion. The names *Arrius* and *Piso* should not be seen multiple times within important statements in the New Testament, and the numbers associated with it should not, in *any* way, create the names Arrius, Kalpurnius, Piso, and Flavius, but when the '*rules*' of the Hebrew, Latin, and Greek languages are known, that is what we have. Arrius is only known publicly in history as 'Flavius Josephus', and after his father's death, his immediate family, for 73 years, do not appear with the name *Piso* in public Roman history, the Piso name only appears again when Arrius' grandson, Antoninus Pius, becomes emperor, and even then, they are known only as of the Antonines. Before Antoninus took the throne, the Pisos were in the background busy writing the New Testament scriptures and subtly gaining even more power over the then known world.

There was no Christianity or Christians in terms of our understanding from the Gospels, these terms were not used before and during the time of Nero, they only appeared after, by individuals of the Roman aristocracy who were all related to each other, and who had motives for backing this new religion which would become the largest in the world. The Roman claims of persecution of 'Christians' would give the impression of Christian martyrdom for future generations, which it did, meaning the religion would be seen as moral and worthy of following, because it created the impression there were those who were willing to die for it; another crucial factor that attempted to make this religion appealing to people was the removal of the Torah requirements, such as circumcision and the dietary requirements. However, regarding persecution, there were some later emperors, such as *Diocletian*, who could be considered as having persecuted 'Christians', but this was only the case when trying to suppress the spreading of it by those who were trying to promote and support it.

As the year 300 approached, those who had been claiming the throne of Rome were becoming divided and aware of how being an emperor had become a fatal position to be in, so solutions were needed. Some members of the aristocracy were in favor of devoting more time and attention to promoting Christianity, others, however, were opposed to it. *Diocletian*, *Galerius*, *Maximianus I*, and *Constantius Chlorus* were in favor of the old religions of the Roman Empire and wanted to suppress Christianity or put it on the back burner. Others, though, such as Constantine, wanted to promote and establish it as the official religion of Rome. Some stories of "persecutions" were complete fabrications, whilst others were embellishments of the disagreements between those royals who wanted to promote Christianity, and those who did not.

The historical evidence does not point towards a tiny band of illiterate individuals converting a powerful pagan empire, it points to those in power converting their empire. Today it is well known, if not entirely accepted, that Christianity uses components borrowed from much earlier religions, such as the *virgin birth*, *God as the father*, the nickname *'the Lamb'*, *the Way and the Light,* and *Only Begotten,* which was a nickname given to a favorite son. By backdating the Jesus story, it meant the New Testament became an intricate mix of fact and fiction, resulting in biblical scholars seeing no reason to search for the answers in the time of just before the Flavian dynasty and after. Backdating the story by 40 years fit into the Judaic prophecy of a coming Messiah, and it allowed the authors to create propaganda around their enemy, Nero. The Romans wanted to be seen as Gods and mostly they were, by conquering civilizations and then replacing the heads of statues with sculptures of their heads, making the people of those conquered civilizations worship them.

This did not work in Jerusalem however, the Jewish people worshipped scripture, not statues, and so rightly refused to accept any Roman emperor as their God, which led to a very long war. The scriptures were written in a way that would make the common people believe the accounts had come from people like them, and not by those who were trying to manipulate and control them, then, years later, those in power would claim to be "converted" and would then proceed to spread this new religion far and wide, often in violent ways. In the end, this religion was a product of those who received a level of education far exceeding that of what the common people did, if any at all. Education was limited to the upper classes and clergy who became synonymous with power, in Britain, for example, the studying of the classics carries the prestige of the posh schools, and the children of the aristocracy were, and are, taught how to rule from a young age, whereas society is taught how to work.

My final view is that if Arius Piso did exist, then he was a very elusive man, and as a result of his name not having been given fully in history, for some, the information in this book may not be strong enough evidence to be convincing, which is understandable. The important thing to keep in mind then is the motive: these families desired to retain their power which was under threat, so they built a type of power that could not be simply taken away; psychological. Arrius also shows traits resembling that of a psychopath, it is no secret that the most common trait of a psychopath is pathological lying, for them, it is a means of covering up their behavior to get what they want. Many individuals of a psychopathic nature are found in positions of power and authority, resulting mostly from their enormous sense of self-worth. Arrius was a royal, a confident, arrogant royal, who lied to get what he wanted, and he had powerful support, which resulted in a lethal combination that, in the end, meant the Roman aristocracy emerged victoriously and is the reason this religion has lasted so long, because of the immense power it had behind it.

TIMELINE OF EVENTS

The beginning of the long war, with the Jewish changeover from the Seleucid leadership to the Hasmonean leadership

(circa 135 BCE)

|

The war between the Hasmonean leadership and the Pharisees

(circa 50 BCE-under Julius Caesar)

|

Herod 'The Great' installed as 'King of the Jews' by Rome

(40 BCE-4BCE)

|

(Jesus is stated to have been crucified-33 CE)

|

Collaboration between the Sadducees, Herodians and the Caesars

(circa 30 BCE-6 BCE)

|

The Roman committee to create a new religion

(under Emperor Tiberius, circa 14-37 CE)

|

The dissolution of the official committee to create a new religion

(under Emperor Claudius or Nero, circa 50 CE)

|

The Zealots begin their rebellion

(August-September 66 CE)

|

The twelfth legion of 'Cestius Gallus' is defeated at the Pass of Beth Horon

(October-November 66 CE)

|

We are told "Flavius Josephus" commands the Jewish forces in Galilee

(December 66 CE-May 67 CE)

|

Emperor Nero is assassinated and Vespasian eventually becomes emperor of Rome, and we are told "Josephus" is captured

(January 67 CE-December 69 CE)

|

The siege at Jerusalem takes place and the Second Temple is destroyed

(March–September 70 CE)

|

The final siege at Masada takes place

(Spring 73 CE)

NOTES & REFERENCES

JOSEPHUS AS A PEN NAME

Thrasea Paetus' wife Arria the Younger was a relative of **Persius the Poet**.

Supporting information – (**Suetonius**, Lives of Illustrious Men, On Poets — Persius, pg. 497, 499).

Tacitus does mention that **Thrasea Paetus** and **Arria** may also have a son (Arrius Piso). He says –

"To touch Nero with shame for his infamies (an evil or wicked act) was an idle dream, and it was much more to be feared that he (Nero) would exercise his cruelty on Thrasea's wife, his daughter, and **other objects of his affection**." He doesn't mention Gaius' and Arria's son directly, but he does suggest the possibility that one exists.

Then to further hide the existence of this son (**Arrius**), **Tacitus** says –

"Arria, who aspired to follow her husband's (Gaius) ending and the precedent set by her mother and namesake, he Gaius (Thrasea Paetus) advised (her) to keep her life and not to deprive their **child** of **her** one support". **Tacitus** said this because at that point **Arrius** was in exile, so he was not there to support his sister. It also indicates that 'Fannia' or F.Arria, did not or would not have a husband at that time.

Note – Arria's mother (Arria the Elder) had committed suicide with her husband after the revolt of Lucius Arruntius Camillus Scribonianus against Claudius in A.D./C.E. 42 had collapsed)

Supporting information – (Tacitus, *Annals*, Book XV 1, XXVI).

There is a lot of information about the Piso family in an article titled 'People in Pliny', by Sir Ronald Syme, *Journal of Roman Studies*, 1968–69, pg. 144, 146, 148.

Such as –

1) A. Caecina Paetus, suff. 37 C.E., of Patavium.

2) P. Clodius Thrasea Paetus (also of Patavium), who married the daughter of the above A. Caecina Paetus.

3) Arria the Younger as the wife of Thrasea Paetus.

4) C. Fannius (Caecina. Farrius/Arrius Piso) as a barrister who wrote the biographies of Nero's victims. To quote: "*Supposed relative of Fannia, the daughter of Patavine (P. Clodius) Thrasea Paetus by marriage with Arria, the daughter of A. Caecina Paetus.*"

Relating to the above source and mentioned earlier: suff. 37, cf. Groag in PIR-2, F 116. Sir Ronald Syme says – "*Why she should be called* "**Fannia**", *no clue.*" He is right, we would think a daughter of an "**Arria**" would carry the name of her own mother, somewhere, and she does, she is '**F' Arria/Annia** with **r's as n's**.

Supporting information for **Thrasea Paetus** and **C. Caecina Paetus**; "*Domitius Corbulo,*" by Sir Ronald Syme, *Journal of*

Roman Studies, (post-1969), his source was **Pliny the Younger**, Epp. III, 16. 7 ff.

As **Caesennius Paetus**, Arrius Piso married Vespasian's niece, who was most likely his first wife.

Supporting information – "*Some Flavian Connections*", **Gavin Townend**, (*Journal of Roman Studies*), 1961. Also see Sir Ronald Syme, *Tacitus*, 595, n5.-ref. for **Caecina Paetus** and **Arria the Elder**; Dio Cassius, 7. 407E

Polla, the wife of Lucan the Poet is referred to as 'Queen' by Martial. Note that '**Polla**' is the feminine form of '**Pollo/Pollio**'.

Supporting information–Martial, Book X, LXIV.

Arria mentioned by **Martial** (I. XIII).

Pliny the Younger mentions Arria in Epist. III, 16.3.

Tacitus speaks of Arria (Tacitus, *Annals*, XVI).

'Ihrasea' is mentioned in **Juvenal** (Juvenal, V36, Loeb Classical Library Edition).

Thrasea Paetus, **Arria the Elder**, **Arria the Younger** and **Fannia** are all mentioned in the **Annals of Tacitus**; Book XVI, XXIV, pg. 373; Book XVI, xxv, pg. 375-377; Book XVI, XXVIII, pg. 379-381; Book XVI, XXXIV, pg. 387. Read through books: XVI, XXIV, XXV, XXVI, XXVII, XXIX, XXXIII, XXXIV, XXXV (Loeb).

Appian's Roman History, mentions a **C. Philo Caesennius (Paetus)**. 'Paetus' is inferred (concluded from evidence) the same way that '**Piso**' would be when the name '**Frugi**' is used. 'Frugi'

refers to a name used by Lucius Calpurnius *Piso Frugi*, a name used by Roman men of the gens. Calpurnia during the Roman Republic and early Empire. They were descendants of Lucius Calpurnius *Piso Frugi*, who was consul in 133 BC, and who established the addition of **Frugi** (*Frux in Latin*) as an agnomen, a fourth name, occasionally given as an honor to an ancient Roman citizen, which was passed down through the family and means 'fruits of the earth'.

– gens. (plural 'gentes'), means a family consisting of all those individuals who shared the same nomen and claimed descent from a common ancestor)

History records that both **Arria the Younger** and '**Fannia**' were alive when Nerva became emperor in 96 A.D/C.E. They had been in exile under **Emperor Domitian** and **Arrius Piso** as '**Caesennius Paetus**' was the governor (president/king) of **Syria**, as several of the Piso ancestries were noted for being '**governors of Syria**'.

Supporting information – (**Flavius Josephus**, *The Jewish Wars*, 11, VII. 59; or **Flavius Josephus**, **Whiston** translation, pg. 597).

Montanus:

'**Montanus**' aka **Arrius Piso**, is "*spared out of consideration for his father*" when '**Thrasea Paetus**} is killed."

Supporting information – (this is found in the *Annals of Tacitus*, XVI, 33, Loeb Classical Library. '**Montanus**' is found in 'People in Pliny', Sir Ronald Syme, *Journal of Roman Studies*, 1968 – 69, pg. 149-150. Also in Tacitus, *Histories*, III, 35. 2; and in Tacitus, *Annals*, Book XVI, XXIX, pg. 381, Loeb Classical Library. /

Book XVI, XXXIII, pg. 387, Loeb Classical Library. '**Montanus**' is mentioned in *Juvenal*, IV. 107, 131, Loeb Classical Library. Also ref-"*The True Authorship of the New Testament*," in "The Proof of Josephus as Calpurnius Piso," pg. 20, Abelard Reuchlin, 1979, 1986).

Arrius Antoninus:

'**Arrius Antoninus**' was proconsul under Vespasian in 69 A.D/ C.E.

Supporting information – ('*The Consulate of the Elder Trajan*', by John Morris, *Journal of Roman Studies*, Vol. 43-45, 1953-1955, pg. 79-80. **Josephus**, BF, 4, 9, 2 (499), **Tacitus**, *Histories*, II, 1, cf. 1, 10; **Suetonius**, '*The Twelve Caesars*', under 'Titus', 5. He is also in the *Historia Augusta* by this name, he is the grandfather of emperor **Antoninus Pius**. And it appears that **Antoninus Pius** and **Suetonius** are the same person. – Reference – *Piso Christ* – 'Suetonius as Emperor Antoninus Pius'.

Also see '**Marcus Aurelius**' (A Biography), Appendix 2, '**The Antonine Dynasty**', B: **Antoninus Pius**, pg. 242, Birley, published by Yale University Press, c. 1986).

Annius Varus:

In the '*Historia Augusta*', '**Annius Verus**' is given as the great-grandfather of **Marcus Aurelius** (ref-Marcus Aurelius, 1. 4). This '**Annius Varus**' (Arrius Piso) was obviously the founder of the '**Annii Verii**' (i.e., the Antonine Dynasty). You can find quite a bit of information regarding this family and the names that they used in the work titled '*Marcus Aurelius*' (**A Biography**), Appendix 2, '*The Antonine Dynasty*', C: ANNII VERlI (pg.

243–244), by Birley, pub. by Yale Univ" c. 1986. **Arrius** is **M. Annius Verus** (even the '**M**' is provided for the '**Marcus** in Marcus Antonius'),

Supporting information – (ref-'*People in Pliny*', Sir Ronald Syme, JRS, 1968–1969. pg. 137).

Annius Gallus:

'**Annius Callus**' is in **Plutarch's** '*Lives*' *under* '*Otho*'. And **Juvenal** also mentions a '**Callus**' in his works (**Juvenal**, VII. 144, Loeb Classical Library Edition).

Supporting information – (Tacitus, ll, *Histories*, Book II, XLIV, pg. 233; and **Tacitus**, II, *Histories*, Book II, XXXIII, pg. 215; as well as **Tacitus**, II, *Histories*, Book 11, XI; and **Tacitus**, II, *Histories*, Book 1, DOCXVII, pg. 151).

Cestius Callus and **Gessius Florus**:

The Roman writer **Martial** mentions '**Cestius Callus**' in his works (**Martial**, XLII, 2., Loeb Classical Library Edition). **Arrius** ('Josephus'), speaking about '**Gessius Florus**' (i.e., himself as Roman General and procurator of Judea) says –

"*... where the case was really pitiable,****he was most barbarous, and in things of the greatest turpitude he was most impudent.*** *Nor could anyone****outdo him in disguising the truth; nor could anyone contrive more subtle ways of deceit than he did.*** *He indeed thought it but a petty offence to get money out of single persons; so he spoiled whole cities, and ruined entire bodies of men at once, and did almost publicly proclaim it all the country over, that they had liberty given them to turn robbers, upon this* *condition, that he might go shares with them in the spoils they got."* (ref-*Josephus*, pg. 484, Whiston).

Antonius Primus:

'**Antonius Primus**' is found described in **Tacitus**, Histories, Book II, LXXXVI, pg. 299. And in the works of '**Flavius Josephus**', '**Antonius Primus**' turns into '**Antonius Julianus**'.

Church father **Origen** says that to find out about the destruction of the Temple, look in (the works of) **Flavius Josephus** and '**Antonius Julianus**', implying that 'Antonius Julianus' was a contemporary historian with 'Flavius Josephus' and well-known. But there was not any historian known as '**Antonius Julianus**', it was just another alias name of **Arrius Piso**, and so it would appear that Origen was also aware of what Arrius Piso was doing.

Also worthy of mention, is the fact that Josephus calls himself 'Joseph' (as in the father of Jesus), on pg. 427 of the works of Flavius Josephus, Whiston Translation.

And about the 'signs' that the Temple and Jerusalem would be destroyed, he says – "... ***the signs were so evident***..." and that "... **(the Jews) *did not regard the denunciations that God made to them***" ('God' in this case being **Arrius Piso** himself).

There was a **"starresembling *asword*** <which stood over the city **(of Jerusalem),** that continued(lasted)***for a whole year.***" He is referring to his own 'sword' or 'weapon', i.e. 'Jesus', which he was using to defeat the Jews and which "stood over" the city (of Jerusalem), that continued (lasted) for a whole year. At the end,

where he says "lasted for a whole year", he could be referring to his position as Roman procurator in Judea.

'Josephus' (Arrius Piso) states further... "... **as if they had been ready to (play as)/be "actors" against them.**" ref-*Flavius Josephus*, pg. 602, Whiston.

"**Some of them be took themselves to the writing of fabulous narrations,** *some of them endeavoured to please the cities of the kings by writing in their commendation: others of them fell to finding faults with transactions, or with the writers of such transactions,...*" "*...and thought to make a great figure by so doing, And indeed these do, what is of all things the most contrary to true history; for it is the great character of true history,* **that all concerned therein both speak and write the same things; while these men by writing differently about the same things think they shall be believed to write the greatest regard to the truth.** *We therefore,[who are Jews,] must yield to the* **Grecian writers** *as to language and elegance of composition...*"

Remember, when Arrius says "We therefore (who are Jews)...", he is pretending to be a Jew, so what he means is that the authors of the New Testament wrote differently about the same thing and people do regard it as the greatest regard to the truth. The Jews did have to 'yield' to the 'Grecian writers' (the Roman Royals) because they had no choice.

Supporting information – (*Flavius Josephus*, pg. 608, in '**Against Apion**', Whiston).

"**As for myself, I have composed a true history of that whole**

war..." Josephus calls it a "**war**", not a "**revolt**" as most others do, he also says; "*I **acted** as general...*"

Supporting information – (*Flavius Josephus, pg. 609, in* "**Against Apion**", Whiston).

Josephus (Arrius) says; "*...**and as for the History of the War, I wrote it as having been an "actor"myself**...*"

Supporting information – (*Flavius Josephus, pg. 610, in* '**Against Apion**', Whiston).

"*I say nothing of such kings as have been famous for piety (a quality of being religious), particularly of one of them whose name was**Cresus**...*"

Now '**Cresus**' can acrostically be part '**C(h)r(ist)**' and part '**(J)esus**'... **Supporting information** – (*Flavius Josephus, pg. 628, in* "**Against Apion**," *Whiston translation*).

Sir Ronald Syme

Sir Ronald was a highly regarded and respected scholar of classical Rome, he taught at Oxford University and was regarded as the greatest of modern historians on ancient Rome. As well as the *Journal of Roman Studies*, he wrote many books and papers regarding his research and knowledge of that time, including 'The Roman Revolution' and a biography of the historian Tacitus.

Reference for Sir Ronald Syme's work can found in the following –

(Tacitus as Neratius Priscus) *Tacitus: Some Sources of his information*, JRS, page 68, Sir Ronald Syme 1982.

The Composition of the Historia Augusta: Recent Theories, JRS, Sir Ronald Syme 1972-73.

(For Arrius Antoninus) *The Consulate of the Elder Trajan*, JRS, vol. 43-45, page 79-80, by John Morris 1953-55.

(Calpurnii Piso descent from Numa) *Calpurnius Siculus and the Claudian Civil War*, JRS, T.P. Wiseman 1982.

(On the family of Licinianus Frugi Piso and ancestors) *Piso Frugi and Crassus Frugi*, JRS, Sir Ronald Syme 1960.

(Information on Arrius (Antonius Primus) being Flavius Silva (Bassus), *Antonius Saturninus*, JRS, Sir Ronald Syme 1978-80.

(Information on nomen and nomenclature) *People in Pliny*, JRS, Sir Ronald Syme 1968-69.

(Pliny and Trajan's ancestry, and the Piso's conspiracy) *Domitius Corbulo*, JRS, Sir Ronald Syme post-1969.

Oligarchy at Rome: A Paradigm for Political Science, JRS, Sir Ronald Syme. Examines the structure of an oligarchy that was in place and running the Roman Empire.

Empire and Biography, JRS, Sir Ronald Syme. Gives genealogical data relating to the Roman emperors.

'Piso Frugi and Crassus Frugi', regarding the family of Licinianus Frugi Piso and ancestors, JRS, Sir Ronald Syme 1960

SELECT BIBLIOGRAPHY

'Young's *Analytical Concordance of the Bible*'

Africa, Thomas W, *Rome of the Caesars*. New York: John Wiley & Sons, Inc, 1965

Baron, Salo, A *Social and Religious History of the Jews*, Columbia Univ. Press, N.Y., and Jewish Publication Society, Philadelphia: 1952

Berry, George Ricker, *The Interlinear Greek-English New Testament*. USA: Zondervan Publishing House 1976

Birley, Anthony R, *Marcus Aurelius, a Biography*. Yale: circa 1986 & Birley, Anthony R, *Marcus Aurelius, a Biography*. Routledge: 1993

Bruno, Bauer, *Christ and the Caesars*, 1877 – Online Version

Clough, A.H, *Plutarch's Lives*. Boston: Little, Brown, and Company 1888

Deiss, Joseph Jay, *Herculaneum: Italy's Buried Treasure*. New York: Haper&Row 1985

Feldman, Louis H., "*Josephus: Interpretative Methods and Tendencies*" found in Evans, Craig A. and Porter Jr, Stanley E. (editors), *Dictionary of New Testament Background* Illinois: IVP, 2000

Graham, Lloyd M, *Deceptions and Myths of the Bible*. UK: Bell Publishing Ltd 1979

Hannay, James Ballantyne, *The Rise, Deline, and Fall of the Roman Religion*'. London: Kessinger Publishing 2010

Hay, Malcolm, *Europe And The Jews: The Pressure of Christendom Over 1900 Years*. Chicago: Academy Chicago Publishers 1992

Helms, Prof. Randel – *Professor and biblical scholar 'Gospel Fictions'*

Helms, Prof. Randel, 'Who Wrote the Gospels'

Holland, Richard, *Nero: The Man Behind The Myth*. England: Sutton Publishing 2000

Hone, William, Editor.*The apocryphal book of 'Barnabas, Lost Books of the Bible'*. New York: Bell Publishing Co.1979

Huntsman, E.D., "The Reliability of Josephus: Can He Be Trusted?". Bringham Young University Studies 36, no. 3: 1996

Jellicoe, Sidney,*Studies in the Septuagint: Origins, Recensions, and Interpretations: Selected Essays, With a Prolegomenon (Library of Biblical studies)*. New York: Ktav Publishers and Distributors Inc 1974

John, Michell, 'City of Revelation'. NY: Ballantine Books 1972

Josephus, Flavius, *The Jewish War*, Loeb Classical Library Edition

Josephus, Flavius, *Jewish Antiquities*, Loeb Classical Library Edition

Juvenal and Persius, *Loeb Classical Library Edition*: 2004

Martial, *Epigrams*, Book 2. Loeb Classical Library Edition: 1993

Mason, Steve, *Flavius Josephus Translation and Commentary*, Volume 9, Life of Josephus: 2001

McNeil Cooke, Ian, 'Sun Disc to Crucifix': 1999

Pei, Mario, *The Story of Language*. London: Unwin Brothers Limited 1966

Piso, Roman, & Gallus, Jay, *Piso Christ*. USA: Trafford Publishing 2010 (details a wealth of important research material)

Rajak, Tessa, *Josephus, The Historian, and His Society*. London: Bloomsbury Academic 2002

Reuchlin, Abelard, *The True Authorship of the New Testament*. USA: 1986

Rohl, David, *A Test Of Time: The Bible – From Myth To History*. UK: Century Publishing (A Channel 4 Book) 1995

Schiffman, Lawrence H, *From Text to Tradition, a History of Judaism in Second Temple and Rabbinic Times*. New York: KTAV Publishing House 1991

Schulz, Regine, & Seidel, Matthias, *Egypt, The World of the Pharaohs*. UK: Konemann UK Ltd 1998

St. Augustine, *City of God, Modern Library*. Random House: 1950

Strong, James, *The New Strongs Exhaustive Concordance Of The Bible*. Nashville, Tennessee: Thomas Nelson Publishers 1990

Suetonius, *Lives of the Caesars*. Oxford University Press: 2000

Suetonius, *The Twelve Caesars*. Penguin Classics: 2007

Syme, Sir Ronald, A chapter called 'The Bogus Names' in the book *Emperors and Biography – Studies in the Historia Augusta*. UK: Oxford University Press 1971–Syme says that to understand Ancient history more completely, a simple superficial reading of ancient *historical literature will not be enough.* This is because the 'borrowing' of ancestors names to create alias names was a practice used in ancient Rome, so deductive logic needs to be used in order to have a realistic understanding of the period.

Syme, Sir Ronald, *Journal of Roman Studies. (post-1969)*

Tacitus, *The Annals of Imperial Rome.* London: Penguin Classics 1974

Tacitus, *The Annals,* Loeb Classical Library edition 1989

Tacitus, *The Histories,* Books 1-3 Loeb Classical Library Edition: 1989

Tacitus, *The Histories,* London: Penguin Classics 2009

Tannahill, Reay, *Sex In History.* USA: Scarborough House/Publishers 1992

The Younger, Pliny,*the Letters of Pliny the Younger (Letters and Panegyricus),* Loeb Classical Library edition: 1989

The Younger, Pliny,*the Letters of Pliny the Younger.* London: 1963

Townsend, Gavin, *Some Flavian Connections, Journal of Roman Studies.* 1961

Tropper, Amram, *Rewriting Ancient Jewish History: The History of the Jews in Roman times and the New Historical Method.* New York: Routledge 2016

Walker, Barbara G, 'The Woman's Dictionary of Symbols and Sacred Objects'. San Francisco, California: Harper 1988

Whiston, William, *The Complete Works of Flavius Josephus.* London: George Virtue, 1841

William Poole, Gary, *"Flavius Josephus"*, Encyclopedia Britannica

ABOUT THE AUTHOR

Henry Davis is an independent historical researcher with a passion for ancient history, whose knowledge of early Christianity is self-taught. Although Henry had wanted to embark on a formal education studying the Classics, he suffered from extreme anxiety and felt he could not do so. Instead, he decided to learn everything he could himself, with help from family and friends, who had achieved degrees in Classical studies. Since embarking on his self-educated journey, he has read the work of leading historians and scholars, including *Dame Mary Beard, Tom Holland,* and *Sir Ronald Syme*, to name only a few. He has of course also studied the work of *Tacitus, Suetonius, Pliny the Younger,* and *Flavius Josephus*, again, to name only a few classical works.

You can engage with Henry on Twitter at @HenryDavisCC

Learn more information regarding this investigation at https://www.henryhdavis.com/

If you would like to share your thoughts regarding this book, you can do so here: (US) http://www.amazon.com/review/create-review?&asin=B07J46545B or

(UK) http://www.amazon.co.uk/review/create-review?&asin=1789265576

Printed in Poland
by Amazon Fulfillment
Poland Sp. z o.o., Wrocław